PRAISE FOR
*YOU CAN MAKE IT BIG WRITING BOOKS*

"If you are ready to be a bestselling author, *You Can Make It Big Writing Books* will guide the way."

—**Rick Frishman**, president of Planned Television Arts

"*You Can Make It Big Writing Books* is inspiring, richly informative, realistic, fascinating, and, above all, encouraging. This remarkable book is all writers will ever need to fulfill their creative potential and attain their dreams of success."

—**Joel Hirschhorn**, two-time Academy Award Winner, coauthor of *Titanic Adventure*

## About the Authors

Jeff Herman is founder of The Jeff Herman Literary Agency, one of New York's leading agencies for writers. He has sold hundreds of titles and represents dozens of top authors. He is the author of the bestselling *Writers Guide to Book Editors, Publishers, and Literary Agents* and co-author of *Write the Perfect Book Proposal.*

Deborah Levine Herman is Vice President of the agency. She's a writer, an attorney, lecturer, and a spiritual motivator. She's currently authoring *Writing as a Spritual Journey.*

Julia DeVillers is Editor-at-Large for the agency, a freelance writer, and author of several books.

# You Can Make it Big Writing Books

A Top Agent
Shows You How
to Develop a
Million-Dollar Bestseller

*Jeff Herman*
*Deborah Levine Herman*
*Julia DeVillers*

PRIMA PUBLISHING

PRIMA PUBLISHING and colophon are registered trademarks of Prima Communications, Inc.

Library of Congress Cataloging-in-Publication Data

Herman, Jeff.
    You can make it big writing books : a top agent shows you how to develop a million-dollar bestseller / by Jeff Herman.
        p.      cm.
    Includes index.
    ISBN 0-7615-1362-0
    1. Authorship—Marketing.  2. Authors and publishers.  3. Books—Marketing.  4. Bestsellers  5. Authorship.  I. Title.
PN161.H48      1999
808'.02—dc21                                                          99-23995
                                                                          CIP

99  00  01  02  HH  10  9  8  7  6  5  4  3  2  1
Printed in the United States of America

---

**How to Order**

Single copies may be ordered from Prima Publishing, P.O. Box 1260BK, Rocklin, CA 95677; telephone (916) 632-4400. Quantity discounts are also available. On your letterhead, include information concerning the intended use of the books and the number of books you wish to purchase.

---

**Visit us online at www.primapublishing.com**

# CONTENTS

# Acknowledgments

We are grateful to the authors and publishing professionals, who generously and enthusiastically shared their time and wisdom to inspire us all. For editorial and administrative support, thank you to Susan Silva, Andrew Mitchell, Mandi White, Donna Bowen, John Nees, Allison Gentile, Johanna Haney, and Dawn Nocera.

To my wife Deborah Herman, for insisting that this book be done. My colleague, Julie DeVillers, who's never met a deadline she couldn't beat. And our editor, Susan Silva, who knew how to wait, how to demand, and how to be grateful.—Jeff

I would lovingly like to acknowledge my father, Stuart H. Levine, (March 23, 1932–April 9, 1999), who taught me the value of thinking "big."—Deborah

All writers should have as supportive a family as I do: David DeVillers (the history reader), Robin Rozines, (the mystery reader), Jennifer Roy (the inspirational reader), Amy Rozines (the business reader), Virginia Quinby (the spiritual reader), and my daughter, Quinn DeVillers (the future reader).—Julia

# INTRODUCTION

So you want to make it big writing books? You want to see your name on the cover of a book, do the talk show circuit, have book signings, and receive the adoration of all. You want tons of cash, a beach house, and even want to be featured in the Oprah book club. Well, everyone has his or her dreams. What separates the dreamers from the doers is the single-mindedness to do whatever it takes to reach the goal.

Some people are born into writing success by being so gifted that no matter what they do, the path will find them. Although they still have to produce, they are not so bothered by the trivialities of breaking down the publisher's doors. The publishers find them.

The other 99 percent of writers have to have more going for them than just talent. In these pages you will hear some stories of the greatest writers of our time. Many are living legends. They all have something you want: they have made it big writing books. These writers are giving you the greatest gift a person can give to another: the benefit of their experience.

Some of these stories represent the American dream of rags to riches. Some are more like riches to more riches. In the following chapters you have the opportunity to see into the lives of people who have blazed the trail for you. Their stories are extraordinary, but more importantly for you, they give insights that can be extremely valuable in plotting out your own writing career.

Making it big writing books has to become your mission if you are going to succeed. It isn't like any other job. You have to have a good marketable product and you have to be tough. The better the product, the more savvy the writer, the better the odds. It is a very simple equation.

After you have read how others have done it, close the book. If you are still totally committed to this goal, reopen it and read Section II, which covers the industry nuts and bolts. Every serious writer needs to know how the publishing industry works and how each dollar of revenue gets divvied up. You need to see that you are only one layer in a complex production system and that every layer requires nourishment for a successful outcome. If you understand how the industry works, you will be more likely to create a product that people will buy.

You will learn how to put together a manuscript or nonfiction book proposal. You will learn to write queries that jump out of the stack. If you are willing, you will learn what you need to become a professional.

Not everyone will make it over the walls to the closed publishing world. But if you have what it takes, this book will help you substantially increase your odds.

Pay careful attention to publishing industry protocol. There is a way to do things and ways not to do them. Don't put your book out of the running by errors in presentation or process. You have enough strikes against you. This section of the book includes what you need to know to:

- Find an agent
- Keep an agent
- Find a publisher
- Package your own book

You will learn how to hit the ground running–not whining. Most first books do not bring in the top-dollar advance. When you become more sophisticated about the industry in general, you will realize that a modest advance is not necessarily the measure of a book's ultimate success. If you believe in yourself enough and persist, you can push your book to the top.

Many writers are under the misconception that having a book published is the end of their road, that they can sit back and wait for everyone to run out and buy the book. In Section II you will learn what to do for yourself after your book is in print. Publishers will bring your book to the bookstores, but you can make it a true success. Too many writers want everything now. If you have an inflated ego and assume the publishing world is waiting to roll out the red carpet for you, you will be vastly disappointed. In fact, you're likely to fall flat on your face. The "Chicken Soup for the Soul" legend started with a $1,000 advance. You will learn to see the bigger picture and to build your success through know-how and your own efforts.

Some of the most prominent book publicists in the industry will give you their secrets for creating bestselling books. They will also tell you what you can do to keep your career skyrocketing, building one success on top of another.

You can learn the tools of making it big writing books but will still need some secret ingredients to help you along the way. Originality, tenacity, creativity, credibility, personality, and some attitude will give you that extra push. You can do it. You can be the one who is responsible, the one who grabs destiny by the throat and proclaims: "My will is my fate. My hunger is my fuel."

# AUTHORS WHO
# MADE IT BIG

## SECTION ONE

## CHAPTER 1

# The Marathoners

A common lament of the author is "But I can't find my book anywhere in the stores!" In an age of books coming into and going out of print within months, the Marathoner is someone to be truly admired. The Marathoner is the author whose books and talent have staying power. Like Sandra Scoppetone, they have published acclaimed books for decades. They have weathered changes in reading trends like Jennifer Blake, whose gothic novels spanned the '70s, historical romance in the '80s, and contemporary romantic suspense in the '90s. And, like Pulitzer Prize–nominated Loren Estleman and Charles Ghigna, they have picked up an award or two along the way.

No matter how long their writing careers have lasted, and how many books they have published, for the Marathoners, the joy of publishing their first book remains fresh. "There's holding that first book in my hands once it was printed in book form," says Zilpha Keatley Snyder. "I will always remember that with a great deal of pleasure." "Having written my first book, I took great pride in going to the library and looking it up in the card catalog," said Patricia Rushford. After 29 years as an author, still the best thing that has happened to Meg Chittenden was, "I got an agent! I got published!"

The Marathoners show no signs of slowing down. Jennifer Blake looks forward to a "golden anniversary" in the business. "In the meantime, I only want to share more of the stories that clog my brain."

Charles Ghigna, too, has no intention of stopping. "I look forward to continuing to ride this magic carpet for as long and as far as it will take me. Writing, especially for children, is one of the most honorable professions in the world. It is one of the few professions that allows you to dream, that encourages you to dream, and to capture those dreams on paper and to make them come alive in the minds and hearts of others."

## CARMEN RENEE BERRY

*Carmen Renee Berry is a well-known bestselling author and speaker. As a former therapist, and now a nationally certified body worker, she has dedicated herself to the integration of the body, the emotions, the spirit, and the mind in promoting healthy lifestyles for people of all ages.* Girlfriends for Life *is Carmen's twelfth book. Her other books include the bestselling* Girlfriends *and* Girlfriends Talk About Men, The Girlfriends Keepsake Book, Coming Home to Your Body, Is Your Body Trying to Tell You Something?, *and* Daddies and Daughters.

Ever since I learned to read, I wanted to create books. I started my first manuscript at the age of nine, a story about a haunted house, I recall. The manuscript was never completed, but the dream had been born.

It's interesting looking back on it now, how strong that desire was for me. I watched many television shows but never dreamed of working in television. I saw films and never saw myself making movies. But when a book was in my hands, something magical stirred within me. I loved to read, but more than that, I wanted to create these small packages of inspiration and information. Writing is something I have to do.

I made the transition to publication in the mid-'80s when my life collapsed in on me. In tears, looking at what I saw as a series of losses and bad decisions, I vowed that my life would be redeemed through writing. Like Scarlett O'Hara clasping dirt in her fist and vowing, "As God is my witness, I will never be hungry again!" I vowed I would have no unpublished pathology. Rather than resent what I had lost, I plunged myself into reflecting on and making sense of my past mistakes. From that passion, all of my books have sprung.

I don't remember any one person discouraging me. However, I found it hard to tell people, until I was actually published, about my dream to be a writer. Perhaps this is true of any dream, especially in the arts. I live in Southern California, where they joke about people saying, "I want to be an actor" or "I write screenplays," when in fact they wait tables or teach for a living. A lot of people have dreams, but so few seem to actualize them.

> **Writing is something I have to do.**

The most discouraging aspect of writing came from publishing itself. My first two years of trying to get published were brutal—two agents and enough rejection letters to wallpaper my living room. It is very hard to break into the club.

How I became a bestselling author is still a mystery for me, not a formula that can be arbitrarily recreated. I don't believe bestsellers can be forced on the public. To write a book a lot of people buy, a variety of things have to line up—a topic that hits people on an emotional level, putting into words what they felt but hadn't been able to articulate; a book structure that fits the topic; a great title; a publisher who believes in the book and puts energy and lots of money into packaging and promotion; a "break" of some sort, that magical something that no one can control. All you can do is be ready for the ride if you're invited.

The best thing that happened to me was meeting my mentor, Roy Carlisle. Without his support and editorial genius I would not be where I am today. He taught me how to "worry" over a concept until it takes on a life of its own, creating its own structure in which to live. He taught me how to write the kinds of books I want to write. I have always known that when he told me something was good, I could believe him (he certainly let me know when something wasn't!). He's been a part of my writing from my first contract, and his influence cannot be understated.

The two most difficult aspects of publishing have to do with the business side. First, I've had a similar experience with four different publishers, in which my editor has been fired or has taken a leave of absence when the book is released, leaving no advocate for it inside the company during the marketing phase. It is very painful to have "one of my children" ignored, lost in the politics of a publishing house, and therefore not properly promoted and sold.

The second difficulty for me has been the promotion aspect of publishing. I've done everything—television, radio, print. I've been on *Oprah, Montel Williams, Sally Jesse Raphael,* and hundreds of local shows. I am an introvert who loves to write. My vision of being a writer was writing, not being a television star; to communicate with a reader, not a media audience. And I like to stay at home, not travel at neck-breaking speed from interview to interview back to the airport to the next hotel to the next interview. Ugh!

The most surprising thing? That publishing is a business that doesn't care one hoot about my "art"—only what sells. I have two pieces of advice. First, recognize that publishing is a business while writing is an art form. Getting published does not speak to how well you've honed your writing skills, but to how well you've honed your "getting published" skills. They are different, and published authors must be skilled in both their craft and the business of publishing.

Second, get lots of support while starting out. Know who your friends are, and when you hit disappointment or rejection, let them help you recover and try again. This is important for many reasons—first, most writers don't get published because they give up before they get in print. But those who have support are better able to withstand the obstacles. Perhaps most importantly, once you do get published, people who never noticed you before will want to be close to you, simply because they now see you as important to their ends. If you have friends who loved you when you were "nobody," you can trust them to stick by you during the inevitable ups and downs of publishing.

Perhaps the most thrilling for me was hitting the *New York Times* bestseller list a few years back. Looking at it, I'd say that most of my childhood dreams have been realized. Yet I keep discovering and creating new dreams. I've always published nonfiction and would like to try my hand at fiction, an entirely different process, so it feels like starting over again. I also would like to get into other aspects of book creation, such as painting covers (I'm a closet artist) and designing layout. Even though I have more I'd like to accomplish, I do feel satisfied with myself, like I've been blessed in my efforts. I believe that anyone who has exceptional success not only worked hard, but had help along the way.

> ...I'd say that most of my childhood dreams have been realized.

## JENNIFER BLAKE

*Jennifer Blake is the international bestselling author of over fifty books, translated into seventeen languages, with worldwide sales approaching 22 million. She made the* New York Times *bestseller list for the first time in 1977 with* Love's Wild Desire. *Other titles include* Royal Seduction, Love and Smoke, Tigress, Fierce Eden, Shameless, *and* Garden of Scandal. *A recent project has been the Turn-Coupe Trilogy, titled* Kane, Luke *and* Roan, *which examines the manners and mores of a small Louisiana community. She has received numerous awards for her work and was honored with the position of Writer-in-Residence for the University of Northeastern Louisiana. Blake has been called "the Steel Magnolia of women's fiction" and a "legend of the genre" in a career spanning three decades. Her Web site in www.jenniferblake.com.*

I love history. I might have been a history teacher if I'd taken a different path, so the historical novels have always been a joy. Many of my contemporary stories explore the dynamics of family life, something that's always been important to me. Writing in a variety of genres is lovely because it helps keep me involved creatively and is a constant challenge.

You might say that I stumbled into writing by accident. While growing up I was always in awe of writers and the kind of life they led. Still, the idea that someone basically self-educated and living in a small, isolated community might interest a publisher was beyond imagining. I was an avid reader from childhood; later, as a young mother with three preschool-age children, books became my entertainment, my solace, and my tranquilizers. Then one night I had a dream in historical context. It was so unusual that I sat down and wrote out the scenario. The process was so enthralling that I continued with it as a hobby, writing small stream-of-consciousness pieces, bits of poetry, and short stories. My first sale was a poem for which I was paid the munificent sum of one dollar. As minor as that accomplishment might have been, it represented a major validation. From then on, there was no holding me back.

> **My first sale was a poem for which I was paid the munificent sum of one dollar.**

When I was fourteen, a science teacher, Mr. Crow, made much of both my IQ test results and my ability to concoct and put a story on paper. All children know instinctively where they stand in intellectual ability compared to their classmates, but before that time I had no idea that I might be above average beyond my small rural school. The idea was disturbing then—no teenager wants to feel different. Only in retrospect do I see it as pivotal.

One or two people said privately that I'd "never do anything" with my scribbling, but most were mildly positive. It was generally seen as a harmless pastime that kept me occupied and out of trouble. The fun of it, and the clamor of the stories in my head, kept me motivated.

I was in the right place at the right time when the romance genre exploded. I'd been writing "gothic" romances set in Louisiana that featured colorful historical detail and some degree of sexual tension. The market for this kind of story went into a steep decline around 1974, not long after the publication of *The Flame & the Flower* by Kathleen Woodiwiss. Because of my writing background, I was asked to submit a proposal for this new sensual historical romance genre she'd created almost single-handedly. The story was published in 1977, just as this genre boomed, and became my first *New York Times* (NYT) bestseller.

The worst event for me was the decline of the gothic market. I'd written seven or eight of these romantic suspense stories, with steadily growing advances and sales, then the bottom dropped out. I wrote another gothic before I realized the problem, then did a paranormal mystery suspense tale, a murder mystery, a light historical on the order of a Georgette Heyer Regency novel, and a contemporary romance. Nothing sold. The dry spell lasted so long that I thought it was the end for me as a writer.

Most surprising was being met at the airport by my editor and a limousine when I flew to my first ABA convention. This was my first inkling of the true importance of making the NYT list. Until then, I was so far out of the loop in my small Louisiana town that I had little clue.

Then I realized exactly where I figured in the scheme of things while standing in an ABA publisher's suite. I, the bestselling author, was holding a pile of cocktail napkins, like a handmaiden, while L.A. Rams quarterback Jim Plunkett, who thought he might write a book, autographed them for a crowd of adoring fans.

I have chosen my topics on instinct primarily, according to what interests me as a reader and citizen of the world. That said, I'll also admit to hard thinking about what readers like and don't like, what might pique their interest in the way of unusual historical incidents or subjects of universal fascination in the media. Once or twice, I've accepted a suggestion from my agent with good results.

I've used a computer program from time to time to create characters and explore their internal and external motivation and how they apply to my plot. That's about it. I write in my office surrounded by computer, printer, scanner, copier, Caller ID, fax machine, coffee warmer, and other such devices with their miles of electrical cords. Writing was once so simple—a pen and paper and a comfortable chair. I sometimes feel something good has been lost.

> **Once or twice, I've accepted a suggestion from my agent with good results.**

Write for the joy of it. Your pleasure and fascination with the process will shine through, creating the same feelings in the reader. If it isn't fun, don't bother. It isn't worth the sheer, slogging labor; and the lack of creative spark will almost guarantee failure.

I look forward to a "golden anniversary" in the business. In the meantime, I only want to share more of the stories that clog my brain and, perhaps, a bit more of my own peculiar insight into what makes life worth living.

How do I maintain my success? Luck, instinct, persistence, and the eternal quest for the exact phrase and perfect word to say what I mean. By believing, sincerely, that the process of transferring the stories and images that I see in my mind's eye onto paper so that readers can see them, too, is the greatest joy—and the greatest job—going.

## LOREN D. ESTLEMAN

*Critically acclaimed and versatile author Loren D. Estleman has been called "the absolute best in the hard-boiled business." Since the appearance of his first novel in 1976, Estleman has published forty-two books, including the Detroit series and many historical westerns. He is best known for the Amos Walker mysteries that put him in "the top echelon of American private-eye specialists." He is also the author of* The Wister Trace, *a critical study of twenty-nine classic Western novels. His pastiches pitting Sherlock Holmes against Dracula and Jekyll and Hyde have made Estleman a cult figure among Sherlockians and horror aficionados for twenty years.*

*Estleman is an authority on both criminal history and the American West. He has been nominated for the Pulitzer Prize, the National Book Award, and the Mystery Writers of America Edgar Award. He is the recipient of seven national writing awards, including three Shamuses from the Private Eye Writers of America, and Three Golden Spurs from the Western Writers of America. He is vice president/president elect of the Western Writers of America.*

Writers are born. W. Somerset Maugham once defended his penchant for transcribing real-life events into his stories by insisting that he had no natural creative talent, but I consider this response disingenuous, as it takes creativity to recognize a compelling story and then present it in an entertaining format. Beyond that, I would say that most writers are drawn into the Life against their better judgment. Most ways of earning a living are more effective, although few are as enjoyable and satisfying.

My journalism training (six years high school and college, 12 years practical experience) has been extremely valuable. It taught me discipline, economy of language, and observation, and exposed me to a cross-section of humanity that I continue to employ almost 20 years after I left my last newspaper job.

No one tried to discourage me, although several people did urge me to develop other skills that would allow me to earn an income while waiting for my writing to pay off. I took this advice, which gave me a strong fallback position that has allowed me freedom to write what I wanted, how I wanted, without fear of starvation.

A fellow in Maine plagiarized an old story of mine some years ago. I lost a good deal of sleep thinking about him parading around on my legs, but had the great pleasure of exposing him. I consider this kind of criminal the worst, as even murderers tend to come up with their own plan, which gives them legitimate pride of authorship.

Years ago I used some observations on the recording business given me by the owner of a recording studio for a magazine interview, putting them in the mouth of a character in a novel. When the book went to audio, the company that had bought the recording rights leased his studio for the taping. When he heard his words coming out of the reader's mouth, no one would believe that he had originally spoken them until I came down to the studio and backed him up.

My mother, always one of my strongest promoters, insists upon telling supermarket clerks, doctors, and complete strangers in my presence that I'm a writer, and I have to spend the next ten minutes telling them about my work. It's like giving away puppies.

My topics generally choose me. I have more ideas than I have the life span to use. I write four to six hours per day, five days per week; weekends are optional. I use manual typewriters. I have a partnership with them that I would never find with a computer. I write in a study that I designed myself when my house was built in rural Michigan, with floor-to-ceiling bookshelves and long shallow drawers, ideal for storing manuscripts.

I attribute the fact that I write historical Westerns and contemporary crime novels to my ability to bring something fresh to each project. By alternating them, I never get bored. I refer to this phenomenon as literary crop rotation.

## SANDRA SCOPPETTONE

*Sandra Scoppettone is a successful feminist author spanning different genres, writing crime, mystery and suspense, and young adult novels. Her crime novels are* Some Unknown Person, Such Nice People, Innocent Bystanders, *and her most popular, the series featuring lesbian private investigator Lauren Laurano include* Everything You Have Is Mine, I'll Be Leaving You Always, *and* Gonna Take a Homicidal Journey. *She also writes novels for young adults such as* Trying Hard to Hear You, The Late Great Me, *and the Edgar nominee* Playing Murder. *Her mystery and suspense novels, origi-nally written under the pseudonym Jack Early, are* A Creative Kind of Killer, Razzamatazz, *and* Donato & Daughter. *In the '60s, Scop-pettone collaborated on* Suzuki Bean *and* Bang Bang You're Dead *with Louise Fitzhugh, writer of the children's classic* Harriet the Spy. *In the '70s, Scoppettone wrote the third-ever young adult novel to include gay characters,* Trying Hard to Hear You, *and the third-ever young adult novel to portray lesbians,* Happy Endings Are All Alike. *Her 1976 young adult novel about teenage alcoholism,* The Late Great Me, *was made into an Emmy award–winning After School Special and remains in print today. Her Web site is www.imt.net/~gedison/scoppett.html.*

The first two books I had published were picture books. One, called *Suzuki Bean*, is sort of famous. It was in 1961 with Louise Fitzhugh, author of *Harriet the Spy*, whom I knew personally.

Louise was an artist long before she became a writer on her own. She had a studio around the corner from me on the lower east side, and occasionally I would sit for her. And we would talk about doing a book together. One day she handed me all these drawings of Suzuki. I took them home and spread them all out on my bed. Then I sort of pasted them up, and wrote the story underneath, and sometimes there were blanks. Then I gave it back to her, and she filled in the drawings. We then did it in a more professional way, gave it to our agent, and it was sold to Doubleday in 24 hours. Of course, I thought that was the way it would be the rest of my life. We were kids then, in our twenties.

> **When *Suzuki Bean* was published, it was very well received.**

When *Suzuki Bean* was published, it was very well received. It was meant to be a book for adults, but it crossed over. Kids saw very different things in it and loved it, too. It was in print for 20 years, which was amazing. Louise and I did another book later called *Bang Bang You're Dead.* It was definitely for children, an anti-war book. Louise, I believe, was picked by the *New York Times* for best illustrations, but the book wasn't well received. The *Hornbook* hated it because kids said things like "puke-face." It's ridiculous anyone would think that way.

That was my only time with picture books. Then I went on. As a playwright, I did plays (I was an O'Neill winner in '72), television stuff (never a feature, though), and movie scripts. Then I went on to write five young adult books that were pretty groundbreaking. The first one, *Trying Hard to Hear You,* was about homosexuality (boys), so it certainly got attention. Then I wrote one about alcoholism called *The Late Great Me,* which stayed in print forever. Of course, people do accuse me of trying to write hot topics, but that isn't true. I do what interests me. I'm a recovered alcoholic (sober now for 26 years) so alcoholism interested me, especially about children. That's why I wrote it, not because it was a hot topic.

> **Of course, people do accuse me of trying to write hot topics, but that isn't true. I do what interests me.**

And I'm gay, so that interested me, too. Although I was really writing about rape, the two girls in *Happy Endings Are All Alike* happened to be lesbians. *Playing Murder,* my final young adult, was a mystery. But in between these, I did adult novels.

My favorite book, and the one that brought me a great deal of money at the time, was called *From a Nonperson.* It was my first adult novel and was based on a true case, a 1931 unsolved murder of Star Faithful. I decided to solve the crime fictionally. Two stories are going on—Star Faithful's story, on which I did a great deal of research, and another based on my father's family.

As I said, *From a Nonperson* brought a great deal of money, but critically, forget it! Bad. Rona Jaffe reviewed it in *The New York Times* Sunday section. She didn't slam it, but wasn't enthusiastic. It didn't sell that well, but had already been bought in paperback; that's how I made the money. It was published in such a sleazy way, you wouldn't believe it, but it's been sold all over the world. Everything I wrote then was crime-oriented, always my interest.

Then I went into a writer's block for about two years. I don't know what happened, but suddenly the voice of this first-person private-eye male, Fortune Cinelli, came into my head. I decided to write under another name, especially because it was first-person male. (Men seem to get away with this, but women don't.) I chose the name Jack Early and wrote *A Creative Kind of Killer*. No one, except my agent and my editor, knew who Jack Early was. And interestingly enough, it was nominated for an Edgar, and a Shamus, which is a private-eye thing, and won. It got wonderful reviews, as if I were writing differently, but I wasn't. You know what I'm saying . . . . Of course, there's no way to prove it, but it's pretty suspicious. The second Jack Early book was *Razzamatazz*. It got rave reviews and Jack Early was likened to Elmore Leonard and all kinds of others. No one would have said, "Sandra Scoppettone is like Elmore Leonard." Never! I obviously did not accept the award in person. By the time I wrote Early's next book, it leaked who I was. It was made into a television movie, unfortunately, though Dana Delaney was wonderful in it. Then I had another little lapse, sort of a writer's block, for a year or so.

I wanted my name back, so I wrote the first of the Lauren Laurano series, about a lesbian private eye. It was the right time for that to be published—the beginning of lesbians being acceptable for a minute.

I was lucky enough to publish five books in that series before that fifteen minutes was over. When I wrote the fifth book, I knew it would be the last. I never intended it to be a series. Then it was picked up as a series, exposed me (in a good way), and sold all over the world. Cybill

Shepherd wanted to make a film of it but, of course, couldn't get anyone to do it because happy lesbians are not acceptable.

I didn't want to write anymore. I find writing a series absolutely a nightmare. Even before I wrote a series, I said nobody should write more than four because it really gets stale. I don't think my fifth book is very good. Writing about the same people over and over again is so boring—not challenging in any way. I'm writing another book, a non-series piece, and I have to go back to using a pseudonym (I'm not going to tell you what it is) because I'm now associated with lesbian novels. Isn't that nice? Also, I will do better financially because everything is by the numbers now. No matter how good my next book is, if I put it under my own name (let's forget the lesbian part of it), whoever is interested in it would ask Little Brown, who published the Lauren Laurano series, what my sales figures were and decide what to give me as an advance. It has nothing to do with the work. It's disgusting. And you can quote me on that.

## ZILPHA KEATLEY SNYDER

*Zilpha Keatley Snyder is an award-winning writer of children's books. She is the recipient of three Newbery Honor Book awards for* The Egypt Game, The Headless Cupid, *and* The Witches of Worm. *Since her first book,* A Season of Ponies, *was published in 1964, she has published thirty-six stories. Her audience is primarily children ages nine to thirteen, but she's published two books for young adults, four picture books for younger children, and a book of poetry. Her titles have been named as Notable Books by the American Library Association, Best Books by the School Library Journal, and have also been honored by the American Library Guild. In addition,* The Witches of Worm *was nominated for the National Book Award,* The Headless Cupid *was the U.S. selection for the international Hans Christian Andersen Honors List, and* The Egypt Game *was awarded First Prize in the* New York Herald Tribune *Spring Book Festival.* The Changeling *and* The Headless Cupid *received Christopher Medals from the Catholic Educators of America, and* The Headless Cupid *was voted to receive the William Allen White Award by schoolchildren in Kansas. Her books have been published in translation in thirteen foreign countries. Her Web site is www.microweb.com/lsnyder/home.html.*

I just finished my thirty-sixth book. I don't write anything but fiction if I can possibly help it, because for me the fun of writing is letting your imagination become real. Some of my books that are out now are fantasy—sort of borderline fantasy, fairly realistic but with a touch of the mysterious. Others are entirely realistic, but even those have some mystery, something outside the usual. I've just always liked that kind of ambiance so I have books set in the Middle Ages, a trilogy set in the future, and pretty much everything between.

My best-known books are the three Newbery Honor Books: *The Egypt Game, The Headless Cupid,* and *The Witches of Worm.* Three other books are about the family in *The Headless Cupid.* My more recent well-known books are *Cat Running,* which came out about four years ago and has done very well; *The Trespassers;* and *Libby on Wednesday,* inspired by meeting kids at school who were serious writers. I like to have a small session with those who write not because it's an assignment; the teachers know who they are. All five main characters in that book are loosely based on kids I've met when visiting schools. My husband has the nonfiction gene, so I twist his arm to do my business letters.

> **I had always thought I would write what we all think we're going to write— The Great American Novel.**

My educational background for writing comes from being an avid reader since a very early age: good, bad, and indifferent. If it's there and legible, I read it. That was a big help in my writing because, even if you don't realize it, you absorb writing techniques as you read. As far as formal education, I took journalism and all the literature courses in college, but never had a course called creative writing. Towards the end of my college years I realized I better not depend on writing to make a living right out of college, so I prepared to teach. I taught school for nine years, during which time I got married and had kids of my own.

The way I sold my first book was rather unusual (I don't think it would happen nowadays). The last year I taught school was the first time I thought of writing for kids. I had always thought I would write what we all think we're going to write—The Great American Novel. But suddenly, I thought it would be fun to write something for my class that year—the kind of book I would have liked at that age. I couldn't decide between two favorites: horse stories (I grew up with horses, so they have always been terribly important to me) and my favorite kind of fantasy—the kind often done well in England, where the story starts realistically and the next thing you know, you're sliding into some sort of fantasy world.

I wound up writing both at once—a manuscript about magic horses. I showed it to our school librarian, who was much more knowledgeable about children's literature than I was. I sent it to one place and never sent it anywhere else. It isn't quite as grand as that, though, because what I got from the editor at first was a long, long letter telling me what was wrong with it—it wasn't really long enough for the age level, but was more a long short story. She liked a lot of things about it, such as character development, and made all kinds of suggestions. At the end she had written, "We are interested in what you're doing here, and since you are working on it more, we'd like to see it again." Of course, I was delighted. And two rather complete rewrites later, it was accepted and published. I never did receive a form rejection slip.

When I won my first Newbery award in 1967, I think my editor called to tell me. I remember her saying not to talk about it for twenty-four hours because it was going to be formally announced or something. I was very pleased, but too new to children's literature and not exposed enough to the New York publishing world to be as elated as I might have been.

I always remember holding that first printed book in my hands with a great deal of pleasure. Letters from kids. A kind of feeling of serendipity when you are writing along and experience a breakthrough, an epiphany when you suddenly have a new insight into what you're doing and can't trace it to anything in your background. It is an exciting feeling—one of the nicest things about writing as far as I'm concerned.

I have had books where the initial kickoff idea came from a dream, most often a dream I had as a child. Several books have come from memories of games I played when I was a child. I had games for everything—to get the chores done so they wouldn't be so boring, for walking to school. I entertained myself by taking an interesting bit of reality, my reality, and building upon it that sometimes got me into trouble. My mother used to say, "Just tell it; don't embroider it!" I have written books that started from brief meetings with an interesting kid, such as Amanda, a particular girl who at the time was very angry at the world, at her parents, and was using her interest in the supernatural to sort of get even with them. That is pretty much what Amanda in *The Headless Cupid* was doing. Alex in *Libby on Wednesday* is quite close to the boy who inspired the character. I always expected to hear from them saying, "Hey, did I have anything to do with this?" But I never have.

I visit bookstores, go to librarian conventions and children's literature conventions around the country, but I'm trying to cut back. After all, my first book came out in '64. I am just finishing something now, then will take a long vacation—clean out closets and that sort of thing. But generally after about two or three weeks, I get antsy and start writing again. I somehow feel better when I'm writing. It's not only a great hobby and escape, but if you can't sleep because you're worrying about something, you just say, "Well, I'll

> **I always remember holding that first printed book in my hands with a great deal of pleasure.**

think about that tomorrow, and in the meantime, I'll think about what's going to happen next in my story." I look forward to my next good idea and kickoff point.

My reader response has been wonderful. In the last year or two, I have been getting a lot of e-mail from readers. About half the time, they are older readers who find my Web page and discover I have an e-mail address. Perhaps they read my books a long time ago and write to tell me about that. They wouldn't take the time to write unless they'd been real fans. I get funny e-mail letters, too. For example, I got a letter from a middle school boy asking me to send him a very, very, very long summary of one of my books. Then he said, "I'd read it myself, but I don't have the time." So I wrote back and said something to the effect of "I don't have time to write your book report." I didn't hear back from him.

> **But generally after about two or three weeks, I get antsy and start writing again.**

I think the most important thing is to read—all kinds of things. And if you are really serious, read a story through just for fun and excitement, then go back and notice things like dialogue and how the writer gets a character from one place to another. Notice transitions and how they explain the character, not by saying that he has a bad temper, but by showing it. Another thing that has been very helpful to me over the years—I have met kids who are doing this—is to form a small support group. Find two or three others who are serious writers and set up a time to meet and read what you're working on to each other and critique it. I think journal-keeping is also a good idea—not the kind where you have to write every day, which is usually not very creative (you find yourself writing mundane things about the weather and what you had for dinner). I mean the kind in which you write about important events in your life, or what makes you feel strongly. Usually, it is a secret journal when you do that.

## MARGARET CHITTENDEN

*Maragret Chittenden is the author of* How to Write Your Novel *and 28 suspense, mystery, romance, and mainstream titles. She has written three children's books and over 100 short stories and articles. Her latest mystery series,* The Charlie Plato Mystery Series, *features continuing characters with different ethnic backgrounds. The books in the series are* Dying to Sing, Dead Men Don't Dance, Dead Beat and Deadly, *and* Don't Forget to Die *(recently released in July 1999). Her novels have made* Waldenbooks *and* B. Dalton's *bestseller lists, and have been reprinted abroad. A noted lecturer, Chittenden has spoken at writers' and readers' gatherings in Washington; British Columbia; Oregon; Massachusetts; New York; California; Illinois; Nevada; Texas; Minnesota; Hawaii; Washington, D.C.; and Japan. She is a member of Mystery Writers of America, American Crime Writers League, International Association of Crime Writers, Romance Writers of America, Sisters in Crime, and DorothyL, the online mystery digest. She is on the faculty of the Hollywood Network and writes a column for* Murderous Intent Mystery Magazine. *Her Web site is www.techline.com/~megc/biopage.html.*

I started writing short stories and poems when I was six. I always wanted to be a writer, but was such a worshipful reader, I thought writers lived on Mount Olympus with all the other gods and an ordinary person couldn't be one. When I found out that wasn't true, I became one!

Winston Churchill said, "I got into my bones the essential structure of the ordinary British sentence—which is a noble thing." I grew up in England and my education gave me the same advantage.

Mostly, nobody encouraged me. Though I did well in English composition and short story writing, nobody ever suggested I could be a writer. There were the naysayers who said that nobody's accepting articles from unknowns right now, nobody's publishing short stories, and so on.

I sold the first article I wrote, "The Legends of Easter," to the Sunday supplement of my local newspaper, saw my byline and was hooked. I didn't sell another thing for a year, but figured if I did it once I could do it again. Plus, I wanted it badly! When I didn't sell any more, I wrote "The Story of Santa Claus." That sold, so I wrote about New Year's Day, April Fool's Day, and Hallowe'en. This led to my being asked to write a children's book on "Merrymaking in Great Britain," as part of an around-the-world holiday series.

When I wrote short stories for children, I chose topics that came up in talks with my children—things of interest to them. When I wrote romance, I went to places I'd always wanted to visit and looked around for stories. I was convinced stories were waiting for me in all major places of interest in the world; I just had to go there and find them. So I'd interview police officers and newspaper reporters and people I ran into, and the story would develop from those things.

Now that I'm writing a mystery series, I use things that happened to me or my family or friends, or that I read about in the newspapers or magazines. The first mystery began with an earthquake in the San Francisco Bay area—my daughter was living there at the time. Fissures opened up in the earth. I could imagine a skeleton popping up in one. My daughter's pet rabbit was scared stiff, literally, so the rabbit went into the book. I've always written from life, though everything gets changed to fit the story.

The funniest thing that happened to me (comparatively early in my career) was that my daughter's orthodontist asked me how many books I'd sold. "Five," I said. There was silence, then he said, "Well, maybe you'll sell more next time."

The best thing that happened? I got published! I got an agent! I've been able to keep writing for the last twenty-nine years!

The most embarrassing thing was sending one of my short stories to *Alfred Hitchcock Mystery Magazine.* I thought it had a really neat twist ending. When it came back, I saw a written note on the rejection slip. I got very excited, as I'd heard that was a good sign you were getting close. It said, "Were we supposed to be surprised?" Makes me blush every time I think of it.

I strongly believe in sticking to a writing schedule, though sometimes life interferes and I have to bow to it. I aim at working from 10 A.M. to 5 P.M. five days a week, with a break for lunch. I've done that for 29 years. I look upon writing as an art, a craft, a business, and a job. I don't believe in waiting for the muse to visit me; she's more likely to visit when I'm actually writing.

I started out using a yellow legal pad and a ballpoint pen. I wrote a lot of articles and short stories and three books that way, typing them up when I was finished, then editing them on the typewriter. Finally, I realized this was not very professional, so I made myself switch to composing on a typewriter—first a manual, then a portable electric, then an IBM. Then I switched to a dedicated word processor, when they first came out, and finally to a computer. I love computers. I have one for work (writing); one for communications and making promotion items and checking out stuff on the Web; and a laptop. I also own two scanners, a laser printer, a color inkjet printer, a fax machine, and a copier. My office looks like the command deck of the starship Enterprise.

I started out with a small desk in the corner of the master bedroom and graduated fairly quickly to a small room of my own. For the last ten years I've had a large office that we built over our garage. When I need a break, I wander around looking out at a small freshwater canal, trees, a lot of ducks, geese, pheasants, occasional beavers, and deer. But I could probably write in a tent. I've been known to plug my laptop into our car's cigarette lighter and persuade my husband to drive around while I finish the last few pages of a book during a power outage, after using up the batteries.

> **I've always written from life, though everything gets changed to fit the story.**

I hope to be sitting in front of my keyboard writing until the moment I die. I hope to try other kinds of books. I've always liked variety. I'd like to do more short stories. And I'd like to keep writing on my mystery series as long as somebody wants to read it. And there's always that *New York Times* bestseller list to aim for!

I hope to maintain my success by working hard, by keeping up with what's going on in the book world (easier now that we have the Internet), getting out and promoting, speaking at conventions, doing signings, sending out promotional materials, being accessible for interviews, and answering *all* fan mail.

> **Revise, revise, revise until you are sure your work is as good as you can do.**

Write what you want to write, but be prepared to tailor it for the market if you want someone else to read it. Create a place where you write, so that when you go there you automatically feel like writing. Try to write every day in the beginning—even if it's only a page or so. Write the very best you can at all times. Make sure your grammar and spelling are correct. Don't rely on spell checkers, and never use software grammar checkers. Revise, revise, revise until you are sure your work is as good as you can do. Research the marketplace. Then send your stuff out and keep sending it out until there's nowhere left to send it. Never, never give up.

## ELIZABETH WINTHROP

*Elizabeth Winthrop has written more than 45 fiction books for children of all ages and one nonfiction picture book. She has garnered many awards for her outstanding work.* The Castle in the Attic *and* The Battle for the Castle, *two of her novels for middle readers, have been nominated for over 20 state book awards. She is also the author of two novels for adults,* In My Mother's House *and* Island Justice. *Her books have been translated into many languages and five have been selections of the Junior Library Guild. She twice won the PEN Syndicated Fiction Contest as well as the Open Voice Award for her short stories, and "Golden Daughters" was included in Best American Short Stories in 1992. She has a Web site at http://www.absolute-sway.com/winthrop.*

My best-known book in the children's field is *The Castle in the Attic*, a time travel book for eight- to twelve-year-olds. It was nominated for 23 state book awards, and won in Vermont and California. It sold well over a million copies and is optioned for the movies. It's the story of a boy who goes back in time to the thirteenth century to rescue someone he cares about. It was published in 1985, when whole language was introduced to the classroom. It is read in the classroom, which gave the book a huge boost. I've done 10 years of touring to support the book and to talk about all of my books—at school visits and so on.

I received a lot of fan mail asking me to write a sequel, so about eight years later, I published *The Battle for the Castle*, about the same characters with a different problem. Now they're clamoring for a third book, which I am pretty sure I will do, but it's not on the front burner right now. I also have a very popular book called *Shoes*, a board book for very young children. It's also published in cassette and book form, and in a big book for teachers. It's a rhyming book—very simple rhymes for two- to four-year-olds, with illustrations by William Joyce. "Shoes for sliding; shoes for hiding; High top shoes for horseback riding." A funny thing about me is that I truly write for all ages.

I was born into a family of writers. I love to tell the children that I have a great, great uncle who wrote 37 books and also happened to be President of the United States—Theodore Roosevelt. His sister, my great grandmother, was a published poet. My grandmother wrote all sorts of journals, letters, and columns. My father was a journalist (he wrote the back page of *Newsweek*). My uncle was a syndicated columnist. I have a huge tradition in the family. I think what influenced me most was coming home from school in the afternoons and hearing my father's old Underwood typewriter. I thought, he doesn't have to go to an office, people come to see him, he interviews people, he thinks, he writes. This is a cushy job! (My father wanted to brain me with the typewriter when I said that!) I lived with a man who supported six children as a writer so it seemed a very viable profession to me. I also loved to tell stories. I told stories well verbally, but writing let me tell them on paper.

I went right through Sarah Lawrence, taking one writing course after another and studied with people like Grace Paley, E. L. Doctorow, and Jane Cooper. That was a real encouragement to me, made me feel I was in a viable profession.

I had published ten to 15 books by 1985, but *Castle in the Attic* popped me up into the top. It definitely pushed my career to a new level. My greatest thing is having my two children in their 20s think it's fun to tell friends that I wrote *Castle in the Attic*.

A lot of writers, in the beginning and often throughout their lives, write and teach. I teach occasionally at writers' conferences, but have found that the children's books balance the longer projects for adults. For example, right now I'm starting a new novel for adults, but I may well write a couple of picture books so I have a project finished; I send it in, get a contract, and get some money in. Also, children's books sell much, much longer than adult books. They stay in print—not as long as they used to, sadly enough, but longer than adult books do. They are still available in hardback a couple years after you publish them, which is also not true of adult books.

My worst thing is cosmic. It's what's happened to publishing. That's truly what I despair about. The gross change, the increased power. I really support and care deeply about independent bookstores because I think they have sold my books better than anybody has. They sell books because they really read them, not because the publishers pay them to put books in the front window. I have to admit that I'm quite discouraged by the situation as it now stands. I'm glad I'm not trying to make it as a writer now. I'm glad I have an established reputation.

When you go out and visit schools, one of the toughest things is facing a group of 150 kids. I love kids, and I have terrific crowd control skills, but I've found that children are incredibly literal and don't forget small details the way copy editors do. I once went down to Texas, and a little boy in the learning disabled group raised his hand and said, "I want to know why in your book *Lizzie and Harold,* Lizzie has green shoes. And on all the other pages, Lizzie has black shoes." The illustrator, by mistake, had left off one of the overlays. Nobody caught it—not me, not the illustrator, not the copy editor, not the editor. I actually had the editor write him a letter, suggesting that he might want to be a copy editor when he grows up. There are often small inconsistencies that children can catch.

> **I told stories well verbally, but writing let me tell them on paper.**

There's a little bit of me in every character I write, a little bit of me in every villain and every hero. To be able to write a book, I must imagine myself into the head of the character, walk in their shoes a mile. If I cannot do that, then I cannot write the book. Someone suggested I do a woman very high up in the corporate ladder who was being dissed by her fellow workers. It did not appeal to me because I was never in that position. I couldn't imagine myself into her shoes. I've noticed that most characters in my adult novels are their own bosses. That's the kind of life I live—I am my own boss—so in that way, they grab me.

Setting is also very important to me. I have to be able to bring myself into a certain setting—a house of my grandmother's, an attic, the house of my childhood. This creates problems because people often think that if you use a setting that's familiar to them, people who walked around on that setting are the characters in the novel. It's not true. It confuses a lot of readers and is frustrating for a lot of writers. If you make the setting absolutely real on West Something[th]

Street in Manhattan and make the character of the doorman a certain way, that doesn't mean it's my doorman. It's a complicated issue.

When I'm on a book, I work best in the morning. It's not actually an hourly schedule. It's a page schedule. I play a little game with myself. If I write five pages, I'm fine. If I write ten, it doesn't count for the next day, but if I write three, I have to make up two the next day. I am my own boss, so I set my own schedule and deadlines. I don't work that well under deadline, either. I tend to write my books, then try to sell them, which is the despair of my agent, I'm sure. But it makes me feel creatively free and sovereign to do it that way. It may not be smart financially, but it holds the most integrity for me.

> It's what's happened to publishing. That's truly what I despair about.

I use a journal. I write for thirty minutes before I get out of bed, which is a tool I picked up from *The Artist's Way,* the Morning Pages. I thought it would diminish what I wrote during the day, but I've found that it clears out a lot of the junk that has accumulated during the night. I go to museums, and I took painting courses, which fed my creativity in a different way. I also write in a journal in a different way, where I talk to myself, noting a book I want to read or describing a character, because it keeps my skills up. It's a way of practicing my craft.

For children's books, I've done school tours. I created a Web site, a huge project to provide all the content, and had some terrific Web site designers. It's a living, breathing thing. I've learned that you have to keep it current so people will keep visiting. I went into it with trepidation, because I didn't want it to take away from my writing. I write a newsletter for kids and one for adults—in an erratic sort of way—and probably will write them for a year. I'll talk about the state of publishing, what I'm working on, my struggles as a writer. I've done an enormous amount of thinking about groups that would be interested in my books who might not normally get them because they're fiction. For example, *Island Justice* is about emotional abuse, so I contacted domestic violence organizations and alerted them to the book, and many talked about the book in their newsletters. I think the book did well because it had that kind of support behind it, not just the publisher's. But it took so much time that I hope I don't have to do it again.

Readers have responded with enthusiasm and disarming honesty. The best ones are always the kids who say, "I liked *The Castle in the Attic,* but I didn't like the rest of your books." I sometimes get letters from people who are very upset about my topics; they wish I would write happier topics.

For my next book, I'd like to go short and deep—try to make it more focused, shorter (250 pages), and go deeper with two characters rather than dealing with a whole cast. Also, huge sales. Honestly, I would like my name to be as well known in the adult field as it is in the children's fields.

## CHARLES GHIGNA

*Charles Ghigna, also known as Father Goose, is an award-winning poet, author, and nationally syndicated feature writer. He has written more than twenty books for children and adults.* Returning to Earth *was nominated for a Pulitzer Prize in 1990. Other titles include* Plastic Soup: Dream Poems, Speaking in Tongues: New and Selected Poems, Wings of Fire, Father Songs, *and* Riddle Rhymes, *which received a full-page, color review in* The New York Times *and was, along with* Tickle Day, *the American Booksellers Association's "Pick of the List." Ghigna's poems for adults have appeared in hundreds of literary magazines and anthologies. His translated poetry appears in Italy, Germany, France, and Russia, and his verse has been featured on national radio and television programs. His poems for children appear in* Cricket, Highlights for Children, Ranger Rick, *and many other publications for young readers. He has received numerous honors in addition to the Pulitzer Prize nomination. His Web site is www.inkspot.com/author/ghigna/who.html.*

I think I always wanted to be a writer, but didn't know it. I wrote a silly story in the third grade about a talking freckle on a boy's face. My teacher made a big deal about it. My parents used to make me stand in front of the couch and read it to their friends who came to visit. The story caught on and kept getting longer. I was finally invited to read it on the air at the local TV station. When I got back to school some of the kids made fun of me. I stopped writing and started playing baseball all through high school and on the local American Legion Team. I loved baseball. I even went to spring training camp in Fort Myers, Florida, and tried out with the Pittsburgh Pirates. I'm still waiting to hear from them.

Besides that wonderful third-grade teacher who liked my freckle story, I had a very good high school English teacher who let us do a lot of creative writing. By the time I entered college, I had developed a love of literature, particularly poetry, and could recite many poems of Frost, Millay, Teasdale, Wylie, Sandburg, and others.

**Get yourself a notebook and write in it every night for two weeks. Then stop—if you can.**

Most people, including my family and friends, did not know for many years that I enjoyed writing poems every night. I began keeping a journal in high school. After a few weeks I became hooked, staying up late most every night writing my private thoughts in my journal. I kept it under my bed and pulled it out after everyone in the house was asleep. I even took it with me when I camped out or spent the night at a friend's house. It became like a best friend to whom I could tell all my secrets.

The best thing was getting a poem published in *Harper's* while I was a student in the writing program at Florida State University. The next best was having a book of my poems nominated for a Pulitzer Prize. The third was getting a four-book contract from the Walt Disney Company to write children's books. But the greatest thing of all is having a loving wife and two wonderfully inspiring children.

The worst thing? The death of my mother. She was the most inspiring, creative kid in the world. She taught me how to look at things and how to have fun with language—and with life.

The most surprising? Discovering a poem of mine was made into a jingle and aired on ABC's *Good Morning America.*

And the funniest? Listening to children try to pronounce my last name!

My topics tend to choose me. And I'm glad they do! I like writing about nature, animals, sports, and the joys of childhood.

I write every day—almost all day—whenever and wherever I can. Besides the computer, I used lots of yellow legal pads, notepads, scratch paper, hotel stationery, and anything else I can get my hands on quickly. I also like using dark #2 pencils, and buy black Stanford Calligraphic pens by the dozens. I don't try to do the neat calligraphy with them; I just like the way the words look playful and bold on the paper. I write everywhere—mostly at my computer or on the rolltop desk next to my computer desk. I also write a lot on the pad beside my bed, on yellow legal pads while waiting in airports, and in the car while waiting to pick up my son from school and from sporting events.

Here's some advice for aspiring authors: Get yourself a notebook and write in it *every* night for two weeks. Then stop—if you can. If you can't, you're a writer. And no one, no matter how hard they may try, will ever be able to stop you from following your writing dreams. Enjoy those dreams. Follow them. Make new ones. Share them. Write of your passions, your loves, your fears, your joys. Find your writer's voice by listening deep inside. It's that little voice that says in a low, soft whisper, "Listen to this . . . "

I look forward to continuing this magic carpet ride for as long and as far as it will take me. Writing, especially for children, is one of the most honorable professions in the world, one of the few that allows you to dream, encourages you to dream, and to capture those dreams on paper and to make them come alive in the minds and hearts of others.

I do a program for schools called the Poems and Pranks of Father Goose, and a lot of talks for teachers and librarians. I do three or four a month, 30 or 40 a year. I visit the schools and do two programs of my show, which is anywhere from 45 minutes to an hour, depending on the age group—usually assembly programs in front of large groups of kids, sometimes in front of bleachers in a gymnasium. I literally start acting out my poems, tell them how the ideas came about, and let them know that poetry can be about anything and everything, and isn't just for sissies and grandmothers anymore. I do two shows then spend the rest of the day in the library as classes come in. The teachers bring the children in with little sticky notes with their name and the books, which I sign to them personally. I have been doing so many lately that schools prefer that I send four or five hundred bookplates before I get there. I usually do that in my spare time, while I wait for my computer to boot up, and when I get to the schools they can peel those off and stick them inside the book. Rather than spending all that time signing, I can use the afternoon for visiting, and doing questions and answers, which is a lot of fun. And sometimes as a follow-up, I do workshops with teachers to teach them how to get started. Some of the same tips are on the Classroom Fun page of my Web site.

I get a lot of feedback because I am at schools all the time and they usually read the books before I get there. I have sacks and sacks of really nice e-mails and letters I send to a collection archive at the end of each year. They keep all my manuscripts, letters, and correspondence—anything that has to do with my writing—which is nice.

I don't think I ever sat down and said, "Boy, I would like to be a poet." I can hear my father saying, "You're going to be a what?" Actually it was about in tenth grade that I really fell in love with poetry. I wrote a love poem to a girl, and she gave me a kiss on the cheek. I thought, "Poems are a good thing." I do my poetry in print to tell kids that we all have a poet inside us that wants to come out and see the long-tailed dragons and the flying ships, rather than just cumulus and cirrus clouds. So I really got started in the tenth grade. I became like the little boy who couldn't go to sleep until he said his prayers, only I couldn't go to sleep until I wrote in my journal. I tell kids who ask if they can be a writer, "It's a real simple task: buy a journal, keep it under your bed, and pull it out just before you go to sleep every night. Write whatever you want for ten or fifteen minutes (don't worry about spelling or punctuation, just write!) and put down a time and a date. Let it be like a best friend you can tell your secrets to.

What I have been writing for thirty years, mostly University Press collections of poems that nobody ever reads, are anthologized in a lot of good books and published in some nice magazines like *Harper's*. But a couple of years after my son was born, I started dabbling with children's poems and sending them out. It is interesting that I have been writing all my life for the adult market (actually, literary publications is really not a market) and my day job was as a teacher, but I went to writing for very young children. Now there is this no-man's-land (in regard to poetry) called young adult; very few books of poetry are written for the ten to 14 or 16—not quite adult—market. They still want to

> I wrote a love poem to a girl, and she gave me a kiss on the cheek. I thought, "Poems are a good thing."

hear about subjects that interest them, but in a more mature way than little rhymy poems (I shouldn't call them that because I put my heart and soul into those!). They are ready for free verse, but with a nice melody and a poetic surprise.

For my newest book, I chose sports heroes, some of whom have been sort of unsung, and have written portraits of them in poetry. I write it in present tense, as though they were still alive.

It is easier for me to write poetry than prose. I guess I'm backwards from most people. Here is a poem that will also be anthologized in the new Random House, or Knopf 20th Century

Treasury of Children's Literature: "She takes you to the fields and shores, to anywhere you please, follow it and trust your way, with mind and heart as one, and when the journey's over, you find you've just begun."

## PATRICIA RUSHFORD

*Patricia Rushford is the author of some 32 books in fiction and non-fiction. Most are self-help books dealing with issues such as parenting, women's issues, and aging parents. She started writing in her 30s as therapy to help her through a difficult time. Therapy turned into a career when her first book,* Have You Hugged Your Teenager Today, *was published within her first year of writing. Rushford has degrees in counseling and nursing, and feels this gives her the opportunity to help people in difficult life situations. She credits writer's conferences with helping her develop her skills in creating characters with depth and stories with a high level of realism.*

I always loved to read, but never considered myself a writer or a storyteller. I began writing while I was in my 30s and had gone through depression. While trying to play the role of superwoman, going too fast and flying too high, I suffered massive burnout. That's when I began writing poetry. I never considered writing as a career, only therapy, but I got hooked and felt God was pulling me in that direction. I attended some writer's conferences to learn the business and within a year sold my first book, *Have You Hugged Your Teenager Today.*

My own insecurity as to whether or not I could make it was probably the greatest hindrance to my writing. But I promised myself and God I'd give it a shot, and look what happened.

What kept me motivated? Money. Deadlines. That and encouragement from others and editors who wanted more books. For fiction it was a matter of just plain wanting to write mysteries.

Selling my first book and realizing I could do it was the best thing that happened. My editor was wonderful and actually taught me how to write a book. I would send chapters in and he would send me tapes—editing, encouraging, telling me to back off on the lectures and tell more stories.

The worst was realizing that having a book come out didn't mean instant success. It's a wonderful feeling to have a book come out—like having a baby. Then you realize not everyone is interested in your baby. I was also disappointed to learn that a lot of the promotion falls to you. Two of my books, *Have You Hugged Your Teenager Today* and *What Kids Need Most in a Mom* ended up being good consistent sellers. The teen book stayed in print from 1983 to 1995. The publisher released it

> **I never considered writing as a career, only therapy . . .**

again just last year and it continues to sell well. The mom's book was published in 1986 and never went out of print. I recently undated it, to be released in time for Mother's Day.

I took great pride in going to the library and looking my first published book up in the card catalogue. I had a Library of Congress number and was under contract for two more books. I held my head high and felt an air of self-importance—until I felt a cool rush of air just below my belt line as I walked outside. My zipper was open. Pride goeth before the fall.

I chose my nonfiction topics by simply looking at publishers' as well as people's needs. The need for new and updated parenting books and how-tos on all kinds of subjects is always there. The key is to find a hole and fill it. For fiction, I just plug into ideas floating in my brain. Sometimes it's triggered by an article I've read, or the story ideas just pop in.

I have a desktop and a laptop. On warm days I go outside with my laptop. Rainy days I snuggle in my recliner. I use the laptop for the more creative and new writing and the desktop (office) for editing.

The best advice is just to do it and don't be afraid of rejection. Know that rejection letters are part of the business; don't let them be a hindrance. Becoming a writer is generally not accomplished overnight. It takes time and perseverance and lots of hard work.

## The key is to find a hole and fill it. For fiction, I just plug into ideas floating in my brain.

Keep your name out there. I have done mailings, book signings, flyers, and have joined organizations such as Sisters in Crime, Mystery Writers of America, Romance Writers of America, and Society of Children's Book Writer's and Illustrators. I also do a lot of speaking and teaching at conferences. Publicity never hurts.

But along with that, it's important to take time out and take care of yourself and your family. I've been known to write to the exclusion of everything else and have to back off occasionally.

## CHAPTER 2

# The Heavyweights

The heavyweights. They are often household names. They have a devoted following of fans who wait anxiously for their books to come out. Like Barry Sears and Dave Pelzer, they have books that stay on the bestseller lists for enviable periods of time. Like Nelson DeMille and Lois Duncan, they have movies made of their books starring celebrities. The vocabulary from their books become part of the daily lexicon, like Mark Victor Hansen's *Chicken Soup for the Soul.* Like Charlotte Vale Allen, their books sell in the millions. They have been on *Oprah*—more than once. The Heavyweights are the authors every aspiring writer wants to be.

The Heavyweights all remember the moment they felt they had made it. Nelson DeMille first felt he had made it "big" when "our guys auctioned my manuscript and said to me, 'Sit down.'"

Naura Hayden remembers the first time she was on the *New York Times* bestseller list. "It was like a dream. I never thought it would happen. I was on cloud nine. The *New York Times* is the peak—when you know you have made it to the top."

"I had already decided that even if my book didn't make the bestseller's list, I was going to celebrate—reward myself for writing a great book," says John Gray. "So I bought a new car and went on vacation. Then on vacation I went out to get the paper—every Sunday I check the bestseller's list—and my car was dinged, a dent in the side. So I picked up the paper and thought, "So what if my car has a ding? I'm a bestselling author!"

The Heavyweights may have made it big, but they don't take their success for granted. "Authors do not make themselves bestselling authors," says Dave Pelzer. "It is the audience—the people who read the books, the folks in Norfolk, Virginia, or Hayes, Kansas, or the backwoods of Florida."

## JOHN GRAY

*John Gray, Ph.D., is author of the runaway bestseller* Men Are from Mars, Women Are from Venus, *which has sold more than six million copies in the United States and millions more in 40 different languages. Other Mars and Venus books include . . . in the Bedroom, . . . Together Forever, . . . in Love, . . . on a Date, . . . Starting Over, and . . . Book of Days. His newest book,* How to Get What You Want and Want What You Have, *incorporates material he presented on Oprah's "Personal Success" series. An internationally recognized expert in communications, relationships, and personal growth, Gray is a popular speaker and frequently appears on radio and on television shows, including* Oprah, Good Morning America, The Today Show, Politically Incorrect, Larry King Live, *and many others. He has been profiled in numerous newspapers and magazines, including* Time, USA Weekend, TV Guide, People, *and* New Age Journal. *In 1997, his work was the focus of a two-hour ABC special, "Men Are from Mars, Women Are from Venus, But We Have to Live on Earth," hosted by Barbara Walters. Gray's syndicated column,* Mars and Venus, *is published in a number of U.S. newspapers. His Web site is www.marsvenus.com/aboutJG.html.*

I self-published a few books before *Men Are from Mars.* Then an agent saw that my books sell, found me, and sent me to New York to write *Men Are from Mars, Women Are from Venus.* I went on the *New York Times* bestseller list—in the top four slots—and never went off for four years. Six months before that I went on the *Pub-*

*lisher's Weekly* list at number 13. I remember exactly when that happened. There had been an Oprah show, and they were expecting a big response. The book had been a slow starter, and the publisher was ready to put it out in paperback and can it. Then it hit that spot and I was so happy—I mean *so* happy. I thought, it's going to have a chance, it's going to have a life! It was on that bestseller list for four weeks, and the whole time, they were out of print. You can't have a book out of print in hardback when it's on a bestseller's list!

> **The book had been a slow starter, and the publisher was ready to put it out in paperback and can it.**

That was in August, and they had printed paperbacks for January that they were ready to release. I said, "No! My book was a bestseller in hardback, and you have no right to do this." So they printed some in hardback. They did get a bunch of orders in January but none in the fall because it was out of print. Then I had a *Phil Donahue Show,* and the book went right on the list. I could never find it in bookstores. I'd ask when they would be getting more in, and they would say, "Well, it's no longer in hardback. It's going to be in paperback in a few months." The bookstores were simply waiting for it.

This actually turned in my favor because it was a very strong word-of-mouth book and people wanted it. I think there was a certain alchemy between people wanting it and it not being available. People wanted it more. My agent told me that being sold out can be really good because it creates more desire for the book. It can be the opposite. If bookstores have huge stacks of books nobody is buying, they think the book isn't selling, so send them right back.

What bookstores think about your book has a lot to do with whether people buy. If people keep asking for a book the store doesn't have, they call other bookstores to see who does have it. That creates this perceived demand. It sounds like everybody wants this book because one person or ten people are calling around looking for it. But I was extremely frustrated. I had a bestseller, and where were all the books?

I was never a good writer in school. I didn't like writing and never thought I'd do anything that involved writing. Although I have become a good writer over the years of writing books, it was a struggle, an agony—an agony into ecstasy is my writing process. It has gotten much, much easier in later years. I'm a teacher first and teaching is not hard for me. The challenge was getting the ideas I was able to develop easily into written form. That was difficult.

> **I want to make a difference in the world; having a bestseller will help that, so I want a bestseller.**

My books address an issue that is very timely. I did market research on popular books and found that people were not finishing my books before *Men Are from Mars,* because they were too dense—meaning readers have to think a lot.

So in writing *Men Are from Mars* and other books since, I took this angle: I want people to read this and *not* have to think, so I gave lots of examples that did the thinking for them. For example, when I made a point that women need to talk about their feelings to feel better, you would have to stop and think, "Is that true? Have I experienced that? Why would they need that?" I would look at my thinking process to validate that point, and put that into the book. I took the work out of reading it.

What makes a big seller is writing about something a lot of people are interested in and writing in such a way that a lot of people can relate to the subject. In my field of self-help, many writers have done fairly big. A million in sales is a fairly successful book. Mine is now at 13 million. I reach out to so many because I focus on normal people. Most people like to feel they are normal—not alcoholic, or had a dysfunctional childhood, or are from a specific minority group with a particular problem. I focused on the problems of humanity in general, addressing normal people—all men and women—instead of a specific group. I spoke on a subject—how men and women relate differently—that's timely and interested everybody in some way. I think that's why more and more people buy a book, not necessarily the actual skill of the writer (it might be in fiction, but in nonfiction it's your subject matter).

In the '50s, not everyone would have read this book; it wouldn't have been that interesting. Everybody kind of knew men and women were different, but society has changed in the direction of men and women being the same. I came back to remind us, to make a correction, that men and women are not the same. Generally when I think of books that influence lots of people, there will be some resistance at first. Yet the new always piques interest.

A book of mine that just came out covers another trend, the new wave of the future. It kind of repeats what happened in the '60s, people's optimism about their ability to create peace in the world. I am meeting lots of resistance by some people, who either say they're against it or they think it's old stuff.

When you have resistance, you have a chance of reaching the mass market. No resistance means the idea is already there, so nobody is interested in hearing you say it. Overcoming that resistance reinforces your own self-beliefs. Truly believing in everything you say—the value, the impact, the usefulness, and the quality—helps other people believe in the usefulness. To the extent you believe in yourself, others will believe in you. To the extent that others resist, you are forced to believe in yourself to keep promoting.

One advantage I have over most writers is that my temperament is not so much a writer's temperament. Many writers (but not all) are introverted and don't have the natural ability to promote. That comes easily for me. As a teacher I am promoting my ideas; I can be out there. But to sit down quietly and write this book—with no audience, nobody to respond to, and nobody looking at me—was a real challenge for me. When you have an audience right there, you pick up all their cues—what they like and don't like, what is going over well and what's not. That's how I develop my ideas—in the audience—then I write about them and develop them even more. The more you promote something, you lean against that resistance. I had ten years of developing and promoting the ideas of *Men Are from Mars* before the book actually came out.

Every technique I used to become an author is in *How to Get What You Want.* One technique is talking about it, doing constant media, and promoting (you've got to be promoting); another is thinking. People think success with books is all about marketing, but it's about how much you think about your book every day. The power of success lies in the quiet time before and after acting. I teach people how to meditate on success.

When my book went on the *New York Times* bestseller list, I had already decided that even if it didn't make the bestseller's list, I was going to celebrate—reward myself—for writing a great book. So I bought a new car and went on a vacation. Then on the vacation I went out to get the paper—every Sunday I check the bestseller's list—and my car was dinged, a dent in the side. I just picked up the paper and thought, "So what if my car has a ding? I'm a bestselling author!"

It is the life, a joy to achieve your goals; but it does take enormous patience and persistence. My project to become a bestselling author became my daily meditation for six years, from the beginning of my first book in 1984 until 1992. Eight years later I actually got on the list. As a writer I was making it my practice every day to focus on what I really want. I want to make a difference in the world; having a bestseller will help that, so I want a bestseller. I always put the highest value first, then the second value (having a bestseller) that will allow me to accomplish that goal.

## NELSON DeMILLE

*Nelson DeMille's novels have appeared on bestseller lists throughout the world. His books have been Main Selections of the Book of the Month Club and the Literary Guild. His first major novel,* By the Rivers of Babylon, *remains in print as do all his succeeding novels:* Cathedral, The Talbot Odyssey, Word of Honor, The Charm School,

Gold Coast, The General's Daughter, Spencerville, *and* Plum Island. *Forthcoming is* The Lion's Game. The General's Daughter *is a major motion picture starring John Travolta and Madeline Stowe.*

I think I was born a writer. In high school and college I would always get papers back that said, "You write well." And I was actually accused of plagiarism once, which was a serious form of compliment. An English teacher in college insisted I must have plagiarized the whole thing. That's how good it was.

Probably my year in Vietnam was my most educational experience. It was unlike anything I had done before or since, and that is when I started keeping a journal. I got the idea of writing The Great American War Novel. A fellow officer I served with went back to his job in New York publishing, and we got together after we both came home. He was working for a small paperback publisher that was looking for a New York City Police procedural novel series, and I really had no fiction-writing experience, but I thought I would give it a try. I wrote *Joe Ryker NYPD,* which was the beginning of the series actually. I did about six or seven books, all paperback originals. At the time, series were big and cop books were big—you know, the Serpico era, Batman and Robin. So I broke into writing by writing in the most commercial genre there was, and I broke in writing paperbacks, which few people do today. That was the easiest way to get published—jump on the bandwagon of something publishers perceive a need for, take a small advance, and agree to a paperback original. But it's easy to get stuck there.

Nobody discouraged me, and I think that was because the first book I wrote I published. I think it might have been discouraging if I tried for years and failed. But there was no time for people to discourage me.

> **I got the idea of writing The Great American War Novel.**

Bernard Geis was a packager and co-publisher (he co-published Jacqueline Susann's *Valley of the Dolls*). He would take up-and-coming young authors, and it was easier because I had published a paperback. We conceived my first novel, called *By the Rivers of Babylon,* and sold it to Harcourt Brace for $400,000 in 1977—more money than I had ever seen.

> **I think a lot of writers fall into the trap of taking something that would make a good magazine article and try to make it a novel.**

We came up with the idea together, I think the way Frederick Forsyth sat down to write *The Day of the Jackal.* I sat down with Bernie Geis and his editors and we banged out an outline, came up with a novel that had all the commercial elements—we were strictly looking at the commerce of it.

I first felt I made it "big" when Geis auctioned it and said, "Sit down—I have great news." That was the summer of '77, and *By the Rivers of Babylon* became a Reader's Digest Condensed and the Main Selection of the Book of the Month Club, which was amazing for a first novel.

Just in a general way, the best thing my writing career brought was the ability to run my own life the way I want. I think every author dreams of having the resources to write professionally and full time, without having to think about money.

My second book, *Cathedral,* was also successful, and the perception was that I had beaten the second-book syndrome. But my third book, *The Talbot Odyssey,* was not as successful, and this turned out to be my second-book syndrome. My publisher, that had published *Cathedral,* didn't want my fourth book, *Word of Honor.* It was published by Warner Books, and was extremely successful. Revenge is sweet.

In terms of sales, my last book, *Plam Island,* was the biggest. In terms of literary success, meaning literary criticism and review attention, it was *Gold Coast*. *Gold Coast* was taken most seriously as literature, even compared favorably to F. Scott Fitzgerald's *The Great Gatsby*.

I think the most surprising thing was getting a Main Selection from the Book of the Month Club and Literary Guild on almost every book. I'm always surprised that, out of all the books they have to pick from, they pick mine.

I sent the manuscript of *The General's Daughter* under a different name to one literary agency, and they said they would read it for a fee. Then they sent it back saying it showed a lot of promise, and I should continue writing. My agent and I laughed about that.

Choosing topics was easier a few years ago. I was always able to fall back on a cold war or a military topic. It seemed there was more to write about in the '70s and '80s, and I just picked topics that interested me at the moment. The only book that was sort of purposefully put together was my first, *By the Rivers of Babylon*. Every other one had a different genesis, but all were something that struck me at the time. I think a lot of writers fall into the trap of taking something that would make a good magazine article and try to make it a novel. A book really has to have depth. It has to resonate, and it absolutely has to interest the author. If the author gets bored, the reader gets bored. My books are very eclectic (critics say no book is the same as the next one), and I think it's going to stay that way.

I stick to a writing schedule only during the last four months before deadline. I am very erratic until I realize I have only four months to go, then I just do the late term-paper thing—write about six or seven days a week, ten hours a day. And I can usually complete a book in 90 to 120 days, because it is already researched and the first third should have been done. The first third takes me over a year to do, and the last two-thirds I can usually finish in three to four months, when I really swing into a schedule. Before that, I am totally erratic.

I write in a small writing studio outside of my main office. It's in a medical building so I'm totally anonymous; nobody knows who I am. There is no name on the door, no phone, nothing but a desk and a chair, and writing pencils, a sharpener, a coffeepot, a few reference books, and maybe a thesaurus and an almanac. That's it. Very sparse. I don't type (I don't know how). I use number one pencils because they are soft, and yellow legal pads; everything is handwritten. My assistant can read my handwriting, and she inputs it on the word processor.

I do the usual 12- to 15-city tour for every book, and I do radio, TV, newspapers, and a lot of book signings, which I think is a good thing, especially for independent bookstores, especially for the hardcover.

I've done *Good Morning America, Today Show,* all the national morning shows, and a great deal of local TV.

I really like the radio interview—the 30-minute format. It's so much more in depth than the 30-second sound bites you get on TV. In print interviews, the press can do what they want after you leave—make you look like a great guy or a bad guy. But live radio is really the best. I do like a few TV shows, like Charlie Rose, but most of TV is sound bites and not very serious for authors.

I'm looking forward to doing other kinds of writing and to doing more magazines, more nonfiction—not books but nonfiction magazines, essays, opinion—and maybe the screenplay I've been asked to do. I would like to stop writing novels. After the one I'm working on, then two more, that's it. My contract will be up with Warner Books, and if I could afford it financially, I don't think I would do any more novels. You get burned out. This will be my tenth or eleventh, and then two more to go, so 13. I don't know why novelists like Clancy or Danielle Steele, who made a fortune, keep turning them out; it's a lot of work. And also most novelists should know when they are ahead and quit then—before they make fools of themselves—because that's what happens at the end. If your publisher and agent come back strong and say one more, one more, your career peaks and starts to go down. And you try to come back with one more, not go down on a low note, but you should know when the high note is and quit.

I would say one thing that has helped me in my career has been living in the New York area. From the beginning I was able to interact with other agents and publishers and go to literary and social events, and I felt like I knew a lot of people in the business who were there to help. There is this perception that you can sit in your house wherever you are and write. That is true sometimes, but you know, like the painters who used to go to Paris at the turn of the century, I would say to an aspiring writer in America, move to New York. You don't have to stay forever, but if you are serious about publishing, especially novels, you have to get into the world where they originate. You have to know these people, do face time, go to cocktail parties and have a bunch of drinks, and do your routine—a little shmoozing goes a long way. It is a very personal business, and you can't be totally anonymous.

> **It is a very personal business, and you can't be totally anonymous.**

Fan mail is fun to read; it's very rare that I get something unkind. Most letters are very positive—people thanking me for giving them enjoyment. That is always a great feeling.

## MARK VICTOR HANSEN

*Mark Victor Hansen is called the Master Motivator. An innovative entrepreneur and leading expert in the area of human potential, Hansen has given over 5,000 presentations worldwide and is in high demand as a keynote speaker and seminar leader. He is also the co-creator of the Chicken Soup for the Soul series, called "The publishing phenomenon of the decade" by* Time Magazine. *The series collectively sold over 30 million copies in North America alone, making it among the most successful publishing "franchises" in America. His book and audio programs have made a profound difference in many lives. Hansen has also written such books as* Dare to Win, The Aladdin Factor, *and* Out of the Blue, *and popular self-published titles such as* Visualizing in Realizing, Sell Yourself Rich, *and* How to Achieve Total Prosperity. *A member of the National Speaker's Association since 1974 and a Certified Speaking Professional, Hansen has appeared on many television shows, including* CNN, Eye to Eye, QVC, *and* The Today Show. *He has also been featured in* Entrepreneur, Success, Forbes, *and other national magazines; the subject of hundreds of newspaper articles; and a guest on over 500 radio talk-show programs. His Web site is www.chickensoup.com/mark/mark.htm.*

Writers should pick the market first, then pick the topic. In other words, find a market that no one else is touching. When we hit the teenage market, our publisher said, "You guys have blown it this time. Teens buy CDs, concert tickets, and clothes." Well, we sold 5 million of *Teen 1* in the first eight months, and 2 million of *Teen 2* in two months, which is a record. Then we sold 750,000 of the journal, and now have the bestselling journal of all time.

My whole principle of teaching is, "Grow rich in your niche." Pick niches that no on one else is doing. Although 35 publishers originally said, "Hit the road, Jack," we just keep going. And we have 74 more niches that I think are bigger than the ones we already hit. The media keeps telling us we have peaked, but we haven't peaked at all. Our 20–20 vision is to sell a billion books by 2020, and at the rate we are going and growing and glowing, we will pull it off.

> **You have to write a great book first, then you have to spend 90 percent of your time marketing and hustling.**

When we published our first book, everybody in New York turned us down. It wasn't that people didn't like us; they just didn't see the vision we did. They said, "No one buys short stories or we would be selling short stories." We said, "We're not selling short stories; we're selling heart-touching, soul-penetrating stories." We knew, but they didn't know what they were doing, as far as I'm concerned. A lot of publishers come up to us and say, "We're sorry we didn't see your vision and take it."

So then we went to BEA (Book Expo Association) ourselves, going from booth to booth, and Health Communications finally said, "We will read it overnight." And they said, "We cried all over our silk shirts. We'll try it if you guys promise to buy the 20,000 books if we don't sell them." We were so sure they would sell that we said, "Sure, we'll do that." Selling 20,000 books, as long as you have some sort of platform mastery, is no problem.

Today we are at 44 million books sold, so we have been serious.

Every author has got to have a vanity number, a name acronym. Ours is 1-800-SOUPBOOK. We went through 228 names before we got to that (CHICKEN was taken by Kentucky Fried). The point is that when you are on radio interviews, most people listen on early morning drive time, which is when 80 percent of books are sold. They can't remember seven numbers by the time you get to work, but if you say 800-SOUPBOOK, they go soupbook, soupbook, and they got it.

Our phones ring off the hook. We did media that no one else did. We interviewed the 101 bestselling authors—Dr. Ken Blanchard, Dr. Barbara De Angelis, Wayne Dyer, James Michener, Scott Peck— and asked, "What do you do?" and they all told us. Then we set in order the 1,094 different experiences we wanted to have, and be, and do, and for the most part we have done all of them.

And now we have just written a 25-year business plan called the Kick Ass Business Plan. You have to write a great book first, then you have to spend 90 percent of your time marketing and hustling.

Right now we are buddying up with the best people in the world. Diet Coke will send 50 million cases of Diet Coke a month with our *Chicken Soup for the Couple's Soul.* They are working with us in the Boy's and Girl's Clubs, and the books we sell—maybe millions—go toward getting kids off the street and out of risk. We have promotions scheduled for the next couple of years, and each one is bigger than the last. My cliché is that massive marketing time plus massive exposure equals massive sales. We try to be in front of a mass of people every day in bright, new, and interesting ways. There are a lot of brilliant writers out there, but they ought to bring the same creative brightness to market their books.

We have the most widely read Web site in the world, www.soupserver.com, and 500,000 people get a free newspaper from us every day. It will go to a million one day. We have grown organically through word of mouth.

There have been a lot of surprises with the writing. First is the power of the story. We are really in the business of storytelling and story-selling. When I went to China, the head of Buddhism wanted me to do a 30-minute interview. She said that a story is the only thing that goes from one heart to another. Every writer, in some way or another, is in the storytelling business. If all writers tested their stories the way we do (have 40 to 100 readers read and grade them mercilessly), then their copy would be better. Most writers do not get to have focus groups. Why not test it on somebody else before you put it in the marketplace?

The surprise to me is that our books and stories have absolutely universal appeal. That was our plan—to make a living classic and become part of the literature scene. You don't have to go very far, though, to have people tell you that we are not part of the literati. (Jack should be; he's smart, graduated from Harvard!)

We are both professional speakers. I taught Jack how to do the stories at the end of talks that would get a standing ovation. He had the idea for the book and we put together 60 great stories and called all of our author peers and said, "What are the stories that got standing ovations?" Then the next phase, we were smart enough to say in the front of the book, "If you have a great story, tell it." America doesn't have a great forum to tell its stories.

Another surprising thing is that I went from a $2,000 speaker fee two years ago to $20,000 an hour now. That will probably rise even more as I get more famous, and we come out with the movies, the TV show, and everything we have coming up. What is astounding is that the more money I get, the less time they give me. And I think, "Gosh, I had less to say here and they paid my full fee; now I have more to say and they pay me more to do less." They pay for me because I'm a celebrity.

When you're on a radio show and they really like you, they will expand your time from half an hour to an hour, to two hours if they have the time; or they will say, "Can we call you back tomorrow?" There has never been a day that we haven't done media—at least one a day, 20 some days. We have to thank Scott Peck for that. He had the number one bestseller, made 40 million dollars, and said, "You have to do media every single day, no matter what." We bought it and do it.

> **It has to be a labor of love, and you have to really want it, so your desire is white hot.**

There is enough media out there for all of us. *New York Times* actually has five bestseller lists, and there's the *USA Today* bestseller list, *Publisher's Weekly,* the Christian Book bestseller list, and *Entertainment Weekly.* There are enough lists that everybody can be a bestseller. We decided we didn't just want to be a mega-best seller; we wanted a mega-bestselling series. We are never going to do hardbound books. We aren't going to do fiction yet. I don't know where authors become so naive to assume that they are going to come up with something colossal and make it work. It took five years for it to happen to us. It has to be a labor of love, and you have to really want it, so your desire is white hot. With white-hot desire, a lot of things happen.

We're doing TV now—26 one-hour shows that dramatize our stories. The first show had everybody in it—Jack Lemmon, Martin Sheen, Paula Abdul, Leeza Gibbons. They are going to air it twice a week and think that at least a million people will watch every week. It could be like the next Cosby Show (I'm not making this up; I'm quoting them). We visualized this seven years ago. It should bring a lot of our books that no one has ever seen up to the surface.

Young writers have to be careful; they want it to happen fast. I have a book out called *Future Diary,* which says you have to have many goals because different goals have different gestation rates, and you can't push the edge of the envelope more than it's willing to get pushed.

The funniest thing happened when my wife and kids and I were out to dinner at a four-star restaurant. My little eleven-year-old looks across the table at a husband and wife about 80-something years old, who were looking bored as far as she was concerned. Then she goes over, unannounced—doesn't ask dad or mom's permission—and starts telling them stories. And the guy pulls out a 20-dollar bill and says, "We needed those stories, thank you very much." I think the guy thought she was just a little street urchin. Anyway, my daughter comes back and says, "Boy, Dad, this stuff really pays well." She didn't go over hustling; she just went to make them happy.

> **Most people have a great talent, but haven't spent the time finding that talent, where they are unique.**

That's what I've been saying: stories sell. Both of my daughters, Melanie and Elizabeth, have stories. I believe everyone has a story. If I had time to sit with each person for an hour, I could find that story. Most people have a great talent, but haven't spent the time finding that talent, where they are unique. I think I am unique as a writer, and a speaker, and maybe most unique at seeing markets that absolutely no one sees but me.

Building geodesic domes was my first job. In graduate school I was research assistant for a brilliant guy named Buckminster Fuller. I was there when he re-wrote *Intuition* 14 times, took it to the staff members, and we gave him our opinions. Here was the smartest guy on the planet asking us what worked and what didn't.

When Ken Blanchard had breakfast with Jack and me, he said, "You guys have to get all your books tested for the marketplace." He was doing a book with Norman Vincent Peale on situational ethics and gave us each a copy. When I read the book, I saw three major thought holes. The last thing I want to do is offend my friends, but they had major thought holes. I wrote up a 12-page dissertation on where I thought they screwed up, then called Jack and said, "Do you think I am right in this?" He said, "Yes, I think you're right. These guys are just older and have a different position, but their position is wrong." My thoughts ended up going into the book and they thanked me. But my point is, if you are writing a book, give it to the best people in your marketplace. It is much better for someone to reinvent your paragraph or sentence so it will flow flawlessly *before* you get edited than to get attacked in the marketplace.

I think the only thing that works at the bookstore level is hand-selling. Most authors are intrinsically shy, and want to stay in their bungalow writing, but they have to spend some time pressing flesh, getting pictures with people in bookstores. If you get that going, people will start helping you out. You have to take it to a level that when people are asked, "Have you read a good book?" they say, "Yeah, *Chicken Soup*."

## DAVE PELZER

*Dave Pelzer is the* New York Times *bestselling author of* A Child Called "It": An Abused Child's Journey from Victim to Victor. *The book chronicles the unforgettable and horrifying account of one of the most severe child abuse cases in California history—Pelzer's own story. He has also published* The Lost Boy *and has a third book in progress:* A Man Called Dave. *Dave Pelzer travels throughout the nation promoting inspiration and resilience. His efforts and accomplishments have resulted in personal commendations from Presidents Reagan and Bush. In 1993 Pelzer was chosen as one of the Ten Outstanding Young Americans (TOYA) and in 1994 was the only American to receive The Outstanding Young Persons of the World (TOYP) award. He was also a torchbearer for the Centennial Olympic Games. His Web site is www.bookbrowse.com/nonfiction/reviews/pelzer_dave.html or www.davepelzer.com.*

I never went out to write an abuse story. I went out to write a story about the indomitable human spirit. The backdrop was people trying to help this kid, and the subplot to the backdrop was, unfortunately, abuse. I thought if I can write it as a kid, keep it very gripping, keep it very short, and edit it as a child, it would work. I mean, kids have a certain text involved; they don't speak in four-syllable terms. It might be choppy, but more visual. I tried to analyze a story from a child's point of view.

I started out speaking as a comedian, helping kids who were abused and in foster care. As I was speaking, people were telling me that this was a very unusual story. "You speak about resilience. Can you write a technical manual-type book?" I thought, no, I'm not a doctor. To me writing is sacred. It's like John Steinbeck walking into hell leading the cardinal valley for goodness sake, or Monterey. To me, Steinbeck lives the story rather than making something up. So, I came up with an idea, "What if I can do the writing of my story, what I experienced as a young person, but make it more a story of a kid who didn't quit rather than a story of abuse."

My first book was printed for the first time in 1993, but it was never published. There was no ISBN in the Library of Congress; it was never even formally copyrighted. It was printed on the twentieth anniversary of my rescue. What I was going to do is give my teachers this book as a gift, as a way of saying thank you for standing up and rescuing me because they are the ones who called the authorities. They received the first official printed copies of the book.

I had a friend who had heard of Jack Canfield, and Jack had heard of me. We gave the book to Mr. Canfield, and he passed it on to his publishers. Three or four people were spellbound with me. Someone within the publishing house did say, "Hey, it's all make-believe. Dave made it up." Another person said it was nothing but a manual on how to brutalize children. Unfortunately, those two people had not read the book.

It was officially published in September of '95. Our book numbers weren't high at first—an average of 300 to 400 books a month, maybe 1,000. It was continually growing and growing, yet our book numbers were stagnant. The problem was that for every one person who bought it, an average of 43 people would read it. I would receive 500 to 700 pieces of mail a month, then 850 pieces. I'm going, "Oh, my gosh. It's a hit." People were saying they passed it around, mailed it to their friends. By the time it made the *New York Times,* it was October of 1997. I was in LA doing a little talk show thing when I found out about it. I've been fortunate in my life to win awards, but this news came so out the blue, I was stymied when I heard it.

I never wrote the book to be in the *New York Times.* To me, it's so sacred. It's like when I received a call saying, "Dave, I'm going to nominate you for the Pulitzer Prize," I'm like, thank you very much. Then it hits me. As of this conversation, we've been on the *New York Times* for 69 weeks, off it for a total of eight weeks here and there because of New Kids on the Block or Leo DiCaprio kicking our little butts. But it's an international bestseller. I'm the first author to have two books simultaneously in the *New York Times* and trade paper. The joke is that there was no push involved whatsoever. If anything, we had things against us. Authors do not make themselves *New York Times* bestselling authors. It is the audience, the people who read the books, the folks in Norfolk, Virginia, or Hayes, Kansas, or the backwoods of Florida.

It's sad that you have to be a bestselling author for people to take you a little bit seriously in this business. The fact was that a small publishing house in Florida, not a New York publishing house, published the book; it's beyond me because right now we're receiving just under 4,000 pieces of mail each month. We have a Web site and get asked 300 questions a day. It's getting out of hand. What I try to do is put out there the best project possible. It's nice, but it's almost like a beeper you're tied to in a sense.

> **I started out speaking as a comedian, helping kids who were abused and in foster care.**

I am a comedian, which is kind of unusual. Some people think, "Oh my god, Dave, you were abused, so you must speak so seriously." Then I come out like Robin Williams/David Letterman doing impromptu storytelling. I do a lot of work in the areas of child abuse. I can do a six-hour program with no notes whatsoever on the psychology of abuse, the perpetrator's point of view, how kids are resilient. And yet I'll do 74 different Robin Williams–type characters. One woman said she laughed so hard she relieved herself. I work with kids, do programs on kids and responsibilities, issues they face—a "you can do it" kind of thing.

> **Look at the bigger picture. Don't write to get the big deal; write to write.**

I have commendations from three presidents, which is pretty cool. You go out there and speak in a humorous way, but in a way that can teach them something as Americans. I work very hard at what I do—extremely hard. And my speaker friends say, "Oh Dave, we're jealous," because I get an average of two to four interviews every single day. If you fill a pipeline, people come to listen. I think one of every thousand people in America has heard about Dave the Funny Guy, or Dave the child-abuse guy, or Dave the Americana resilience guy. It's slowly paid off. I've been doing this for many years because I did volunteer work when I was in the armed forces to the point that I'm flying active duty. That's difficult because I'm out of the country working my butt off, and I was the California Volunteer of the Year.

It's just nice to have a message people can read, and 99 percent of those who do get the message. You can look me up at Amazon.com under the reviews, and I think we've got about a hundred 95's, one or two 3's or 4's or 1's or something. We're doing pretty good.

To me, my message is timeless because it takes me six hours to write one single paragraph of a story. I analyze every word, even "is" and "are" because "is" is more like a verb to me; it's more action. I keep thinking, why would people want to read this? Or how does this tell the story? That's very hard in the production of the story. But, then again, I'm out there doing it. I've been on Montel Williams at least three times and Leeza, Sally, the View, and Dini Petty. These people always want us back. We never call them. Whatever we want, we can do. People say I am so damn funny, especially when they had the preconceived notion that I'd be boring. You just come out shooting, hitting, fighting in a sense and in a way that people can relate. I say, "Here is what I learned that made me a better person," and people listen.

It took me two years to talk because I was locked in the basement and wasn't allowed to speak. But everything in my life I have been fortunate enough to earn, such as people's respect and dignity. The biggest lesson I learned as an author was that I had a few things against me, but the writing is pure. I didn't make it overnight, and I'm glad because I am the leading author this fall. I'd *better* be good! I'm extremely thankful for the small number of people who initially believed in me and for the people who read the books. Without them spending money on my book, I'd be nothing. One person stood on a desk at a conference room and said, "You *have* to read this book!" A lot of people pushed this book, and the numbers started to show.

It's funny when people write and say, "I'm 86 years old and I think you're cute," or when kids write and say they had a problem and they're getting over it now. A few months ago, I was in Rochester, New York, in the middle of a blizzard, thinking that not many people are going to show. All of a sudden I see a mob. One person starts to stand up and clap, then a few more stand until they all stand and clap. I start to cry. I think it's all this stuff building up from the past few years. People see me and say, "This guy made it after all he's been through without any help. What do we have to complain about?" This is the only story out there that doesn't have the victim mentality.

I don't hate either of my parents. There's not a lot of baggage there. I'm not in therapy. I sort of carry on. I don't deserve the applause;

I'm overrated at best, but it's so wonderful when you have old ladies drive to see you.

I'm not about child abuse. I'm about resilience and Americana. My fourth book's going to be an unusual self-help book. Books five and six are going to be like Robin Williams and Doctor Gray writing books about the opposite sex. I'm a storyteller. What I like about writing is taking people on a journey. They think it's about one thing, abuse, then they discover, oh my gosh, it's about resilience. But, if you go back to page one, it was always about that. You change their perception, and that's what I like about writing: You take people on this beautiful journey, and it's very hard to do with words, but hopefully they close the book a little bit wiser than when they opened it.

The best advice I can give any writer is tell a good story. To me there are two different writers. There are writers who have great mechanics, but some of these lose a focus of the story because they are so worried about their text and verbs and adjectives. I would rather write a story that I can edit myself or have the editor help me out. But, if you have a good story and tell it from the heart, that's important. You should not write for money because unless you sell a gazillion million books, you won't get a lot of money. You hear a lot about *Publisher's Weekly* and Hollywood deals with six- and seven-figure advances—pie-in-the-sky stuff. And then there's something called taxes involved, and agents, and everything else. Look at the bigger picture. Don't write to get the big deal; write to write.

## BARRY SEARS

*Barry Sears is the author of the popular Zone series of diet and health books. Trained as a research scientist, Sears' career in academia and biotechnology turned into a successful writing career by a simple twist of fate. "My first book was a case truly of serendipity," according to Sears. He was working with an editor's physician on a number of projects. The physician was treating the editor's chronic fatigue syndrome with Sears' now very popular Zone diet. The diet was so successful that the editor called to ask Sears if he wanted to write a book. The result was an astounding success. The noted lecturer and author is humble about his talents: "I went into science because I couldn't write, so it is the irony of ironies. I don't consider myself a good writer, but I do consider myself a very, very good teacher. And most of what I write is the transition to the written word of lectures I give around the country."*

The whole Zone series of books I've written deals with a fairly simple concept, trying to keep hormones within the sweet zones—not too high, not too low. And the only drug that can achieve that is called food. So we are looking at food as though it were a drug. And in reality food is a vastly more powerful drug, probably the most powerful drug you will ever interact with. The books show that the hormonal rules haven't changed for 40 million years and are unlikely to change tomorrow.

> **The fact that anyone bought the book always surprised me.**

People ask all the time, "How do you get a book published?" I don't have the foggiest idea, because the editor came to me and said, "Do you want to write a book?" It was like being discovered at Schwabs.

A lot of people looked at the book as primarily a diet book, but it was really written for cardiovascular physicians. The fact that anyone bought the book always surprised me. What I think set the book off was a radio call-in talk show I did with Dennis Kreger out in Los Angeles. He had used my program and is also an author with my publisher, Regan Books. He called and said, "I'll put you on the program, but I'll tell you that in my 13 years on the radio, I've never had anyone who talks about nutrition." (Kreger talks primarily about philosophical issues). He said, "Although I am fascinated by the subject personally, if we don't get any calls, we will have to take you off the air." I said, "I understand that." Well, three hours later I was still on the air, and the book went to number one in LA the next week and really took off from there. A case of serendipity.

My background is that of a typical research scientist. I graduated in 1968 from Oxnell College with a degree in chemistry, got my Ph.D. in 1971 in biochemistry from Indiana University, did a NIH post-doctoral fellowship at the University of Virginia Medical School, then became a research scientist at both Boston University's School of Medicine and at MIT. I left the world of academia in 1982 to pursue the wild and woolly world of biotechnology.

I went into science because I couldn't write, so it is the irony of ironies. I don't consider myself a good writer, but I do consider myself a very, very good teacher. And most of what I write is the transition to the written word of lectures I give around the country.

I do a lot of interviews. I look at any type of interview—radio, TV, book signing, whatever—not so much as promoting the book, but as an opportunity to teach to a wider audience. I love to teach, so I usually go anywhere anytime just to talk because I am fascinated by the subject. That is the key: unless you are really in love with your subject, you will probably never be successful. You have to really believe people want to hear what you want to say. And if they don't, you say it anyway.

> **I don't consider myself a good writer, but I do consider myself a very, very good teacher.**

You always want to go through life leaving a legacy of good works. Through a book, you get responses from people who say, "You changed my life." I say, "Stop right there. I gave you the rules, but you had to follow them." On a day-in day-out basis we get letters from people I have never met, but somehow the book has touched them and improved the quality of their life. If that isn't having your cake and eating it, too, I don't know what is!

The best thing is the fact that anybody read the book. Like I said, this is a totally unexpected phenomenon—for both myself and my publisher. The fact that people have read the book, have utilized the program, and have gotten great results has been the most gratifying aspect.

People said, "Oh, the first book is too hard. I don't understand it." I say, "Actually, it wasn't written for you." I wrote the other books thinking, "Okay, can we make it easier, easier, and easier to say?" This isn't rocket science, but people have many built-in barriers. So, going to the essence of adult education, I broke down a complex subject into very simple, easy, digestible formats, so people can say that magical phrase, "I can do this!"

That was the driving force for my next three books, which are basically the how-tos. The fifth book, the *Anti-Aging Zone,* is like *The Zone.* It explores a whole new area, in terms of aging, from a totally different perspective. It is a complex book—make no mistake about it—but the complexity makes the person going through it think, "I understand there is a relationship between all these hormones and how I age; and more importantly, I have the tools right there in my kitchen to turn back the aging process if I choose."

My day job is running a biotechnology company, so writing is just an avocation right now. What I look forward to, like any scientist, is seeing any research I do pay off in terms of benefits to society. So my long-term goal is to put forward this new philosophy of food that has worldwide implications in health care and to bring it to fruition as rapidly as possible. Hopefully that will be achieved in my lifetime; if not, at least I gave it a good start.

I guess the only surprise is that publishing has changed quite a bit. I used to read the books of Thomas Wolfe, and I would read how his publisher spent months, if not years, refining his manuscript. Now you had better deliver a manuscript in more or less its complete form because publishing is more like Hollywood than the old days. They don't have time to build on an audience; the manuscript has to get out there quickly.

Radio is always the medium for me. I like it because you have a lot of time. If your book can be easily condensed, TV is fine for little sound bites, but radio offers time to really explore the subject. You may not get quite the mass audience, but it allows you to refine your thinking, so when you do go onto a media format like the *Today Show,* you have broken down the sound bites to really fit their needs. In many ways you have to be like a politician pressing flesh. You need to get the most salient points out in a way that leaves a lasting impression—so the viewer or listener says, "Gee, maybe I will take a look at that book and make a decision."

The interview I did with Katie Couric on the *Today Show* was a good one. Obviously, being on the *Today Show* is a stressful experience. I looked at a copy of the interview a couple years ago and said, "Wow, I did a pretty good job of getting everything out." You are in a daze right there, but I had a pretty good sound bite down for my two-and-a-half minutes on air.

Now I am working on a book called the *Vegetarian Zone.* Again, I'm looking at it not like a recipe book, but as an exploration of what vegetarianism is—the pros and cons—and how easy it is for a vegetarian to follow the Zone diet. But more importantly, it explores the implications for world health and feeding the world's population as we enter the twenty-first century.

I really don't stick to a writing schedule. I almost write as I catch time. I'll write a lot here at the lab between experiments, at home, and on planes. The key of my writing is not that I have a vision; it's actually the consolidation of thousands (if not hundreds of thousands) of articles. I never forget what got me there in the first place. It wasn't my writing style that made The Zone series successful; the strength of my writing was my ability to search through databases, millions of articles, and see connections where others don't. And then putting those ideas into a format, first in terms of lectures. I try out the themes there, and if it plays well in Peoria, I translate that into the written word.

Every author looks at Amazon.com about every fifteen minutes ("My book dropped to 106. Oh, my god!"). The beauty is that you can get a feel for your audience, though it's a skewed audience.

Wherever I go I end up at bookstores, usually looking at how the books are arranged. I spend an inordinate amount of time and more money at bookstores than I could ever get in royalties from my books sold there. So it is usually a wash.

I was asked to give a talk about success at school once. I said that success obviously is finding and meeting a goal. From that standpoint I was successful fifteen years ago because I haven't said anything different about the role of food in hormonal response, even though nobody listened then. In my own mind, I am very happy with what I have accomplished.

> **You always want to go through life leaving a legacy of good works.**

Relative to the celebrity status, it actually embarrasses my two daughters. I might have an article in the *Boston Globe* and they say, "Dad, you are such a dork." But I think the celebrity status just gives you a bigger platform to speak from. And if you think your message has validity, if you think it will make the world a better place, then celebrity status gives you an advantage. Do I get an extra free cup of coffee here in my hometown? No, the status hasn't paid off in any great ways in terms of my local living.

I enjoy traveling because it is a great way for me to not only teach but to maintain old friendships. Nothing could be more important to mental well-being than that.

For anyone who wants to write, have the story so clear in your head that it just pops off. *The Zone* took me nine weeks to write, but I spent 15 years doing the research. Like all things, you just keep going over in your mind, asking questions, over and over again. When you are ready to write, you are ready to write. That's why I say I have no set schedule. I just sit and read and read, and the thoughts just galvanize; I get a "Eureka." If you get enough Eurekas, you think you can put them down on paper and get an interesting story.

It's an odyssey, like a travelog through the mind, using science as your boat. I write things that are interesting to me, and hopefully they interest other people in the world. That is the bottom line.

The main goal of any writer, even if you never get published, is that you tried to bring a little order out of chaos; that would be success. If someone actually buys the book, that is icing on the cake. I think everyone should try to write one book in their lifetime because it forces you to analyze your own life and figure out, "What is the essence of my time on the planet?" and "How can I make good use of it?"

## JAMES FINN GARNER

*James Finn Garner is the author of the popular, humorous series of books* Politically Correct Bedtime Stories, Once Upon a More Enlightened Time, *and* Politically Correct Holiday Stories. *He also authored* Apocalypse Wow! A Memoir for the End of Time. *The author's comic side emerged around the time he took improv classes in his 20s, a period during which "bad writing wasn't even coming out." According to Finn Garner, his experiences on stage freed him from self-imposed stifling expectations, allowing him to have fun, and it was around that time his comedic talents emerged.*

The news that I had made the bestseller list was faxed to me. My wife was throwing a party for me, for just being published. I thought for the life of me that it was a statistical error; it was just impossible. Then it stayed there for 64 weeks . . .

It blew everybody's mind. The initial print run was 25,000; then it kind of snowballed. I got turned down 30 times for the book, or 29 times. I sent manuscripts everywhere and got letters saying, "Oh the market is saturated" or "The market doesn't exist." I just kept plugging away. I knew no other book was doing what *Politically Correct Bedtime Stories* was doing. But I came to realize that the rejections were just excuses. They were not going to take a chance on an unknown author. After the fact, everyone said, "Oh yeah, I knew it was going to be a bestseller."

I am indebted to the man who bought it, Rick Wolfe. A friend who worked for a publishing firm sent it out under her letterhead, saying, "This has come to my attention and as a courtesy I am sending it on to you." That got me more attention, nicer rejection notes, and then the bid from Macmillan. And I don't know why it actually sold.

Somehow the book didn't offend anybody. It was like people saw other people but not themselves in the writing. I thought liberals would just be chewing me apart, but none of them did. Conservatives thought I was sticking it to the liberals—liberals thought I was sticking it to someone else.

With the bedtime stories, every joke had to work. My stage experience probably helped out with that. You don't want anyone to say, "So what?" And that applies to all writing.

My first books were *Politically Correct Bedtime Stories* and the two sequels, *Once Upon a More Enlightened Time* and *Politically Correct Holiday Stories*. After that was *Apocalypse Wow! A Memoir for the End of Time*, which basically examined a bunch of end-of-the-world theories. I had a lot of fun with that. And I contributed an essay to a really nice book entitled *Home;* I think the sub-title was *American Writers Remember Rooms of Their Own*. I wrote this essay about my father's workroom and how terrible my brothers are about home repair.

When I was in my 20s, I hit this basic stone wall and not even bad writing was coming out. So I decided to take improv classes here in town and mess around on stage. It really freed me up from the stifling expectations I was putting on things. It allowed me to have fun, and my comic side emerged about that time, too.

> ## How do I choose my topics? I hunt them down and kill them.

No one encouraged my writing, that's for sure. My parents were befuddled, and through college I would get looks of contempt. People said, "Well, how are you going to earn a living at *that?*" I should have totally ignored them, but it bothered me. In response I kind of pursued a career in publishing, which was pretty fruitless. I worked hard to get a job in publishing here in Chicago and realized this is boring and stupid. I should have gone to Japan like I wanted to, done fun stuff instead of worrying what everyone else thought.

> **I always write in the morning, and if it is good I keep going.**

The best thing that has happened to me, I would say—in addition to hitting the bestseller lists, which was beyond anyone's imagination—was this: I write my wife a Christmas story every year, and the first one I wrote got printed in the *Chicago Tribune* Sunday Magazine. Her reaction was enough to keep me pumped up for years.

It was a little story about a man who stops by the zoo on Christmas Eve to see if animals talk at midnight. I wrote it one year and the next year it made the *Tribune*. My in-laws bought up every copy in western Michigan, and everyone got really excited, so it made me feel like a writer, like this was something I could actually do.

I've gotten up at 4 A.M. and driven out into the hills of Tennessee, just to talk to a morning television personality who had never read my book, never heard of me, and who broadcast out of a trailer. That was interesting. And we got lost in the hills without a cell phone. That was fun. For one photo shoot—*People* magazine, I think—I dressed up like Red Riding Hood in bed with a man in a big wolf costume—some photographer's assistant. It was about 98 degrees that day, and the wolf costume was made of polyurethane and wood—basically a big rubber outfit. He was in tears by the end of it.

The best review I got early, from the *Washington Post*. I kept expecting the reviewer to say, "Oh, but I'm kidding." He was praising it so inordinately, it was totally embarrassing. I thought the punch line was coming, but it never came. I guess he is a really tough critic so everyone was shocked that we got him snookered. One reason the book really took off and got a lot of newspaper coverage was because journalists have to cover PC issues every single day, so could easily relate to what I was doing. They would write column after column, which got me some coverage. When I have a book come out, I try to place other articles that might relate to the book. I cut a chapter that just isn't fitting into the book, try to reshape it into an article and sell it, just for the synergy of two things at once. Why waste your copy? *Politically Correct Bedtime Stories* was a little throwaway humor book, and it stayed up there through thick and thin. And everybody started treating me nice, which was surprising. I used to be just a mook, now I'm a mook with a book. That's more important.

The funniest part was getting the Japanese translations made, because we exchanged five or six faxes with phrases and words that didn't translate. She was asking me to explain the jokes and explain them again; it just doesn't work. Then after all this back and forth, my editor in Japan sent me a fax saying, "My boss and I are very happy that you are publishing with us, and we are very glad and look forward to being in many bookstores. Here is our press run of x copies and we hope you will give many interviews in Japan and tell us what the book is about." Trying to explain what a tractor pull is to a Japanese audience is not so easy.

I gave an interview or two in Japan while I was on a personal vacation. I met with the publishing firm and some editors, but it was mainly a pleasure visit. But I did travel to Britain and France, which is surprising. In Paris they love writers no matter who you are. They really showed me a good time in France, and the book did pretty well. In Britain, I swear to God, a newscaster said that they had this politically correct thing a few years ago, but it's over now. Last I looked, the rich white guys are still in charge over there.

Next year I'll probably go out to Hollywood to see if we can sell some TV ideas, always a fruitless stupid exercise. And soon, my writing partner here in Chicago and I are going to put out an animated cartoon of one of our stage things, a five-minute short of Smitty Wolfboy of the Yukon. It's an old radio thing we used to do about a naked boy raised by wolves in the Yukon.

How do I choose my topics? I hunt them down and kill them. The bedtime stories arose from some live performances I was doing. I decided to write a silly story and read from my prop book. It's basically whatever you think is interesting, whatever you think is funny. I think the end of the world is a very funny idea, so I wrote a whole book about it. I had a whole year I could not come up with another book idea to save my life; that's when you think you've chosen your profession poorly. You have to get through that and get to the next idea. Now I have two ideas I'm pretty stoked about, and we are trying to work it out with the publishers.

One piece of advice is don't take advice. Two, realize that you have to crank out a lot of bad stuff before good stuff comes. You are the only judge of what you are capable of. I have regretted the times I sent out articles thinking, ah, the editor will help me with this, show me what's wrong with it. They just print what I send, and I realize it's only a 75 or 50 percent effort on my part. That bothers me.

I think taking Latin is the best thing a writer can do because it teaches you how to assemble your language. French is okay if you want to order in a restaurant, Spanish if you want to work in the kitchen; but Latin helps you write. Friends—poets and writers—who ignored it in high school, then took it in college, agree with me. I didn't believe it either, but it is true.

I'm proud to be a satirist—if I can live up to the mantle. Otherwise I'm just like a joke writer—the guys I try to measure myself against.

I think all writers are born writers; they just have to learn how to control their schizophrenia. I read Anne LaMott's *Bird by Bird,* and she talked about going for days hearing conversations in her head and having to stop doing that. And I thought, yeah, that's what I do. I create imaginary conflicts or scenarios and fill in the lines between people. It's not a healthy way to think.

I always write in the morning, and if it is good I keep going. You have to write every day—even though I never do, and most writers say they don't, but you're supposed to say that. (You're supposed to floss, too, but how many people actually do that?) For my writing tools, I bought a *memento mori*, a little Indonesian pencil box with skulls on the outside. You know what a *memento mori* is, right? Medieval writers used to keep skulls on their desks to remind them that life is short. I hope it will keep me from wasting more time.

## CHARLOTTE VALE ALLEN

*Charlotte Vale Allen is the popular and prolific author of 30 plus novels, including the groundbreaking autobiography* Daddy's Girl. *The* New York Times *bestselling author is one of Canada's most successful authors, with over seven million copies of her books sold. Her books have been published in all English-speaking countries, in Braille, and have been translated into more than 20 languages. In 1990, she was the only Canadian listed by the British Public Library system as one of the top 100 most borrowed authors in the UK. In her writing, Vale Allen deals with issues confronting women, and tries to be not only informative, but optimistic as well. "My strongest ability as a writer is to make women real, to take you inside their heads and let you know how they feel, and to make you care about them." Vale Allen wrote* Daddy's Girl *in 1971, but this first book was deemed too controversial to publish at the time. It wasn't until 1980, after her success as a novelist, that the groundbreaking book was finally published. Her Web site is charlottevaleallen.com.*

> Love of writing kept me motivated for a long time.

I've always written things down to find out what I think, how I feel. But the determination to get *Daddy's Girl* published saw me become a writer. I have what I refer to as an "accidental career" because I had fifteen books published before *Daddy's Girl* finally sold. By then, there was no question that I'd found something I liked doing—something that gave me more sense of power and control than anything else.

Love of writing kept me motivated for a long time. Then, when the publishing business turned to something resembling a world-wide asylum, necessity took over.

The best thing that happened was making the *New York Times* bestseller list. The worst thing was being loyal too long with the same publishing houses and the same agent. With hindsight, I realize I should have moved along. Loyalty in publishing has become something of a contradiction in terms.

> **If you feel strongly about your work, defend it, but don't ever make it a deal-breaker.**

Most surprising was being paid hundreds of thousands of dollars in advances by companies that then spent almost nothing to publicize the books. This is astonishing to almost every author, I think. There seems to be no connection between the brains and the money.

Once I was at lunch with my agent and the big cheese of a major paperback house, who had just paid hundreds of thousands of dollars for the reprint rights to one of my books, listening to her tell me how much she disliked the book. My agent told me later I deserved a special award for not beating the crap out of the woman. I didn't go mental until I got home.

I've always been drawn to women's issues. So a newspaper/magazine piece, some dialogue with a friend, a badly done movie or TV show might start me thinking.

Now that I'm also a publisher, I've got to fit the writing into teeny-tiny slots that become unavailable. I've been trying to finish the last book for almost a year (unheard of in my previous life as a simple writer). I write wherever I can. At home I write in the bedroom. At my place in Toronto, I actually have an entire office—an insane luxury, especially since I don't get much free time to write there.

My advice to authors is be prepared to write, rewrite, write, rewrite, then have some editor or agent tell you to throw out 200 pages and write new stuff. Then they'll have you throw out another

200 pages and ask you to put in the very stuff you took out in the first place. If you feel strongly about your work, defend it, but don't ever make it a deal-breaker. Personally I always said, "You don't like the wallpaper? I'll change it. Want different furniture? Fine." If you're a writer and want to be published, you've got to be willing to accommodate, at the same time finding some way to keep your integrity intact. Not at all easy. And have patience. Agents and editors these days take six months just to open a submission envelope.

For me success has always been: You're not a writer if you're not published. So continuing to be published is all too often the best and most one can hope for. Right now, because I dislike what's happening in publishing, I'm reinventing the wheel a little and finding different routes to getting my books to readers.

## Lois Duncan

*Lois Duncan is the author of popular young adult novels, and is best known for her brilliant psychological suspense novels. Five of her novels, including* I Know What You Did Last Summer, *have been made into box office or TV movies.* Stranger with My Face, The Third Eye, *and* Locked in Time, *all young adult novels involving metaphysical subject matter, are her personal favorites. She also co-authored a nonfiction book,* Psychic Connections: A Journey into the Mysterious World of Psi. *Written with William Roll, Ph.D., director for the Psychical Research Foundation, the book introduces teenagers to the world of parapsychology. She also wrote* The Circus Comes Home, *a behind-the-scenes look at life at the Ringling Brothers and Barnum & Bailey Circus. Duncan's hometown was winter quarters for the circus, and her photographer father Joseph Steinmetz's photographs provided the incredible illustrations. Her most personal journey, the account of her search for the truth behind her 18-year-old daughter Kaitlyn's murder, was written in real time as the tragedy unfolded.* Who Killed My Daughter? *was featured on* Good Morning America, Larry King Live, *and* Unsolved Mysteries. *The mystery remains unsolved, but Duncan is hopeful. Her Web site can be found at www.randomhouse.com/features/loisduncan/bio.html*

In 1998, my YA novel *I Know What You Did Last Summer* was made into a movie. I was thrilled. I was the first in line at the box office and settled into my seat, too excited to open my popcorn. The houselights dimmed and an insane fisherman who was not in the story strode onto the screen and started decapitating my characters with a hook. I watched in horror as one character after another (from a book that did not include a single murder) met hideous deaths. This was not easy for me, as *I Know What You Did Last Summer* was one of the books that earned me the Margaret A. Edwards Award "for a distinguished body of literature that provides young adults with a window through which to view the world." As a mother of a murdered teenager, I do not want to be part of desensitizing young people to violence and making blood a trigger for giggling and squealing.

My most embarrassing moment was when I had to phone my grandchildren and forbid them to attend the dreadful slasher film.

I can't remember a time when I didn't think of myself as a writer. When I was ten I started submitting a story per week to one publication or another and having them all rejected, then I began to be published at age 13. Throughout my high school years I wrote regularly for youth publications, particularly *Seventeen* (at ages 16, 17, and 18, I placed second, third, and finally first, in their annual young writers contest). When I was 20 I wrote my first YA novel, which was Dodd Mead's "Seventeenth Summer Literary Award." That launched my book-writing career.

When I was in my late 30s, I was teaching magazine writing for the journalism department at the University of New Mexico and started to get nervous that the Powers That Be might discover I didn't have a college degree. I'd been hired by my friend Tony Hillerman, who was department chairman at the time, and Tony didn't care if I had a degree or not, as long as I could teach. But he stopped chairing the department when his own writing career took off, so I no longer had a champion to guard my guilty secret. I surreptitiously started taking classes under my married name, Lois Arquette, hoping to graduate before anyone found out I wasn't educated. As Lois Arquette I took a class in Juvenile Literature, and we were studying novels by Lois Duncan. It was fascinating to hear the professor (who didn't know my second identity) lecture on all the deep hidden meanings in those stories that I hadn't been aware of placing there. I realized then that a story is as much a product of the reader as the author.

In the beginning, simply the joy of creating kept me motivated. Then once I saw my by-line in print, the excitement of achievement. For the years I was divorced with small children to support, the need to put food on the table, and later, the trying of all kinds of different projects—magazine articles, verse, suspense novels, nonfiction, chapter books, picture book texts, song lyrics, a historical novel, an autobiography—made it fun to get up in the morning. Every day was a new adventure.

> **I realized then that a story is as much a product of the reader as the author.**

The best thing may have been the publication of *A Gift of Magic*, which was rejected by seven publishers before Little, Brown finally accepted it in 1971. That book is still selling well and was a turning point in my career, the first of my books about metaphysical subject matter.

My musician daughter, Robin, and I collaborated on a marvelous book and a cassette of original lullabies called *Songs from Dreamland*. I wrote the lyrics and narrated; Robin wrote the music and did the vocals and instrumentals. It was a labor of love (created for my first grandchild, Robin's first niece), and we were thrilled when a publisher brought it out in a specially packaged gift edition. *Songs from Dreamland* received rave reviews, and the publisher did a second run; but this time somebody messed up and packaged the book with the wrong tape—something called "Frederick and Friends." Needless to say, those who bought it demanded money back. The computer registered the flood of returns, the reason for them. So they yanked it out of print, assuming people didn't like it. That broke my heart, because Robin and I had produced something together, something so beautiful, and were dreaming of a mother-daughter career writing and recording children's songs. We still sell tapes to anyone who wants one. (Want to buy one? Believe me, these are good!).

**Brace yourself for rejection and keep going when you get socked with it.**

I write every day, all day—like going to a regular job, but with breaks to run laundry, or go to the store. I've always used the tools at hand—first a manual typewriter, then an electric, then a word processor, now a computer. In the beginning I wrote on the kitchen table, with babies clinging to my knees. Later, on a desk in my bedroom. Today, with the children grown, I use one of our free bedrooms as an office.

Brace yourself for rejection and keep going when you get socked with it. It's part of the process. Don't wait for inspiration, just sit down every day and make yourself write, whether it is good or not. You can always go back and fix it later. Self-discipline is as important as talent—probably more so.

I maintain success by accepting new challenges as they are offered. I'm now editing short-story anthologies for Simon & Schuster—*Night Terrors, Tapped!* and *On the Edge*—and I just submitted a proposal for a television series. I do all the promotional things that are so necessary to keep your work in the public eye, like speaking at conferences of librarians and English teachers, and personally answering letters and e-mails from young readers.

I want more than anything in the world to be in a position to write a sequel to *Who Killed My Daughter?*, the nonfiction book I wrote to motivate informants to provide information about the still-unsolved murder of our youngest daughter Kaitlyn. That was a book without an ending. I want the murder solved, to be able to give my children closure. (We have an online investigation going at http://www.iag.net/~barq/kait.html.)

## JOEL HIRSCHHORN

*Joel Hirschhorn is the multi-talented author of such books as* If They Ask You, You Can Write a Song, *about teaching songwriting;* Notes on Broadway, *interviews with legendary Broadway composers; and* Rating the Movie Stars, *biographies of movie stars with ratings by Hirschhorn of all their movies. Hirschhorn also wrote* Reaching the Morning After, *the story of his former partner's fight with agoraphobia. His latest book is* Titanic Adventure, *about the first woman in history to dive down to the Titanic. Hirschhorn attended the High School of the Performing Arts in New York. His career began as a concert pianist and has included periods as an artist, singer, and film critic. He has won two Academy Awards, an Emmy, and a Tony.*

I wrote a book about teaching song-writing called *If They Ask You, You Can Write a Song* that Simon & Schuster published. For the follow-up book, *Notes on Broadway,* I interviewed legendary Broadway composers from Leonard Bernstein to Tim Rice to Steven Sondheim. Then came *Rating the Movie Stars,* biographies of movie stars that rated all their movies.

Among other things, I've been an on-and-off film critic for different magazines, so this was my chance to be a movie critic in a whole book. Then I wrote *Reaching the Morning After,* sort of a biography about my former partner and his fight with agoraphobia, which is a fear of leaving the house. And finally, *Titanic Adventure,* with my wife Jennifer Carter, is out.

The second time I got an Oscar I was prepared, but the first time, I forgot to thank my family. I just stuttered around. I didn't sound as bad to people as to myself. All the newspapers had picked a winner, and in order of probability, I came in fifth. A song sung by Michael Jackson came in first, so I didn't think there was any chance I would win. But what I didn't recognize was that his song was the story of a rat, and academy members thought that was beneath their dignity, so Michael Jackson didn't win. And I was from a prestige film, which helped. The second time, my strongest competition was a love song to a dog. So I won against a rat and a dog. What can I say? Life is funny.

When we broke up, my ex-wife became involved with someone who had just gotten out of San Quentin for murder, a heroin addict. The three of us were friends in true Tennessee William's style for a while. We tried for a civilized divorce, but that of course led to disastrous complications. Anyway, he stole one of my Oscars and sold it for drugs. I had to get a replacement. No, this does not make me happy.

I started my career as a concert pianist. I went to the High School of the Performing Arts in New York, and I started as an artist, too, as a singer, a writer. I had a contract with RCA, and for some reason they called me Hathaway and the producer said, "This is your image." So that was my start. But really my career began when I had a hit with a group called Jay and the Americans called "Why Can't You Bring Me Home." After that I had a hit with Elvis Presley called "Your Time Hasn't Come Yet Baby" from a movie called *Speedway*. That was the most exciting thing that had happened to me up to that time, maybe ever, because Elvis is such a legend. I had many hits in New York, but decided to get in to film, so I went to Hollywood and signed with Columbia as a staff writer. I had lots of movies with Jack Lemmon, Henry Fonda, and James Stewart in them.

## I started my career as a concert pianist.

Then I had my opportunity to write "The Morning After" for *The Poseidon Adventure*. Everybody had auditioned for that, and I decided I would give it a chance. The producer said, "The ship is turning over, people are dying, tragedy is everywhere. Make it positive." I panicked, went home, had about ten cups of black coffee, then came in the next morning hardly knowing the thing. The producers looked at me and said, "All right, we'll use it." That completely turned my life around. I was within an inch of thinking, "It's not a job, they're not paying me; maybe I just won't bother to try." I think that reinforced something I thought before: Try for everything; don't give up.

The producer said, "We want Streisand to sing it or nothing" (typical Hollywood). Well, Streisand was not available, and they were desperate. They received a demo from a secretary in Ohio who had never done a record. Her name was Maureen McGovern. The producer said, "Well, we'll try her." The producer and director were both very unhappy about it, then for reasons only known to God (aside from her great talent), it went to number one and changed my life. I won an Oscar for it, and that launched the follow-up, *Towering Inferno.* I won another Oscar for that. And from there, Disney noticed me. Al, my partner at the time, and I went to Disney and they said, "Bring us a proven property." I went to the library and searched desperately through every proven property from Cinderella to Oliver Twist, but they said, "Nope, we're going to do an original." So I did an entire score for *Pete's Dragon,* including "A Candle on the Water," sung by Helen Reddy, which got an Oscar nomination, too. It has been unbelievable.

So along the way, as a parallel career that people knew less, I wrote books. Simon & Schuster approached me because they thought I could say something firsthand about music, rather than just have teachers writing about the subject. Teachers, in my opinion, never emphasize anything practical; they're too academic. As somebody who is in there with all the slings and arrows, I felt I had something to offer. *If They Ask You, You Can Write a Song* stayed in print for 22 years, like a songwriter's bible. It was wonderful.

And following that, *Notes on Broadway* happened because then I went to Broadway. I had a chance to write a script for a show called *Copperfield,* as well as the songs, and the score was nominated for a Tony. Of course, Broadway is a brutal business, but it's absolutely wonderful. Herman Wouk wrote that World War II combat was easier than putting on a Broadway show. Yet you are drawn to it because of the live aspect, and seeing your material on stage is the biggest thrill in the world. We had a wonderful cast, including Mary

Elisabeth Mastriantonio before she made it in the movies; she was just radiant. And the follow-up show to that, the stage version of *Seven Brides for Seven Brothers,* is still touring all over. It's a hit in Europe right now.

My latest book is *Titanic Adventure.* Jennifer Carter was a *National Geographic* producer, and when they decided to bring up artifacts from the Titanic and film it, they had an eight-week expedition at sea. Jennifer was hired to lead the expedition, one woman leading 50 men. That was a challenge, in addition to facing hurricanes and dangerous fogs, and of course going down there, which is also dangerous. One man on board wanted her removed because he thought women were not capable of leading men. That was a problem, but she enlisted the support of everybody on board who thought she was doing a good job and was able to defeat him. Of course, it makes a gripping story about a strong woman who meets prejudice.

I've had enormous success with Internet promotions. There is a great advantage to a subject like the Titanic, which has hundreds of Web sites, maybe thousands, about it. So I struck up e-mail conversations with all these people and told them about the book, about Jennifer. They really became excited because, first of all, the subject is interesting, then they put up Web sites with pictures, displays with Jennifer's picture and mine, and information about the book. If you bring up Titanicdistributors.com, you'll see the incredible work that guy did and a big screen-size picture of Jennifer in her Titanic suit. We have a Web site too, titanicexpert.com, that has received superb reviews, terrific raves from William Buckley who did the foreword. He also wrote such a good review in the *National Review* that it looks like I paid for it.

Jane Seymour, the actress; Robert Wagner, the actor; an author named Richard Ellis, who is a big in the field as far as underwater books; and *Publisher's Weekly* gave us raves, too. If you don't get *Publisher's Weekly,* then you lose all the libraries. I'm glad I didn't realize that because none of the libraries were carrying it, then that review came out and boom, every library in the country bought it. It's sort of equivalent to the *New York Times* and Broadway shows.

The Internet was fantastic in boosting sales, and doing a lot of radio has been very helpful.

A friend of mine said, "Don't be concerned with TV; it gives a lot of publicity, but it doesn't really sell books. Except for *Oprah,* of course. But radio sells books." We've been finding this is true. The Titanic will sort of be a permanent stock item, so that attracted me to it. Aside from that, it's an incredible story about a woman who was a bank teller, had nothing but her dreams of going to sea, her three children, and no money. Going from that to being the first woman to go to the Titanic is sort of a *Rocky* story. People have told me it's the kind of book you pick up and can't put down until it's over. It would be a great movie—like *October Sky,* a someone-risked-everything-for-a-dream story. Everyone said, "You're crazy, you'll never make it, don't bother," but Jennifer didn't listen. She just kept on and became a *National Geographic* producer, and produces films for Imax now. It's all that unstoppable, tenacious feeling that you can do it. So many talented people fall by the wayside; they get discouraged, or grab onto security.

> **The Internet was fantastic in boosting the sale, and doing a lot of radio has been very helpful.**

I'm a great believer in suggestion and visualization, but not in the typical way. I feel that hearing my own voice always motivates me. So if I have a project to do—a book, a television show, a movie, anything—I give myself suggestions, listen to it through earphones, then visualize the completed product. And for some reason that always works—gets the juices going and gets the project done twice as fast. It's my own form of creative visualization. I work better early in the morning on books, when my mind is extremely clear; but, of course, there is no such thing as picking a time when you're on a deadline.

When we were doing *Titanic Adventure,* the publisher said either do it in three or four months, or we wait a year. I didn't want to wait. I'm a person who, when there is a gun to my head, functions twice as well. Writers often find any excuse to keep from getting started, so I said, "This will be finished in three months." I gave myself two months just to make it worse, and would get up in the middle of the night. I don't think I saw anyone for three months straight.

When I was about 19 years old, a vocal coach heard some of my material and said, "You'll never make it." I think many creative people run into that. The greatest lesson in life is to have your own vision and to completely ignore what people say, especially anything negative, because there will always be people who do that, and listening can really derail you. Then a year later I had a hit, and I ran into him. He was really sheepish about the whole thing—not apologetic, but embarrassed. I had an eighth grade teacher who disapproved of everything I did. When I wrote the high school play, she said it really wasn't me, but a collaborator. For years, I heard her in my head as a person who downgraded me. I was waiting until I would have success to tell her about it, but she died before it happened.

For a while, I wasn't sure what I wanted to do. I was playing in nightclubs until four in the morning and not liking it much. My father said, "You've got to make a living while you're thinking." So I became a court reporter. After a couple years of that, I said, "No, this is not for me. You know, even though it's a risk; I have to keep trying until I make it."

## STEVEN MITCHELL SACK

*Steve Sack is the author of popular legal advice books such as* The Sales Person's Legal Guide; The Employee Rights Handbook; *and* The Working Woman's Legal Survival Guide. *Sack also authored* From Hiring to Firing: The Legal Survival Guide for Employers in the '90s; The Hiring and Firing Book: A Complete Legal Guide for Employers; *and* The Complete Collection of Legal Forms for Employers, *published through his own company, Legal Strategies Publications. He never realized he would be an author until he wrote* The Sales Person's Legal Guide *with his roommate his senior year of law school. It was published and released the year he graduated, launching his writing career. Sack wrote another book, and success continued.*

Writing came later in my life. I wrote great papers in college, got straight A's, and got into law school. But I never realized I'd become an author until my senior year, when I wrote a book called *The Sales Person's Legal Guide* with my roommate. It was miraculously published by Prentice Hall in 1980, the year I graduated from law school—a really lucky break. Then my father, who was always instrumental in my success, encouraged me to write another book "because it's always great to follow up one winner with another one."

> **After my first book started selling, it became easier to get my other books placed.**

After my first book started selling, it became easier to get my other books placed. Then I wanted to self-publish, just because there was a niche I wanted to see if I could do. These books were very successful, but I just got too busy as a lawyer.

Nobody discouraged me from writing. In my business, writing books is a smart, strategic move because you get clients. It doesn't detract from your profession. Plus, it's a tremendous feeling to know that tens of thousands of people read your words and find they really help. It's amazing; I am really blessed with that.

My greatest book success is *The Lifetime Legal Guide,* which was commissioned by Book of the Month Club which paid me a very large advance. The book was a main selection, which is incredible, and is now in its third edition. Two separate publishers have distributed the trade rights.

The best thing in my writing career happened when I was promoting my last book, *The Working Woman's Legal Survival Guide.*

I was a guest on a radio show, and the producer thought so highly of me they eventually hired me to conduct and host my own national show. I do *Jobs and Careers with Attorney Steve Sack* through the United Broadcasting Network, live every Sunday from 2 to 5. That was an outgrowth of my book work.

I'm a labor and employment attorney so most of my books center around labor and employment, and job rights. I've used my innovative knowledge of what has not been written out there and my marketing skills. When the publisher goes along with your book, that's proof that your marketing instincts were accurate—the book is worthy of involvement so they'll put up money because it fills a need.

I've stayed motivated by the desire to help other people and for the money. I mean, you don't make a ton of money, although I have on a couple books—several hundred thousand dollars on one, which certainly pays the bills.

I always write my books in my home, only in my home office, on an old 1985 IBM computer, a dinosaur.

I'd tell aspiring authors this: Follow your instincts and dreams. To get into the publishing business and learn the business, to be a self-published author, I attended a lot of seminars, spent three days in California at Dan Poynter's house, attended all the ABA conferences. I bought books by John Kremer on how to publish and promote. It's a learning process. If you're going to do it, you can't skimp on quality. And you have to know what you're doing, or you'll lose your shirt.

> **It's a learning process. If you're going to do it, you can't skimp on quality.**

I'd like my own television show one day, and I look forward to writing more books and to expanding my radio show. I've written 17 books, so if I stop now, it would have been quite fulfilling.

*The Complete Legal Guide to Marriage, Divorce, Custody, and Living Together* was a favorite of mine, because it was outside my specialty, and got me on Oprah. It taught me that I could write on any legal topic for the public. In terms of production and quality, *The Working Woman's Legal Guide* was my favorite. I helped Prentice Hall from soup to nuts, from the cover to the artwork to the layout.

I've been on *Oprah, Sally* four times, *Jenny Jones, Steals and Deals, Smart Money,* all the shows.

In 1988, I got a call from the producer of *Oprah* while I was in my law office late at night. She said, "We are interested in having you on our show. Are you available Wednesday?" I said, "Yes, I'll be happy to do it." She said, "We'll call you at midnight to set everything up." So I went home, told my fiancee, and she said, "You are full of bologna." I said, "Well, it sounded like the producer of *Oprah*." Anyway, 11:30 came and went, 12:00 came and went. My fiancee said, "You see?" Then all of a sudden the phone rang . . ." Hi, Steve, this the producer of *Oprah*." I said, "I'm putting my fiancee on the phone!"

## NAURA HAYDEN

*Naura Hayden's book* How to Satisfy a Woman Every Time . . . and Have Her Beg for More *has sold more than two million copies and stayed on the* New York Times *bestseller list for ten weeks. Ten years later, it made the list again, the first time in the list's history that the same book came back, having never been out in paperback. Hayden has published seven books. Her first book was a vegetarian cookbook called* Low Cal Easy Does It Cookbook, *which had over two hundred easy recipes. The second book,* Everything You Have Ever Wanted to Know About Energy But Were Too Weak to Ask, *sold over 200,000 copies in hardcover. Her third book is called* Isle of View (Say It Out Loud).

I had an idea to do a marriage manual, and came up with the very succinct title, *How to Make Love to a Woman.* But about the time the book came out, a man came out with a book called *How to Make Love to a Woman,* and I thought, "Oh, my god, what am I going to do?" Then I thought, I'll call it *How to Satisfy a Woman Every Time . . . and Have Her Beg for More,* which was tongue and cheek. The title was an act of God; people really loved it. When I first came up with the book idea, I thought it would be a very graphic sexual thing and didn't think I could talk about it on the air. The book took off and was on the bestseller list for ten weeks.

> **Then I just decided I'd re-promote it. I went to my publicist and started to tour the country.**

Then after all the promoting, it survived on word of mouth, selling about 8,000 copies a year for years. Then I just decided I'd re-promote it. I went to my publicist and started to tour the country. I went to 89 cities three times, which is more than anyone in the history of book publishing, and the book was hugely successful the next time around. It sold two million copies.

I was on the *New York Times* bestseller list the first time with my Energy book. I never thought it would happen. I was on cloud nine. It stayed on for about 15 weeks, and that was when the list was ten rather than 15 books. The second time was with *How to Satisfy a Woman,* which was on ten weeks, and it was such a thrill. You might try for it, have it in the back of your mind; but how people react to your book, how many shows you get on . . . was tremendously exciting to me. But the *New York Times* is the peak, when you know you made the top.

I had done *Oprah* a few years before *How to Satisfy a Woman* came out. She had a show in Baltimore, *People Are Talking.* After she did the first part of the interview, we went to commercial and the producer came up and said, "You have to get more graphic or we will never have you on the show again. Be explicit." And Oprah said, "Naura, you do whatever makes you feel comfortable." She was so sweet and such a good person to realize they were trying to brow-beat me. Then I did *Oprah* again when she had the show in Chicago, and I did *Joan Rivers,* who is adorable. And I did *Geraldo.* But the power of Oprah is not to be believed. Just from doing her show once, I sold 200,000 copies.

I started my own publishing company called Bibli O'Phile Books and got all the rights to my books back and get 75 percent of the money from them.

The only work is the selling, promotion. You have to print the books, which costs anywhere from $1.25 to $1.75, depending on how many you print. The part you really have to work at is the promotion. My publicist, Eric Yaverbaum, is one of the best guys in the business—in the world.

With one of my books, I decided I didn't want to go around the country in a plane anymore. I got my husband to rent an RV, which he christened the "mobile," and we went to 52 cities for *How to Satisfy a Woman Every Time.* I would do shows and tell people we were going around the country in the Orgasmobile. My husband would drive right up to the door to pick me up after each show. We got to see the whole country and stayed in trailer parks with little ducks and rabbits and lakes. It was a fabulous, fun experience.

## CHAPTER 3

# The Producers

Look forward to someday publishing a book? Have a little writer's block? Turn to the Producer as your role model. The Producer is the author who has published so many books that others are in awe. Producers don't stop at one book. Like Rosalyn Alsobrook, they turn their books into series. Like Vicki Hinze (also known as Victoria Barrett), they have too many books to publish under merely one name. Like Kathleen Duey, they somehow write several books in only a year. Like the Energizer Bunny, they seem to keep going and going . . . .

The Producers have different inspirations, but no one can deny they are motivated. "I think what motivated me was the dream that one day I would see a book in print. I didn't care if it sold a million copies or no copies, if I got a million dollars or no dollars; I just wanted to see my book in print and hold it in my hands," says Harlan Coben. "Once you have reached that goal, it is no longer any good. Like anything else in life, once you reach that goal, you get hungry for more."

According to Nancy Bartholomew, "What is really important is persistence. A lot of writers I know have talent but don't keep at it, don't put that as their primary goal. To stay focused, I have a screen saver that is a Barbara Kingsolver quote: 'There is no other time to write than now.'"

Ed Gorman says, "Writing made me feel important. It seemed like a romantic calling. When I first met professional writers, they stripped away my romantic notions and forced me to sit down and do the actual work."

And, they are disciplined. "I set deadlines and write at least an hour up to five hours a day," says E. C. Ayres. "I consider ten pages a day a good goal. (Hemingway, incidentally, was happy doing one.)"

Vicki Hinze "doesn't look at clocks very often. You have to write consistently, even during times of crisis and under duress."

They produce and produce, but they seem to fight the drudgery. "I've written everything from historical romances, to contemporary romances, to time travels, to ghost books," says Rosalyn Alsobrook. "Now I'm trying my hand at an inspirational and will soon put together that murder suspense I mentioned. Variety is the spice of life and it keeps the writing from becoming a bore."

## ROSALYN ALSOBROOK

*Rosalyn Alsobrook is the bestselling author of 29 books. Over two million copies of her works are in print, and her books have been translated into seven languages and are available in 18 countries. Her first book,* The Thorn Bush Blooms, *was published in 1981 and she hasn't stopped since. Her latest novel is* Tomorrow's Treasures, *the sixth in the Seascape Romances series created with fellow author Vicki Hinze (Victoria Barrett). The pair met online through Genie Electronic Network's RomEx and crafted the series concept with individual novels, which was uncharted territory for authors. She was nominated for Romance Writers Association's most prestigious Lifetime Achievement Award, featured in* Who's Who in U.S. Writers, Editors, & Poets *from 1989 through 1996, and selected for the 1994 and 1996* International Author's and Writer's Who's Who. *She was nominated in 1994 for The Outstanding Achievement Award presented by the review magazine* Affaire de Coeur *and won the 1995 NOLA Climbing Rose Award and the 1996 RWA ETC Sandy Award for excellence. She recently earned a career achievement nomination from* Romantic Times. *Her Web site address is home.earthlink.net/~ralsobrook/bioroz.htm.*

One time a fellow writer and I were in a local eatery discussing each other's works in progress. My friend was about halfway into her novel, and we were going over different possibilities for the upcoming murder scene. The place was packed with a noisy lunch crowd, so we had to talk louder than usual. Then for reasons only God can explain, suddenly the noise level dropped right as I was saying something like, "I tell you what I think. The best way to kill him is with poison. If you use the gun, you'll have problems later." After that, you could have heard a pin drop. And you could have fried an egg on my friend's red face.

> **Since I wrote my first book at age four, I'd have to say I was born a writer.**

Since I wrote my first book at age four, I'd have to say I was born a writer. My father kept that first work, a masterpiece about an unhappy wall that children color on. It's 13 pages long, one word per page for volume's sake.

I can't really single out any one experience, but I suppose the teacher who influenced me most was my high school teacher, Mrs. Tucker, who encouraged me to flex my writing muscles, whether fiction or nonfiction. The small town where I attended school didn't have any creative writing type courses, nor did Kilgore College when I attended. I have nothing like that in my background.

Being published in the local newspaper starting my junior year of high school, I had lots of people encouraging, not discouraging me. The locals loved my sense of humor, which was decidedly warped for a kid. As for my book writing, I was into chapter ten of my first book before telling anyone other than my husband I was trying a novel. If I'd failed, I didn't want a lot of my family or friends knowing. No one was aware to discourage me. I'm easily motivated. If I want something badly, I keep after it until it's mine. My father had a lot to do with me believing I can do or be anything I set out to do or be. He had incredible faith in me and gave me incredible faith in myself.

When I found my biological mother in the late 1980s, I was able to give her my latest novel on Mother's Day, knowing it was dedicated to the brave young woman who'd given me up for adoption rather than have an abortion. Not only did she give me life; she gave me happiness.

Every time I come up with a new idea that excites me, it's a brand new surprise for me. And, oh, how I loooove surprises!

One funny thing happened when I was writing Chapter 10 of *The Thorn Bush Blooms,* and suddenly the hero was snakebit and all alone. I had to know what a snakebite looked like and what should be done for it to make the scene believable, so I called my father, the M.D. The conversation went something like this:

Me: "Dad? What should you do for someone who's just been snake bit?

Dad, in a cautious voice, "What do you mean?"

Me: "I mean, what do you do for someone who's just been bit?"

Dad, now panicking: "You? Or one of the sons? Which one was bit?" (The man is *not* pausing for a breath, much less a response.) "Hang up and call an ambulance. Now!"

I explained (rather quickly) that the victim was a character in a book I'd been writing on for months, not either of my sons. Nor me.

After that, he commented, "I think you should still hang up and call an ambulance. Give them *this* address. I think I just had a coronary."

> **If you don't believe you can write the book and sell it, then don't bother. You'll never make it.**

I have chosen my topics in different ways. Sometimes something I read triggers a plot idea or something that happens in my life. Sometimes a character comes to me who just *has* to have a story written about him or her.

Until my mother fell ill early in 1996, I wrote from 8:30A.M. until 5:30 P.M. every day but Sunday. Right now, I'm lucky if I can steal five hours a day to write, which is better than last year when I barely managed ten writing days all year, or the year before when I didn't write at all.

I wrote my first book longhand and typed it out on a manual typewriter. I stepped up to a correctable typewriter for my second and third books. By the fourth I had an old Kaypro computer to pound out my novels. I've since had five computers, having just bought a spiffy new one in January. I also have a laptop, but prefer the desktop.

My husband turned our double-car garage into a huge office with a library for me. My writing workstation faces a large bay window that looks out on a country lane and a meadow with woods beyond. My accounting workstation is in a back room and faces a plain white wall, but who needs inspiration when doing accounting work? The IRS frowns on creative writing when putting together tax returns.

I look forward to creating different types of novels. I've written everything from historical romances, to contemporary romances, to time travels, to ghost books. Now I'm trying my hand at an inspirational simply because in recent years I've had to get closer to my God to stay sane. Yet, while I'm putting together a synopsis for the inspirational, I have a murder suspense I want to put together before too long. Variety is the spice of life and keeps the writing from becoming a bore.

Keep writing. Have faith in yourself. If you don't believe you can write the book and sell it, then don't bother. You'll never make it.

## HARLAN COBEN

*Harlan Coben is the author of the popular Myron Bolitar murder mystery series. As Coben describes the series, "Myron Bolitar, sports agent, former NCAA star and Yoo Hoo fan along with his pal Win, the psycho financier, tackle professional sports and murder with snappy repartee and the occasional drop kick." Titles in the series are* Deal Breaker, Dropshot, Fade Away, Backspin, *and* One False Move. Fade

*Away won the 1997 Edgar Allan Poe Award for Best Paperback Original, and the 1997 OLMA (Online Mystery Award), was nominated for a Shamus Award by the Private Eye Writers of America, and "picked up a Dilys award nod" from the Independent Mystery Booksellers. His Web site is cyberjag.com/karen/mystery/coben/newslett.htm.*

I had the worst covers on my books. My first had a bleeding football on it, and my second a bleeding tennis ball, so I became known as the author of the bleeding balls. No woman would touch it unless I begged them to. "Give me ten pages, give me 15 pages, just give me a chance" is more charming than begging. All writers know you have to work hard, do a zillion signings, send postcards out, and do all the things I'm telling you. But the good thing is, if the book is good enough, it will happen; if the book's not good enough, it doesn't matter how much promotion you do.

I think I became a writer, not so much out of, say, perspiration or inspiration as out of desperation. I realized I wasn't meant to do anything else, like say, work. I was one of the later ones. I always love when I am on a panel with other writers, and we're asked, "When did you first know you were a writer?" You get answers like "I always knew," "When I was a three-month-old fetus," or "At the age of six, when the children used to gather around me on the playground while I regaled them with pirate tales of woe." That was not me. I was in college when I got the idea to write a story, and the novel I started then didn't really pan out. It became the usual self-important, pretentious first novel. But from there I got the writing bug, like a virus, then I started writing what I love, which is crime fiction.

I don't believe too much in writing classes and that sort of thing. I think the only way to learn how to write is just to write. To make it sound simple, writing is one of those activities where quantity will inevitably make quality. Rather than taking any course, I would rather write a novel and throw it away if it's no good. The only experience that is really valuable, is that with every book I write I get better, and I think you are always learning.

What motivated me was the dream that one day I would see a book in print. I didn't care if it sold a million copies or no copies, if I got a million dollars or no dollars; I just wanted to see my book in print and hold it in my hands. Like anything else in life, once you reach that goal you get hungry for more. Then the dream is having the book in stores, in windows, and selling more. That was one of the first things that motivated me.

Also, I am the opposite of the tree that falls in the woods and no one is around to hear; I don't exist if you don't read me. I don't believe people who say they write for themselves. Since the days of hieroglyphics until now, writing was meant to communicate, not for yourself. Until you read *One False Move* or *The Final Detail*, it doesn't exist. It's like that old saying, "When one person dies, a whole world dies." When someone reads a book a whole new world is created. That drives me, not the sales or the money. Of course, that is there, but I just want people to read it. I don't care if they get it at the library or steal it; as a writer, I don't exist unless you read me.

> **If the subject matter is your passion, find a way to make your idea work.**

I think I actually started about as low as you can start—with a paperback original called *Deal Breaker*. It had a first print run of around 15,000 and no expectations whatsoever. I had a two-book contract that barely hit five figures, and I'm probably making about 30 or 50 times that now. I had a perspective a lot of the guys who got the early money didn't get. I started off really trying to scrape. Somebody told me that you make readers one at a time, which is a good way of approaching it. When I would go to a conference, I saw everybody as a potential reader.

Those who started out with me or a few years before, and those ones who made the next step, gone from, say, paperback to hardcover, or from mid-list to making some kind of career out of it, were almost always authors who worked hard in promotion. But in almost every case, they were also better authors than those who kept banging the drums. If the book is good enough, it doesn't matter whether you are a nice guy, or have cute buttons and a nice hat; if they don't like the book, the book is going to die out. The good news is that quality does matter.

> **When someone reads a book a whole new world is created. That drives me, not the sales or the money.**

Having a sports agent hero in a market dominated by women buyers, the odds were not in my favor. But *Deal Breaker* won an Anthony, which is voted on by the fans at Bouchercon, probably 80 percent women. They voted for a book that had a bleeding football on it!

My glimmer of hope is that talent does seem to shine through. Of course, authors who get dropped wouldn't agree with me, but I think overall it is true.

I did one book signing with two other authors, and the store had no signs up (nothing!), and literally had three of my books. Miraculously, a lot of us were betting on how many books total we were going to sell. I managed to sell all three books, then went up to the store owner and asked if he had more. He said, "Let me check the computer . . . what's your name again?"

It's also debatable what's good promotional stuff, what's worthwhile, and what is just a waste of time. For example, the Internet was probably a more useful tool a few years ago, before so many people were on. Now every author has a Web site; every author is posting on boards. Every author is checking out Amazon's rankings too often. On one hand, writers should do as much promotion online as they can, understanding that the benefits are limited. On the other hand, you have to be careful not to waste time online. I feel tremendous guilt, if nothing else, when I have the TV on. But the

Internet is just as big a waste of time. Anything that stops you from writing because you are checking boards is bad. Also we tend to check what people are saying about us; sometimes it's valuable and sometimes paralyzing. We tend to forget the 50 good things and remember the one bad thing. When the book comes out I really gear up, get in touch with the stores I know are supportive, and make sure they all have the advance copies. Actually a lot of contacts in the business know me now, and don't really need to be reminded, but I do think it is important to cultivate relationships.

The first couple promotions I nicknamed the Harlan the Whore Tour. I really went around. This is a business, and you have to treat it as such. If you open a restaurant, you're not going to make money the first year, probably not the second or third year. I don't know why writers think their writing should. If you are new with a publisher, and your publisher has given you $10,000 advance, and is printing 5,000 hardcover copies of your book, they are not going to print a $50,000 ad in the *New York Times*. But if I get a $5,000 or $10,000 advance, whatever the figure, I decide to spend all that money on promotion. The money shouldn't be that important to you in the long run. A lot of authors do this. I toured myself a lot, called up the bookstores, sold myself, because the publicist is not going to do it.

I have a little saying for beginning authors, "Publicists are like your appendix—either superfluous or they hurt you." It's not their fault; they don't have a budget for you. Yelling at them isn't going to do any good. Accept that you have to do it yourself. Call a lot of bookstores. I traveled around by myself, driving or whatever. At the beginning of my career I hooked up with two other authors—all young, in our 30s, on our first or second books—and we created a theme tour.

At the time the TV show *Friends* was just starting up, so we used the *Friends* logo, only we called ourselves Fiends, because we were mystery authors. We made a poster and generated some excitement, wrote an article for one of the mystery magazines (a joke travelogue of our tour) to get publicity, and hit the road. Last year Martin J. Smith and Phillip Reed went out together and took their children, rented some sort of van, and went from bookstore to bookstore. So I recommend that.

What I recommend even more is finding and going to the conferences in your genre. For example, at Bouchercon there will be at least 15 to 20 mystery bookstore owners, mystery reviewers, and the mystery magazine people you should make it your business to meet. Plus there are a lot of readers and fellow authors, who are a lot more supportive than people think.

The attitude of mystery authors is that no one has to fail for me to succeed. When I first started, it shocked me how supportive we are of each other. We really aren't in competition. If readers like somebody else's mystery book, then they are going to buy yours. Anything that is good for one raises the whole boat.

From 8:30 to 11:30 A.M., while my almost five-year-old daughter Charlotte is at school, I usually hang out in a coffee bar. My home office has become, with the Internet, phone calls, and faxes, an impossible place for me to work, though it's a good place for me to do the business of writing. I like to go to different spots and also like a little white noise when I work, so coffee bars, like Starbucks, are good places. Of course, you look like a pretentious ass, but that is the price you pay. I am also a streak writer. Writers beat themselves up because they don't produce x amount of pages. I have come to the conclusion that some days I am not going to produce the pages. You still panic, but you know it's going to happen. So if I write a 400-page manuscript, I may write 100 pages in the last week. I wrote 40 pages of *One False Move* in the last day, but I had seen the ending so often in my head that it was much easier to write; you kind of see a light at the end of the tunnel, and you explode. But I try to write a little bit every day.

> **Call a lot of bookstores. I traveled around by myself, driving or whatever.**

We have a TV deal with Fox that would be great if it goes through. I just want to write the best books that I can, and look forward to continuing to grow book by book.

I've actually put my e-mail address in the last couple of books and enjoy hearing from readers. Like I said before, you don't exist as an author until somebody reads your book; and if I can talk to you for 500 pages, you earn the right to talk back to me for a couple of sentences.

## ANNETTE MEYERS

*Annette Meyers and her husband Martin Meyers were once introduced as Meyers & Meyers, The Writing Machines. Annette is the author of the Smith and Wetzon mystery series about two women headhunters.* The Groaning Board *is seventh in the series, and previous titles include* The Big Killing, Tender Death, The Deadliest Option, *and* Murder: The Musical. *She has written the first in the Free Love series, set in 1920 Greenwich Village, featuring poet Olivia Brown as the main character. Martin Meyers began his mystery writing career with the Patrick Hardy series in the '70s. The character is back as part of a collection of short stories called* The Private Eyes. *As Maan Meyers, Annette and Martin combine their talents and write history-mysteries set in New York. The series begins in 1664 with* The Dutchman, *featuring a character of New Amsterdam and the first sheriff of New York. The next five books feature descending generations of the Tonneman family. Their Web site is www.meyersmysteries.com.*

I have three series. The first book in the Smith and Wetzon series was published in 1989. But then with my husband, using the name Maan Meyers, I write historical mysteries set in New York in the seventeenth, eighteenth, and nineteenth centuries. I'm now copyediting the book that is coming out in October, the first of my new series about a woman poet, set in Greenwich Village in the '20s.

I have been writing since I was a little girl and have rejection slips from a magazine that has been defunct for 50 years called *Calling All*

*Girls,* and I've been rejected by *Seventeen,* and have a lot of rejections from *The New Yorker.* Going all the way back, I always wanted to be a writer. It probably is due to a school librarian named Bessie Maclane who, when I was nine or ten and had read every book in the school library, slipped me a Nancy Drew and said, "Hey, I think you might like this." In those days Nancy Drew was not considered proper reading for young girls because it was thought too wild. Also, it wasn't a classic, and you were supposed to be reading classics. So while I did not start writing mysteries until about 1986, I was always attracted to the mystery genre, and read a lot of mysteries.

I was at the Four Seasons Restaurant in New York, an elegant place we new stockbrokers would come for a free drink. I was interviewing a stockbroker who put his attaché under the table, ordered drinks, then jumped up saying he had to make a phone call. I waited half an hour, with his attaché under the table, but he didn't come back. I paid for the drinks and went downstairs to the phone booths, real phone booths with windows and doors. I got halfway across the floor, and saw him huddled over the telephone. I thought, what if I open the door and he flops out dead? Well, he wasn't dead. But I came home and asked my husband (who had five mysteries published in the '70s), "What do you think about this?" He had been after me for years to keep going, so I wrote the scene then decided to write about the extraordinary women I had met in the industry. I figured on a partnership, and the best partners I knew were Holmes and Watson. So I started playing with the Watson name, and got Wesson. I knew one character would be Smith, and I didn't want to use the gun, so I changed the consonants around and got Wetzon. And they go after the top guns. It is a funny series, a crazy New York series.

Doubleday sent me on tour one year, to the Pacific Northwest, with my fourth book, *Blood on the Street.* I was sitting in a mall signing books when this sort of square, very nice woman came in and bought the book, and said, "Would you sign it to my parents?" I said, "Are you sure this is something your parents would want to read?" She said, "Oh, they both love your books because my father is a broker. My mother said she finally knows what he does all day."

I have always told publicists I would do anything, I have even been the published mystery writer at a Republican fund-raiser because they bought books. I have toured pretty much everywhere in the United States, and that's a lot of fun, and of course I do the conventions.

I get tons of e-mail. The latest are from people who don't like when my character breaks off with the police lieutenant boyfriend and begins an affair with an attorney nobody likes. People are asking me to please take her back.

People hate the Smith character because she is so arrogant and egocentric, but I keep saying she is everybody's evil twin. She does awful things that drive normal people out of their minds. When I created her, I did not intend to have her as a continuing character, but the cover said a Smith and Wetzon mystery so I called my editor and said, "You can't do this. I'm going to kill Smith," and they said, "Oh no, you're not." Doubleday decided to send out reader response cards with the galleys, and they could not believe the emotional responses they got, like "Tell Wetzon to get rid of Smith!"

> **Reading and life experience are, I think, as important as talent—and commitment.**

Most of my books were published while I was working full time as a headhunter. I used to work at home on Fridays and work on Saturdays, so I could write two chapters on Friday, print them out, and rewrite them on Saturday, then write two more the following Friday. It was stressful, but I learned to write amid many phone calls and crises. Since I have been a full-time writer, I write five days a week and try to give myself Saturday and Sunday off, unless they need a copyedit by Monday. If Marty was not a writer, too, I would have a big problem with the demands of time by my spouse.

The community of mystery writers is wonderful, just like a family. Of course we compete, but not like other genres. I have talked to writers, fiction writers, and hear that is highly competitive and not very nice.

Read is my advice. Read, read, read! I am an eclectic reader so I read any genre, not just science fiction or romance. Reading and life experience are, I think, as important as talent—and commitment. You have to commit time and stay on a schedule; you can't wait for inspiration.

> **Going all the way back, I always wanted to be a writer.**

I think people assume writers were born with the creative ability, but I learned to write. I grew up on a chicken farm in Thompsonford, New Jersey, which was extremely rural, during WWII. There was little to do except read. I used to read *The New Yorker* in the library and learned to write by reading. F. J. Pearlman and J. D. Salinger were probably the two writers who taught me how to write. I gave up so many times, I can't tell you. But my husband was such a nag, and when I had an idea I just went back and did it. Now I am a Writing Machine.

## PATRICIA POLACCO

*Patricia Polacco is an illustrator, author, and storyteller. She has received critical acclaim for her work, which includes the Civil War era book* Pink and Say, *an American Library Association Notable Children's Books for 1995. Other titles include* Thunder Cake, Rechenka's Eggs, My Ol' Man, Babushka's Mother Goose, I Can Hear the Sun, *and her own photo-biography,* Firetalking. *She has a master's degree in fine arts and a Ph.D. in art history. Polacco reflects her rich heritage and love of storytelling in her many books, which celebrate life in many lands. As a child she struggled with dyslexia, but used her drawing skills to earn her peers' respect. Polacco's Web site is falcon.jmu.edu/~ramseyil/polacco.htm.*

I was born an artist, come from a family of storytellers, and started writing late in life, around age 41. It's just what you end up doing.

Two teachers changed my life. I wrote a book about one, called "Thank You Mr. Felker." I was a child with dyslexia, disnumeria, and dysgraphia. Mr. Felker changed my life by teaching me to read at age 14, when everyone else thought I was dumb. June Steinghart, an art professor in my college, allowed my kids to come to her class when I was a single mother on welfare. Both are deceased now, but they certainly knew what they meant to me.

The person who made my writing happen was my mom. She raised enough money to send me to New York, where I saw sixteen publishers and literally sold all I had thirteen years ago.

The love of doing writing has kept me motivated. There's nothing like it. Seeing the children's eyes, feeling that sense of creativity is like magic. I can't stop.

I'm inspired by life experiences, things that move me. I love stories that demonstrate how truly noble mankind is, about our strengths. The most important heroes are the most unlikely ones.

I'm not a writer who sits down in front of a computer every day. I have to have the "fire in the belly." If I don't, I'll do everything but write, such as garden and shop, although I am on schedule when I do artwork for a book that's already complete. I use an electric typewriter. A story starts out in rockers. I sit in rocking chairs, and have little pads of paper by all the rockers. I put the pads in a manila envelope, then go back and flesh it all out until it becomes a story. I also work in my office at home and in my studio for artwork. I've done it all— national tours (which are grueling), TV, radio, school visits.

> **The love of doing writing has kept me motivated. There's nothing like it.**

My advice for writing children's books would be what has worked for me. Keep your story close to your heart. All stories are circular. You need to take the reader on a journey, then home where they feel safe again.

Next up in my career? Acting. I am currently working on small films and videos for children in my village, and am setting up videos to send to schools. I would love to make them inventive, comedy art films that show consequences, morality, and respect. We are losing ground there these days.

Children like my work very much. People make plays out of my work, and operas by the Seattle Opera Company. My stories have been done for TV, for film. You just sit back and go, "Wow!" It's amazing.

## NANCY BARTHOLOMEW

*Nancy Bartholomew is the author of two series of humorous amateur sleuth mysteries. The Sierra Lavotini series features Sierra Lavotini, an exotic dancer, and her hairless Chihuahua, Fluffy. The novels are* The Miracle Strip *and* Dragstrip. *Her second series, due out in spring or winter of 2000, features Maggie Reid, an aspiring country and western singer with a 16-year-old daughter. The first book is* Your Cheating Heart.

*She is working on a third series featuring a forensic psychologist. This series will have a more hard-boiled, police procedural tone. Bartholomew draws upon her work and life experiences when writing.*

I'm a psychiatric social worker, have my master's in social work, and am in private practice three days a week so I draw upon my work experience in my writing. I did work with drug and alcohol patients, and a lot were exotic dancers and bikers. That helped me with the Sierra series, since Sierra is an exotic dancer. I used to be a country and western singer when I was in high school and college. (I'm not saying I was a good one, just that I was one.) We had a band and I knew a lot of bikers then, so that also helps with this series. And my experience singing on stage helps with Maggie, who is a country western singer. The professional part of me is what fuels the third series, featuring a forensic psychologist.

I came from a family of artists and dancers and writers, and a lot of them had produced books. It was sort of a family myth that you had to produce a book, but I didn't think I had any talent in that area. Then a really good high school teacher just drew it out of me. I dabbled with writing, wrote my own music when I was with the band, and short stories in college, but it wasn't until I had toddlers and felt I was going to go insane that I started writing murder mysteries. I'd be at home without anybody to talk to. I'd get tired of Barney, and pretty soon I was killing off people. I used to wish one of the characters from my books would knock on the front door and say, "Let me whisk you away from all of this." Now if I get bored, I just go to the computer, and people start talking to me, and we have a great experience.

My aunt, Lillian Smith, wrote a book called *Strange Fruit*, which had an interracial romance in it. It got banned in Boston, and all sorts of horrible things happened to her, but it also got produced on Broadway, so she was the big icon of the family.

People would say, "You know you're never going to make any money doing that; it's a hard life." It is a hard life, but when you have to do it, you don't have much choice.

Stubbornness has kept me motivated. The more people told me no, the madder I got and the more determined I was. I think it was Garrison Keillor who said, "If you think you can quit writing, go ahead; maybe you're not a writer. But if you can't quit, and you have to go back to it, then you might as well accept that you are a writer." I thought that was awesome advice.

> I came from a family of artists and dancers and writers, and a lot of them had produced books.

The best thing that happened was sending my first short story off and having it get accepted by *Alfred Hitchcock Mystery Magazine*. I thought, "Wow, if they take me, and they are the best, well . . . ." I went right down to Office Depot and bought a laptop, ninety days same as cash. When I had no cash ninety days later and no other story published, I thought, you know this might be difficult. I paid for that computer for three years at 20 percent interest.

The most awful thing was agreeing to do a signing at a dress shop's fifth anniversary. They set me outside at a table next to a mannequin, and the mannequin got more attention than I did. It was embarrassing.

The most surprising thing has been how very helpful the other mystery writers have been. They welcomed me with open arms when I joined Sisters in Crime. There was no jealousy, no backbiting. I've heard it's not always that way. Mystery writers are a special, special breed.

> **I killed off an old boyfriend, and oh lord, he deserved it.**

I've always read mysteries, so I love them and had no problem picking my genre. A couple of years after I hadn't sold anything but that first short story, I thought, I'm going to Sleuthfest, this mystery writers conference in Florida. And I'm going to enter their short story contest. If I don't even place, I'm going to come back and be the best little social worker there ever was. The night before the short story deadline, I still didn't have a story. And one of my sons asked me to install some computer software for him. And when I did, a little piece of paper floated out that said, "Sierra reveals all." I looked at it and thought, that's a great title. Then I realized that Sierra was the name of the software company. I wrote the story about Sierra Lavotini that won first place. It was awesome! So I wrote a whole book about her, and the objection was, who would read about a stripper? But Sierra is such a compelling character that I don't have any trouble writing about her, or thinking up the trouble she gets into.

For my other series, I was trying to think what other world I know. Actually, when you're a writer, you get to do everything you couldn't do in real life. I wish I'd pursued the singing career with more vigor, but I was a chicken. Maggie Reed isn't scared of nothin' or nobody.

I killed off an old boyfriend, and oh lord, he deserved it. He was such an ultimate redneck that I thought, we'll let him go.

I work and it's really important to me to be there when the kids get out of school. That leaves me Monday and Friday to write in the afternoon. When the kids are home, I'll invite a bunch of their friends over so I can write a little bit. If I'm really going, I'll do a little on the weekend too.

I think what is really important is persistence. A lot of writers I know have talent but don't keep at it, don't put writing as their primary goal. To stay focused, I use a screensaver on my computer that is a Barbara Kingsolver quote: "There is no other time to write than now." Writing is not rocket science. If you read books that tell you how to do it, pay attention to what people tell you, pay attention to your rejections, and are persistent and focused, you'll get published.

I've gotten fan mail that is really cool. All my old boyfriends contact me, saying, "We always knew you'd turn out wonderful. Let's get together when you come to Philly and have lunch." And I think finally, finally I've heard from the boys I couldn't date in high school. It's the ultimate revenge. "So how did you turn out? Oh, you went bald. Maybe that's better than killing you." It's big fun.

## E. C. AYRES

*E. C. Ayres is the author of the popular Tony Lowell Mysteries. His first book,* Hour of the Manatee, *was winner of the St. Martin's Press/Private Eye Writers of America Best First P.I. Novel competition in 1992. Subsequent books in the Florida Gulf Coast–based series are* Eye of the Gator, Night of the Panther, *and* Lair of the Lizard. *His short story, "The Caretaker," will be published in a forthcoming anthology of Florida mystery stories. He is also co-author of* Thief of All Time, *a nonfiction book about Shakespeare and Marlowe, and has written* Red Tide, *an eco-thriller.*

I was an avid reader as a child, and a frequent escapist into the more interesting and safer realms of fiction. But writing didn't interest me until I took a course in literary criticism as a freshman at Cornell

College in Iowa, focusing on the works of F. Scott Fitzgerald. I strongly identified with both the author and his works, and decided I wanted to become a writer. I procrastinated for the next two decades, dabbling in related fields (film and television), but never really tackled the task at hand. I was motivated to make a living. When opportunities in film and television finally dried up (when I turned 40, which no doubt had nothing to do with ageism!), I decided I had nothing to lose by sitting down to write a novel.

The best thing with regard to my writing career was winning the Best First P.I. competition in 1992, for my first book, which included a publishing contract with St. Martin's.

The worst was a near-miss in the film world. In 1982 an old mentor/friend Jack Arnold hired me to develop and write a screenplay based on a classic novel by Sir Arthur Conan Doyle. I wrote a brilliant script, the studio bought it, and promptly removed me from the project (I was naive enough to take this personally). This film was never made (in that form anyway) because, to quote a studio executive: "Who cares about dinosaurs?" The title was *The Lost World*.

> # I wrote a brilliant script, the studio bought it, and promptly removed me from the project . . .

I still have my screenplay, and still think it is brilliant.

The most surprising was that my first book wasn't a bestseller. The funniest was that I ever believed that possible (neither was my second). The most embarrassing? Neither was my third. This is followed by contacts from readers pointing out mistakes, to which I always respond (in vain), "I'm not the editor, I'm only the author!"

I choose issues important to me, that also have "legs." These are primarily social and environmental issues (gun control, over-development and environmental degradation, endangered species, race relations, political corruption). I am frequently stirred by a specific article or editorial in the news.

I set deadlines, and write at least an hour and up to five hours a day. I consider ten pages a day a good goal. (Hemingway, incidentally, was happy doing one.)

My advice is be realistic in your goals and unrelenting in achieving them. Daydreaming is the most dangerous and least productive form of procrastination.

I look forward to my first bestseller, which I expect to come in a genre other than mystery fiction (either mainstream or nonfiction, both of which I am pursuing). Success is a relative term. Just as a Wall Street millionaire no longer feels fulfilled with mere millions and must have billions, being a published author is no longer a sufficiently satisfying goal for resting on one's laurels (and we're not talking millions here). But I remain thankful for the opportunities I've gotten, for the accolades I've received; and I do try to acknowledge those who supported me early on—especially independent booksellers, repeat readers who have taken the trouble to contact me (traveling hundreds of miles to a book signing, for example), and certain reviewers. The bottom line, however, is to keep on writing—no matter what!

## TIAN DAYTON

*Tian Dayton, Ph.D., is an author and nationally renowned expert and consultant in psychodrama and addictions. She has written eight books, including* Heartwounds; The Soul's Companion: Connecting with the Soul Through Daily Meditations; *and* The Quiet Voice of Soul. *Dayton has a Ph.D. in clinical psychology and an M.A. in educational psychology. She has made media appearances on Montel Williams, Faith Daniels, Rikki Lake, Geraldo, and others. Dayton is a faculty member at New York University and a therapist in private practice. She is a Fellow of the American Society for Psychodrama, Sociometry, and Group Psychotherapy, and is also a certified Montessori teacher. She presents psychodrama workshops and training workshops internationally. Her Web site is www.tian-dayton.com.*

Writing is my way of revealing myself both to myself and to anyone out there who can identify. I work things out through writing, unravel my innermost thoughts on a page. As I write, I hear the words being chosen in the front of my mind; it's companionable, in treatment or pleasure. I love to write and cannot imagine writing for any other reason—it's so time-consuming and has so many tedious elements that if you didn't love it, it would be just too much.

> **Write freely and edit brutally. I edit books over and over and over again.**

All my education contributed to the content and direction of my writing, but as a doctoral candidate I learned to love research and to understand writing as a way to synthesize and prioritize divergent thoughts and theory, and integrate it into my own personality so I could use it rather than it using me.

As the youngest of four children, I never had the voice my older siblings naturally had. For a long time I just loved to talk to the paper—to sort of know I had a voice too. Now writing motivates me to research every theory in the field of psychology, so I can stay current and growing in my field.

I had such an easy start with books. I never intended to do more than create a handbook for experimental work that I would have been happy to practically give away. I just wanted people to know about this great stuff. It found its way to a publisher through the hands of Sharon Wescherder, a friend of mine. The publisher picked it right up—which was great and made everything feel easy, sort of fated to be.

I write about what feels pressing and important to me; about what I feel will help my clients, trainers, and students; about important themes that seem to arise in my work—that will help people be happier through knowing themselves better. I write about what fascinates me and what I will enjoy submerging myself in for a couple of years. People inspire me. My children and relationship with my husband inspire me and probably are at the center of my own personal growth.

When my children were young, I used to write at 5:30 or 6:00 A.M., stop to get them out of bed and off to school, then resume until 10:30 or so when I went about the rest of my day—private practice, teaching, and training. Now that they are in college, it's easier to fit writing into my own schedule. Some weeks I have more time than others—for sure, writing takes time whenever you do it.

People think I'm crazy, but I write with pen and paper. I just feel close to my work like this. I am always buying special pens. I love pens and stationery stores. I write all over the place—in my bedroom, library, sitting room, outside when the weather is nice, in all my favorite places, pretty places where I feel comfortable. When the children were small I wrote anywhere I could sit for a while—doctor's offices, airplanes, wherever.

If I have any advice, it is write what you love, what you wish to know more of; write where you want to expand the universe of your heart and mind or your profession, preferably both. Write freely and edit brutally. I edit books over and over and over again. There's no need to get it right the first time (in fact, you never get it right). Learn to live with the feeling that it's always a work in progress. All you can really do is put out your best effort.

Maintaining success is constant work. Once your book is published, a whole new kind of work begins. First you birth the baby, then you raise it, which takes tons of time and effort. Radio and TV are constant for the first few months, then it's maintenance through speaking, training, and so on.

## LINDA JOY SINGLETON

*Linda Joy Singleton is the author of 20 mid-grade and young adult series books. Her titles include* Almost Twins, Opposites Attract,

Barnyard Battle, *and* Almost Perfect. *The My Sister the Ghost series includes* Twin Again, Escape from Ghostland, Teacher Trouble, *and* Babysitter Beware. *The Cheer Squad series includes* Crazy Cartwheels, Spirit Song, Stand Up and Cheer, Boys Are Bad News, Spring to Stardom, *and* Camp Confessions. *She has another three-book series due out in early 2000, a young adult suspense sci-fi series called Sci-Clones. Singleton co-authored a self-published collector Judy Bolton mystery book with the original author, Margaret Sutton. Her Web site is www.geocities.com/Athens/Acropolis/4815/bio.html.*

My most embarrassing moment was when I was the last speaker at a writing conference. Early in the morning I realized I was wearing mismatched shoes. I was *so* upset! I had *no* idea how I'd stand up in front of everyone with such an embarrassing problem. I took out a notebook and listed possible solutions—like sneak to a nearby store and buy new shoes, take off my shoes entirely, or tell everyone mismatched shoes was the new style. When it was my turn to talk, I was *so* nervous. But I went up front, read them my possible-solution list, and everyone burst out in friendly laughter. It was the best speech opening I've ever given.

I was a born writer. No one told me to write. When I started writing around age eight, my parents supported me and enjoyed listening to my stories. I filled notebooks with endless beginnings of stories that I seldom finished, although at age eleven I finished a 200-page novel mystery *Holiday Terror*. I did it again at age 14, writing a long mystery with a teen sleuth named Kerry Blue.

I have never attended a writing class. I do remember a high school teacher telling me to stop rhyming my poems—which caused me to stop writing them. And I have one dim memory of a fourth grade teacher sponsoring a reading contest that really excited me—I think I read over 30 books that month.

There's something inside me that won't let me give up—obsession or desperation, perhaps. I know this is what I was born to do, and I continually challenge myself to try new stories, new markets, and to improve my skills.

My writing career has had two parts. Part One: My childhood writing was encouraged by my parents, then spurred on at age 13 after I wrote a fan letter to my favorite author, Margaret Sutton (author of Judy Bolton mysteries). Margaret became my pen pal, then we met at my high school graduation party. She even showed my stories to her writing classes, which was encouraging and flattering.

Part Two: My husband David gave me the contented, stay-at-home family life I personally needed to become a professional writer. When my kids were out of diapers, I attended writing workshops, conventions, and joined a weekly critique group. My husband helped by watching the kids when he wasn't working and by never complaining about extra expenses. And he continues to patiently listen to my manuscripts when I need critique help.

> **Attend conferences. Join a critique group. And write, write, write!**

The worst thing that happened would probably be the cancellation of two books by HarperPaperbacks one month prior to publication in 1995 because pre-sales weren't exceptional. I know these books would have sold well if given the chance. Time went by, and I'd given up hope for a sale. Then in October '98 my agent got The Call from Berkley saying they wanted to buy my series—*not* the mid-grade series we'd been working on, but my YA suspense Sci-Clones series. A delightful surprise!

When I researched for *Camp Confessions #6 Cheer Squad*, I spent four days at a cheer camp. The coach who invited me decided it was best to keep my "true identity" a secret, so I pretended to be a new coach with my own (fictional) team. I drove the girls to camp, spotted them in practice, and even attended a safety meeting and earned a safety certificate.

I usually come up with a title that sounds like something kids would enjoy. My mind is always on the market, so this also plays a big role in my topic choices. I chose *My Sister the Ghost* because I love ghost stories and am fascinated with twins. I chose Sci-Clones because I was desperate for a sale, and my agent agreed this was a good idea.

I write most mornings after I take the kids to school. If I have a pressing project, I also work on the weekends and sometimes evenings. My cat frequently comes in and sits on my lap while I type. Aspiring authors should read the genre you want to write. Pay attention to specific publications and learn what they publish. Attend conferences. Join a critique group. And write, write, write!

## CHRISTOPHER BELTON

*Christopher Belton is the Japan-based author of* Crime Sans Frontieres, *a crime thriller involving the Japanese yakuza's first ever attempt at computer crime; and* Isolation *(scheduled for publication in the U.S.), a techno-thriller depicting a deadly bacterium genetically engineered for biological warfare purposes and commissioned by the Japanese government. He has also had more than 60 books published as a Japanese/English translator.*

I was introduced to the library at a very early age and discovered that everything I wanted to know was contained therein. The worst thing was the unconditional rejections from agents who never even read my manuscript. I sent hundreds of introduction letters to agents over a period of 14 months for my first book, and throughout that period I couldn't manage to coerce even one to look at the manuscript. None, it seemed, were taking on new authors at the time. Knowing just how beautiful my baby was, I took this mass rejection very personally. I have always liked books that involve a complex story line and jump from country to country, so the natural progression for me was to end up writing techno-thrillers staged in an international setting. I also enjoy the research part of writing and find it easier to write about well-documented topics, as opposed to stories that rely more on the psychology of the mind and the writer's imagination.

I find the delays and indifference inherent with the publishing industry extremely discouraging. It is easy to forget that agents and editors deal with dozens of manuscripts simultaneously; their delayed action tends to bring one out of the clouds with a thump. Thoughts like, "Maybe it is not as good as I thought . . . maybe nobody will buy it . . . ," invariably affect motivation and lead to a sense of being deliberately discouraged.

Self-confidence, determination, and a thorough fascination for the process of research and creation kept me motivated. The best thing

**My advice for aspiring authors would be to never give up.**

with regard to my writing career was receiving my first-ever box of books with my name on the covers. I remember spreading them out over the coffee table and smirking contentedly for several hours (accompanied, I might add, by a bottle of single-malt whisky).

The most surprising was discovering that *Crime Sans Frontieres* had been published with the wrong accent over the first "e" in "Frontieres." My word-processing software did not support the French language, and consequently I forgot about the accent until just before publication. I quickly sent a message to the publisher and heaved a sigh of relief when they acknowledged the amendment.

Sujata Massey, the author of the Rei Shimura mystery series, asked me to act as interpreter during a visit to the Ota Flower Auction in Tokyo when she was researching her third book, *The Flower Master*. We both duly turned up for the appointment, only to be immediately involved in a lengthy lecture on the way the facility operated. I calmly interrupted our docile lecturer and mentioned that all Sujata wanted to know was whether it was possible to murder somebody by locking them in the building's cold storage room overnight. I still chuckle when I remember that poor man's face.

During a book signing tour of Shropshire, England, I was interviewed on BBC radio and asked if *Crime Sans Frontieres* should be pronounced as read in English or with the French pronunciation. This was not an issue I had considered, but thinking the French pronunciation would add a touch of class, I replied, "French." I was then asked to provide the correct pronunciation; to my undying embarrassment, I was unable to. My toes still curl up when I think of that dreadful moment.

Once the research has been completed, the chapter-by-chapter outline perfected, and the biographies for all characters carefully detailed, I usually give myself a writing pace of 2,500 words per day. If I skip a day, then I'll write 5,000 words the following day. If I skip two days, I tell myself I'm a jerk and go back to writing 2,500 words per day. Thus, although I try to write within a schedule, I am not very strict with myself. However, even a 1,000-word-per-day average is very respectable if you think it will only require just over three months to complete a 100,000-word novel. About 75 percent of my energy goes into research and planning, and I view the 25 percent involved in the writing as my reward at the end of a period of hard slog.

> **The job of promoting you lies with you, nobody else.**

My advice for aspiring authors would be to never give up. The road to publication is not an easy path, and you will require every ounce of fortitude and wiliness you can muster. But publishing is possible if your product is good enough and you persevere. And, should you get as far as publication, you must then learn to scream your own name from the mountaintops. Honk your horn, aerate your whistle, chime your chimes, blow your trumpet! If you don't, nobody else will, and the only way to sell books is to make sure people know they are there to be bought. Don't blame the publisher for not promoting you. If they spent large amounts of cash on promoting every author, there would be none left for signing on new authors, and the whole world would be a poorer place. The job of promoting you lies with you, nobody else.

How do I maintain success? By telling everybody how successful I am until they actually believe it.

## VICKI HINZE

*Victoria Hinze, who writes as Victoria Barrett, Victoria Cole, and Victoria (Hinze) Barrett, is the author of novels with elements of romance, suspense, and mystery, in contemporary, historical, paranormal, and time-travel settings. Using her Victoria Barrett pseudonym, she co-created what's believed to be the first author-created, open-ended series of single-title romance novels—Seascape. Beyond the Misty Shore was the launch title for the novels; Upon a Mystic Tide, second in the series, received a 5-star review from Affaire de Coeur; and Beside a Dreamswept Sea was the third novel in the series. Other works include Summer Fling, Seeing Fireworks!, Festival, Maybe This Time, and Mind Reader. She has a Master of Arts in creative writing. Her Web site is www.writepage.com/authors/hinzeb.htm.*

I jumped into writing with both feet because I loved it so much. One question that really nagged at me as a kid growing up was, "What do you want to do?" Well, I wanted to do everything. And writing gives me the ability to be everything—ambassador, attorney, rocket scientist, all different things. It's the most challenging thing I have ever tried to do because you can never master it. I don't care how good you get; there is still plenty to learn. I was business major, then a corporate director of operations with a heavy legal background, which I enjoyed very much. But I wanted more.

Everyone told me, "You're not qualified to write books." I wasn't, and I don't know that you can get qualified to write books. You just have to have a really strong desire and be willing to sacrifice. I wrote a couple of books that, of course, got rejected and shall remain in my closet forever, then I took all the *Writers Digest* courses available. After I sold a few books, I got a master's degree in creative writing, and I do think that helped. I don't think the formal education was essential, but it helped with the discipline.

I am a very persistent person, and the more people told me I couldn't do it, the more determined I was. Some call it stubborn, which I can't deny. The other part was that I absolutely loved it. I woke up in the morning and couldn't wait to start writing. Anything that affects you that deeply, you need to do. When I wasn't writing, I was miserable. I went through a time when I wasn't selling and would get really, really down. I realized it wasn't the writing I was down about; it was the selling. So I asked myself, "Okay, if I never sell a thing, am I going to keep writing or am I going to stop?" Once I made the decision that I'd keep writing come hell or high water, I started selling books—four in six months. I think we are up around 12 or so now. The only thing that changed was my perspective, my mindset. When you let all that negativism keep you down, it carries through to the work. You can't show enthusiasm if you're bogged down with other garbage; you have to get rid of that, and get on with creativity.

> **I don't care how good you get; there is still plenty to learn.**

My first book was *Mindreader,* a Silhouette/Intimate Moments. I had written it as a mystery, but my agent sold it as a romance, so I had to go back and put a romance in it, which was kind of neat. The Barrett books are basically paranormals of one kind or another. They may be time travels, which was a real challenge. I also co-created the Seascape books, believed to be the first open-ended continuity series of single-title romance novels. Now I am writing the Hensley books, which are difficult to describe. They've been called all kinds of things—military thriller, romantic suspense, mystery. I like a story that has mystery, suspense, and romance so all three are in all my books.

Letters from the fans are the best thing that happens to me as a writer. I have read books that really touched my life, that changed the way I look at things, that opened new doors inside my mind. But I never expected a book I had written to do that. When I got a letter saying my book did, it was the most amazing feeling I've had in my life. It made me understand that writers write with passion but also have to write with compassion.

On the Seascape novels, I got letters from abuse victims who told me they hadn't been able to find a way out, but since my characters found a way out, they knew that one existed, so they found a way out. That is pretty potent stuff.

I had started writing the fourth Seascape novel when I went out to the commissary, which is a military grocery store. A young airman and his wife were debating between buying a can of tuna fish and a can of peanut butter; they couldn't afford both. That appalled me, because I had no idea that some military families were struggling so hard. I thought, here this guy puts his neck on the line for us, his wife picks up the slack when he is gone, and they have to debate between buying peanut butter and tuna. That really fired me up, so I wrote *Shades of Gray, Duplicity,* and two more military books since then. Usually that's how it happens. Something comes up that really frosts my cookies, and I have to write about it.

I am very disciplined when it comes to writing, but I don't have a schedule. My day is just as apt to start at 2:00 in the morning as at 9:00 A.M. When I wake up, I'm up, and I work until I can't work anymore that day. An average day for me is putting out 25 to 40 pages. I also maintain a writer's list, where new writers ask questions and I answer them. I don't look at clocks very often. You have to write consistently, even during times of crisis and under duress. It's easy to lock yourself into thinking that you can only write at the computer, or only in longhand on a yellow pad; but I don't believe that. I think working writers write whenever and wherever they can to get the job done. I've written different ways at different times. I do have one little eccentricity about writing. Whenever I am stuck or am writing a particularly emotional scene, I do it at the kitchen table. When I was a little girl, my dad told me that 99 percent of all genius is created at the kitchen table. So that is my little eccentricity. My special place.

I've done a lot of promoting—booklets for writers, for the general public I commissioned an artist to do stained-glass sun catchers. I try to do things that are functional, because then readers keep them. I've done magnets, puzzles with the book on it, T-shirts, and teabags with little notes, "Have a cup of tea and let me tell you about my book." I have accumulated a mailing list over the years. I just sent out a 6,000-piece mailing.

The business background really comes in handy, especially when you are new, because the publisher is less able to go out there and promote you. You have to do it yourself. So, I've done radio and TV interviews, programs with booksellers, such as all-day workshops for their customers, speaking about different topics.

Write. Be persistent. So often writers look at their manuscript in progress, then look at a polished, edited work in a book, and feel their work doesn't measure up. Often it doesn't, but you can't get from A to B without working at it. With every book you write, you are going to learn something—get a piece of wisdom, some new insight on a method, or maybe change the way you look at something. If you gain something, that is growth—which is success, not failure. Maybe an attitude adjustment is what we are looking for, but give yourself permission to fail your way to success. I wrote 15 books and I don't know how many proposals before I sold one. Be persistent; be willing to sacrifice. Had I not failed my way to that first sale, I would not have the 11 books and two anthologies after it. See what I mean? By giving yourself permission to fail, you won't put yourself down be-

> **You have to write consistently, even during times of crisis and under duress.**

cause of somebody else's expectation of where you should be at this time. That takes a lot of pressure off.

I like to experiment with craft techniques, so I am looking forward to mastering the techniques I've started using. I think the only limitations we have are those we put on ourselves, so I'm looking forward to keeping my doors open.

## DEB STOVER

*Deb Stover is the bestselling author of unique works that cross genre and gender boundaries, combining adventure, passion, and humor. Her first six novels were time-travel and historical romances:* Another Dawn, Almost an Angel, Some Like It Hotter, A Willing Spirit, Shades of Rose, *and* Stolen Wishes. *She made her fantasy debut in a* Dangerous Magic *anthology. Stover has received Pikes Peaks Romance Writer of the Year and a Heart of Romance Readers' Choice Award. A charter member of Pikes Peak Romance Writers and Heart of Denver Romance Writers, she is also active in Romance Writers of America, Novelists Inc., Colorado Romance Writers, Front Range Fiction Writers, and Rocky Mountain Fiction Writers. Her Web site home page is www.debstover.com.*

*Another Dawn* is my most recent release. I now tell my children that nothing they do in high school or college will be a waste because this book came about when I stumbled across some notes from a college debate on the death penalty. A newspaper article I'd saved about a young man who survived the electric chair gave me the idea to use this as a time-travel mechanism. Talk about second chances. *Some Like It Hotter* is the book I call "Dirty Harry meets Scarlett O'Hara," and *A Willing Spirit* features a very unlikely hero (the heroine's ex-husband's divorce attorney). I had a lot of fun with this one.

I was born a writer and was a closet writer as a teen. Later I majored in journalism and worked for a newspaper. One day I decided to write what I loved to read. Seven books later, I'm still doing that and wouldn't trade it for anything.

Motherhood has taught me the art of patience, and since New York publishing operates on a different calendar than the rest of the world, this is critical. I think life and living are far more important to a writer than a college degree, though that is certainly an interesting time in most of our lives. Experience is the best teacher.

I heard all the starving-artist comments—which are all true, unfortunately—but I was born stubborn. Writing is part talent, part dedication, and a lot of perseverance. Love and drive kept me motivated. Many people claim they want to write, or they would if they had the time, or whatever. These are petty excuses, in my opinion. A real writer is obsessed and will make the time.

The best thing that happened was the 1993 Pikes Peak Writers Conference, where I met the incredible Denise Little, the editor who bought my first four books. Networking played a crucial role in getting my foot in the door. I highly recommend it.

The worst thing? My first literary agent turned out to be less than scrupulous, which created a lot of problems in the early years of my career. I can't stress the importance of having a good literary agent enough. It took me three agents to find the winner I have now.

The most surprising thing is how much non-writing business there is to being a writer. I spend a lot of time answering correspondence; doing interviews for radio, TV, and newspapers; going to book signings; speaking to readers' and writers' groups. The other truly surprising and fulfilling aspect of this business is hearing from readers. Nothing is better than knowing someone out there is actually reading and enjoying my novels—makes it worth all the headaches.

I was shocked the first time someone walked up to me at an autographing and asked where the bathroom was. My more experienced friends assured me this was quite common, especially at mall signings. The day someone walked up and asked if I was hiring, all I could do was laugh. I had the bathroom thing down pat by then, but this one threw me for a loop.

I think my topics have chosen me in many ways. My first novel, *Shades of Rose*, came about after hearing my father tell my children an Ozark ghost story I'd heard before, but had forgotten. I twisted it just so, and my time-traveling pediatrician was born. Generally, I envision a scene and the characters in a situation. From that situation or scene, the rest of the book evolves.

I get up at 4:30 A.M. so I can write for a couple of hours before my husband and children get up to begin their day. Then I get all three children off to school and him off to the office and return to my computer for the rest of the day. I schedule appointments and errands for the very beginning or end of the day. Any parent who works from home will tell you the hours children are in school are precious. Even on weekends, I do some sort of writing-related activity, but make time for family too.

> **It's easy to get caught up in all the hype of being published, but that will carry an author only so far.**

Finish what you start, find a good critique group (but remember, it's a smorgasbord—take what you want and leave what you don't), always write from the heart and not to the market, and don't surrender. Rejection letters are a rite of passage, not the end.

I'm eager to expand into more mainstream women's fiction, and, of course, I'd like to see my name on the *New York Times* bestseller list one day. I don't think there's an author anywhere who wouldn't like to see her novels portrayed in film.

I maintain success by writing. It all begins and ends with that. It's easy to get caught up in all the hype of being published, but that will carry an author only so far. It's the book that counts. I try to never forget that.

## KATHLEEN DUEY

*Kathleen Duey began writing full-time in 1993 and has published more than 30 children's books in the last five years. Most of these are meticulously researched historical novels for middle-grade kids.*

*She has learned to love deadlines and speaking at schools and writers' conferences—the whole marketing side of her career—almost as much as the pure joy of writing. She lives in southern California in a happy house with the man she loves.*

Writing is an art, but an art wrapped in a business. I think the business part intimidated me most. After years of hoping that my fourth-grade teacher might have been right about me "having a very real aptitude," I decided to chase the dream.

"I am a writer." This statement sounds goofy to you, your friends, and even goofier to anyone steeped in economic reality. Many people try; few succeed. That's the truth. But I was determined to make it from the day I admitted to myself that I was going to try. Determination is key. The people who do make a living writing seem to fit three categories: 1) uncompromising genius types who emerge from MFA programs and take the literary world by its lapels; 2) best-sellers whose competent and entertaining style and topic arena catch the socio-entertainment-popculture wind at the right time to sail into fame; and 3) worker bees who love what they do, believe in the power of the word, write like fiends, and try to tailor their output to amenable markets.

> **I am trained at what I do, yet still have a million things to learn.**

Most of us are worker bees looking for a wind to sail on. I certainly am.

I write children's novels, usually between 125 to 160 pages. Most of them are researched historicals of which I am very proud. I have published over 30 titles in the last four years and am making a living entirely from my writing. Broadening my stance by working with more than one house has been a goal—something I have been working at with a will. I am now working with four different publishers and feel reasonably sure that my income will stay the same or rise—not plunge to zero because one editor quits or moves to another house—so long as I keep working hard enough. For a writer, this is as close to job security as it is likely to get.

I met a man at a party who introduced himself as a neurologist. Grinning congenially, he said he had always wanted to write for kids and explained that he had a couple free months coming up and had decided he would write a book. He wanted to know if I had an agent to whom I could refer him. I said I had an agent, a good one, in fact. Then I explained that I had a couple free months coming up, too, and had always wanted to try my hand at brain surgery. I asked if he knew a program I could complete in my couple of months so I could reach my dream. He looked at me for a long moment, and walked away.

People who assume that writing is a talent that only needs a nudge to blossom into well-constructed novels annoy me. I am moderately talented (I think, anyway), but also have 12 years worth of very hard work into this job. I am trained at what I do, yet still have a million things to learn. That is the fun part. Writers are never as good as they'd like to be, never finished, never bored.

Write, write, write, and show it to people. Everyone's skin crawls when they hand out their work. Everyone is terrified, sensitive, afraid. Do it anyway and don't feel special in your terror. This is a step on the journey, so take it. You must have feedback, at least sometimes. Readers are the mirrors in your dance studio. You have to see what you are doing, watch the technique, the emotion conveyed.

Critique groups can be wonderful and supportive. Beware of giving up the creator's role and writing only to please someone else's sensibility. Even if you respect someone else's ability enormously and benefit from their advice, you must still develop your own skills. Some critique groups degenerate into personality conflicts, self-congratulatory coffee klatches, or chat sessions. If yours does, quit and form another, or work alone. Don't lose sight of the real goal—to write better, continuously, from here to the grave.

I met a man who described himself as a career novelist. I liked the term and pasted it onto my self-image. I write children's novels, mostly historicals, but my career will, I hope, give me room and time to write other things.

Most writers have some strengths and some weaknesses. It is certainly true for me. I can describe anything vividly, make a reader feel like she or he is in the skin of the protagonist. But plotting remains a struggle. I once thought there were writers who "got it all" in the talent department; if there are, I have never met one. I find it reassuring that everyone has to work on weak areas.

I write eight to 14 hours almost every day, but hope to step my schedule back in the coming year or so. I started late, yet am determined to make a solid career, and I stumbled into writing a series of historical novels. These ingredients have combined to create a tighter schedule than I ever dreamed I could manage. It has taught me a great deal and increased my ability to write more polished first drafts.

The best new tool I have discovered is the Internet. I could not maintain my deadline schedule without it. I leave chains of e-mails at universities, museum, and historical societies, explaining my project, my intent, and asking what books I should read. The lists always overlap. This alone saves me months of fishing around for relevant, respected sources. Beyond that, I use the Internet all day long for figuring sunrise times on different dates, what the weather is like in a certain place during a certain time of year, etc. Writers should be online.

My success fantasy goes like this: I am in a bookstore 20 years from now. I overhear a parent saying to a child, "Oooooh, Kathleen Duey's books. I loved these! Hey, this one has a new cover, but I remember it. It's about this boy who has to . . ." Fade to scene of me, back at my computer, probably using voice recognition software to spare my carpal tunnels by then, starting a new book, a smile on my face.

## ED GORMAN

*Ed Gorman has been called "one of suspense fiction's best storytellers" by* Ellery Queen *and "one of the most original voices in today's crime fiction" by the* San Diego Union. *His work has won numerous prizes, including the Shamus, the Spur, and the International Fiction Writer's awards. He has been nominated for the Golden Dagger, the Edgar, the Anthony, and the Bram Stoker awards. Gorman's work has been taken by the Literary Guild, The Mystery Guild, Doubleday Book Club, and the Science Fiction Book Club.*

I became a writer out of necessity. I have no talent for anything else. Much as that might sound like a joke, it is true. The most relevant experience a writer can have, to my reckoning anyway, is reading. Reading and writing are symbiotic. By imitating what you read, you learn not only the mechanics of the craft, but you begin to discover your true voice and how to incorporate your life into your fiction. Fitzgerald told his daughter that a writer is only as good as the quality of writers he reads, and I believe that's true.

> **The most relevant experience a writer can have, to my reckoning anyway, is reading.**

People always encouraged me to write. They figured it was one way to keep me out of the electric chair. Writing made me feel important. It seemed like a romantic calling. When I first met professional writers, they stripped away my romantic notions and forced me to sit down and do the actual work.

The most surprising thing that happened to me was getting a very large movie option for a piece my then-agent deemed "unpublishable." The funniest was getting a marriage proposal from a woman who fell in love with my protagonist, mistaking fiction for reality.

I'm a thrower-away. I just dumped 47,000 words of a novel because I decided it was trash. I choose my topics through trial and error. Once a novel starts to "feel" right, I know I have selected the proper topic or theme. I write five pages a day, 365 days a year. My wife and I are both full-time writers. We each have offices on the second story.

My advice to new authors is to read, read, read. Write, write, write. Getting published is more difficult than ever, even for many established writers. You need talent, pluck, and luck.

I've written two or three novels that are especially meaningful to me, the absolute best I could do at the time. I hope I have one or two more before God takes me.

Success to me is making a good, solid middle-class living while enjoying myself at the machine every day. So far I've been able to do that and consider myself blessed.

## Thomas J. Leonard

*Thomas Leonard is the founder of Coach University, a training organization for business coaching currently in 50 countries. Leonard has published a number of Web sites and has led live workshops in the past and mostly leads TeleClasses now. In 1996, the media discovered Coach University, and Leonard appeared on the major TV networks, large daily newspapers, and made an appearance on Donahue. He also received coverage in a number of other countries. Over 150 stories worldwide were published from February 1996 to May 1997. His books include 36* Module Workbooks of the Coach Training Program *and* The Portable Coach.

If you want to be a writer, you can't not want to be a writer. I believe you have to be compelled to do it. I've always wanted to communicate because I couldn't talk very well as a child. I was frightened of everything, so I invented my own little world. As I began to write, I couldn't write very well because I was so atrophied and my communications skills were so bad; I could barely think, let alone communicate. But I got better. In the past five years I've become truly prolific. I feel like someone born with atrophied legs who is now running the marathon.

The fact that I had coached 600 individuals from 1982 to 1986 gave me something to write about—what worked in their lives, their strategies for success, dilemmas they face, their decision-making processes, changes they made. I began to look at human nature through my 600 clients' eyes and to draw some parallels and conclusions and had lots of material about success and happiness. They were my research.

I started Coach University in 1992 to train coaches because I had enough clients (I started coaching in 1982) and others who wanted to do what I do. Coach University now has 2,500 students in 50 countries around the world. It is the premier trainer of coaches worldwide.

I wrote a piece for a community newspaper in 1981 that got published, and someone on the staff said, "You should try another profession because you're never going to make it as a writer." I was crushed for about a year, but then I got even.

> **I define myself first and foremost as a writer, not as a coach or anything else.**

What made the biggest difference is writing an e-mail broadcast that goes out to about 25,000 people a day. My writing became so much better when subscribers would ask for clarification, or would say "that was good" or "that was stupid." I was getting so much feedback that I let them evolve me, if you will, to become a much better writer. That's how I began to write conversationally rather than just theoretically.

The best thing related to my writing was that I was able to sell Coach University for four million dollars. I had certainly sold the revenue stream that I had built up by 1996, but the core of Coach U was really the intellectual property I had developed out of the writing I had done the previous four years.

I think when Simon & Schuster called me out of the blue and offered me money to write a book related to coaching, that was the most surprising. That was a year and a half ago, and within six months it was in the bookstores.

Two things inspire me. One is what affects people around me—what they are facing, what they are dealing with gives me the pull and the direction that helps me choose what to write on. Another thing is that I've probably gone through the same problems they're facing, so I end up being their voice.

I write virtually every day except maybe Sunday from about 7:00 A.M. to about 2:30 P.M. It's the first thing I do when I get up. I sit in a red leather chair with an ottoman that's incredibly comfortable, my Macintosh Powerbook in my lap, and type that way for eight hours without hurting any part of my body.

We don't promote my books on the Internet. But people who buy the book take a free class from us. When Simon & Schuster asked, I said I probably wouldn't do a book tour. I'm very shy by nature, but I'm powerful in the teleclass and teach on the phone maybe 20 hours a week. People wouldn't know I'm shy—I'm kind of like the Wizard of Oz, who can do lots behind the scenes. I was on a lecture circuit that frightened me after about three years, and I couldn't do it anymore. I don't want the stress of public speaking, but I can teach a teleclass on a dime. I would much rather spend my time writing rather than promoting. I'd rather let the experts do that, or settle for the capillary effect—just let the word get passed around.

> I would much rather spend my time writing rather than promoting.

I'm publishing 38 books this year, all self-published by Coach University Press. A lot is work I've done before, just polished and put together, but it's going to be quite the blitz this year. I've got three writers ghosting parts of it, packaging, and this and that. On the training side, I've got a company called teleclass.com that people can call to take a writing class for a day, an hour, or for ten weeks, depending on what type of class we are offering. That was launched a couple of months ago, and it's doing extremely well.

Standard advice that someone gave me about being a writer is just start writing, whether you're good or not, and then help yourself improve as you read what you wrote. I used to be a dreadful writer, am passable now, and hope to be good in the future. There is a developmental process as well as an evolutionary one. You want to get better at what you do but also want to write about more interesting things. Find people who don't judge you, who don't compare you to the greats, who won't make you feel less than. Whatever your current writing skill, hang out with people who believe in you and your ability to get better. I look back at things I wrote ten years ago, and they seem so lame, but the same people who knew it wasn't perfect back then and knew I had the potential to write well, are encouraging me to continue. Any artist, particularly a writer, needs that kind of support. Don't show your stuff to the public, to people who don't know what it means to be a writer. Show it to those who do understand and ask for their input.

I define myself first and foremost as a writer, not as a coach or anything else. I'm a writer who does other things, but the core of me is a writer because I'm expressing in words. When I'm writing now, I find many different ways to package it—in a book, daily newsletter, electronic tip, audiotape set, real audio, video, licensing program, checklist, or self-test. If you have the ability to write and can write on topics people find interesting, you can package that and find a dozen different ways to make money from it. You are more than just a writer; you are an intellectual factory, an intellectual property developer. There are many revenue streams from the same piece. I would encourage people to build multiple revenue streams around just a single one.

## CHAPTER 4

# The Promoters

The Promoters are the savvy authors who know a secret to making their books sell—putting down the pen and going out into the world of promotion. Speaking engagements, television shows, radio interviews, book signings; these authors are actively involved in the sales of their books. They do their own mailings to bookstores, like Barbara Burnett Smith. Like Elliot and Beatty Cohan, they make themselves available day and night for promotions. Like Willie Jolley, they host their own media shows themselves. Like Jeff Slutsky and Ralph Roberts, their books and business are intertwined. And their efforts have paid off.

Barbara Burnett Smith comments, "I've done everything to promote books but blimp-flying." Everything means glamorous national media interviews and not-so-glamorous book signings where nobody shows up. It means using your own money and licking your own stamps to mail postcards to bookstores. It means doing interviews in the wee hours of the night.

"I always make sure I am available for promotions," says Ann Marie Sabath. "Probably the biggest key for someone who wants to make it big is to be responsive . . . You can bet your sweet whatever that I will always be available, whether it's 6:00 in the morning or 3:00 in the morning."

Authors often are surprised that promoting the book will be mainly up to them. But the Promoters know the deal. "You have the most interest in the book, stand to make the most money, and have thought the most about it, so . . . if you want to make things happen, you have to make them happen yourself," reminds Bob Shook.

## RALPH ROBERTS

*Ralph R. Roberts has been recognized by* Time *magazine as the "bestselling realtor in America." While real estate brokers average seven sales a year, Roberts, the "Michael Jordan" of residential real estate, has closed the deal more than 600 times in one year. He is the author of* Walk Like a Giant, Sell Like a Madman *and* 52 Weeks of Sales Success, *and is co-author of* Chicken Soup for the Disabled Soul. *His Web site is www.ralphroberts.com.*

I have three books out now. The first was *Walk Like a Giant, Sell Like a Madman,* kind of a nuts and bolts success story of my being the top real estate person in the country. The new book, taken from meetings I have, is good for the small business and entrepreneur running a meeting, running a sales force, or just running yourself. My newest book, *I'm Selling It Myself,* will help people market and sell their own home.

The success of my books is greater than I ever imagined, with my first book getting a six-figure advance. Not only did the book succeed, but it brought other books and offers to the table. I'm getting speaking opportunities from around the world—South Africa in a week, where I'll probably exceed $250,000 in income. I'll speak on my books, which means more books will sell and more opportunities will happen.

My first book never went to print, which is true for a lot of writers. I was writing on how to sell real estate, and the market is not broad enough. I had been featured in articles around the world, then because I've had a publicist for about 15 years, was featured in *Time Magazine.* After that, the publishers called me directly and made offers. They asked who my agent was (at the time I didn't have one), so

I said I didn't know what agent I was going to use on this project. I called friends to find the best possible agent I could go to. Then I called this agent and told him I wanted to write a book. He wasn't too interested. I know book people get lots of people calling them on a daily basis wanting to write books. It is not as easy as that. Not only do you write the book, but you have to have the right agent, have it critiqued properly, and be able to present it to the publishing house.

My agent had me fly into New York and do ten different interviews. He said it was up to me to turn on my salesman skills. I had to tell them what the book means and how I was going to be able to help market the book. I'm sorry to say I didn't get behind that first book soon enough, like my agent advised. I was so busy with my own career that I wrote the book and kind of let it sit there. When it was ready to come out, I got all excited again. I'm 42 now, and by the time I'm 60 I'll have published about 20 books and have made millions of dollars. My goal now is to get in the

> **My first book never went to print, which is true for a lot of writers.**

game, get in the big story, and get on the big show—*Oprah.* Get on *Oprah* and just say you are writing a book and it would be a bestseller, instantly.

I, for sure, am not a born writer. I was never extra good in school. I could not have put the books together without the proper means and the proper collaborators. I have five collaborators and I am looking for more people to help me do books.

I think if you want to be the best writer on the planet, you have to hang around the best writers. I hang around Mark Victor Hansen and Jack Canfield and do Chicken Soup books with them. They know I can write and they know I'm successful. Successful people want to hang around other successful people.

The writing industry is very discouraging; you have to have very thick skin and realize that when people say "No," they really are saying

"Know." I've gotten hundreds of letters from publishers telling me no. Someday I want to do a wall with all my form letters saying, "We are certainly interested in your book, but it is not what we are looking for right now." Every time I got one I thought, I'm that much closer to a yes. What motivates me, since I'm in sales and own a company, is putting the stuff in my book right into practice—to motivate my staff, train my staff, for recruiting, and for financial planning. Everything in my books is actually happening. When you read my books, it's like you can actually hear me talking.

> **My book is kind of like a business card now, opening doors I didn't even know were closed.**

I did a tour for my book that I finished in 1997. I just started another tour, which involves radio, TV, print media, and magazines. The key is talking soundly. If you speak and get asked back, that means it was good. If you don't get asked back, it wasn't successful. If you are a great speaker and have great information, but it doesn't come out right to the media, it doesn't get their attention. A writer might make it to a story, but not to the editor's desk. Being a rookie writer, I'm just getting to where we are tying in speaker engagements to a fee and a guarantee that they will buy so many books and other products. Recently we sold 4,000 books to an organization in South Africa. Everyone who signed up for the event will get a book as part of their fee to hear me speak. While I speak, I'll be selling. (They bought my first book too, by the way.) You always want your current book to sell, and that makes your first book sell even better.

I'm doing *Fox News Live* this Saturday, and they are flying me in and picking me up in a limo. I said I wanted to spend the day with my 11-year-old so they said, "Bring her along, too." With the interviews I'm doing for this book, I get in restaurants I couldn't get in, and get upgraded in hotels. My book is kind of like a business card now, opening doors I didn't even know were closed. Endorsing stuff is even possible now. This is totally unbelievable!

If you get fortunate enough to get a book done and do a book tour, it could be the trip from hell. I recently had a five-hour flight to destinations only an hour and 15 minutes apart in the air. We hit such a bad storm that we flew over Philadelphia, and they were thinking of going back to Charlotte. The absolute worst was over-sleeping and missing my airplane to come back home to see my kids. I had to take a flight four hours later.

The most surprising thing about writing books is going to the bookstore and finding only two of your books. Or going into a book-store where people who sell them don't even read books. That's why Amazon.com is doing so well.

The funniest thing that happened to me was one Sunday when I was recording a book into my Dictaphone, coming up with great ideas as we were coming up the driveway in our car. My six-year-old daughter said, "Dad, you are not an author." I told her that Daddy had a book deal I had to get out in a certain period of time. I asked her what she meant, and she said, "Authors come to your school. Then they read the book to you and they autograph them and you order from them." Now she is in sixth grade and I just got asked to speak at her school, so now she thinks I will be official.

I had a collaborator on my second book who put something in about sales and travel agencies. He'd tried putting the story in our first book (it's a great story), but we edited it out. I said I couldn't go around the country and speak about it since it wasn't really my story. We took it out again in the second book, but the publisher missed it and it stayed in. Anyway, an interviewer asked a question about it. That is one downfall of having a collaborator. If you have a collabora-tor, read the book!

I'm a salesperson, so my topics will always relate to sales. I al-ways talk about success, never about failure.

I write in the bathroom, in my hot tub, my steam room, my sauna, on airplanes, at dinner. I carry Dictaphones with me and just write, write, write. Some people write the words down; I put them onto tapes. While you're taping this for your interview; I'm taping it for myself, thinking maybe there's something for me in the future. I try to record important sales conversations and real experiences—like the story of the guy shining my shoes in Chicago, one of the greatest salespeople I ever met. It goes in my "someday" file of about a thousand chapters that are not in books yet. I literally write a chapter or two every day. "They" claim that the older you get the less creative you get because teens are more creative than adults. I find the better I run my company and the more I surround myself with better people, the easier it is for me to write and be creative. Sometimes I just look at my success and write about that.

Once I dreamed about having these things, and now I have them. I had a goal to make a million dollars a year, and I've been making over a million dollars a year since 1988. Some people are so close to success, but they fail to plan or are scared to have the success. I am not afraid of it. I'll take care of it as I get it!

Writers have to practice at it. You have to offer to write a lot for free—articles, PR, press releases. Never give up. You can for sure write a book. I know some stockbrokers and car salespeople who have written books. Even if they're not published, they carry their manuscripts around as sales tools saying, "I wrote this book on how to be the best car salesman." Your customers think, "Wow, you wrote a book!" If you want to be a good author, hang around good authors. At least send them letters and ask what they did and go hear them speak.

> **The first time I saw someone carrying one of my books was totally unbelievable.**

I look forward to writing lots and lots of books, to being on more TV, more radio, more newspaper print. I believe I have accomplished my goal to be the number one salesperson in America and in the world. My goal now is to be the best husband I can be to my wife Kathleen, the best father to Kolleen, Kyle, and Kaleigh. I don't have a goal to be the best writer on the planet. I have a goal to be *one of the best* sales motivators, business writers. I believe Zig Ziglar has been the best speaker on the planet, and I am training towards that. If I am the best speaker, the best presenter, then it is automatic that I will be one of the best booksellers. A lot of writers cannot get in front of 10,000 people. I can. The bigger the crowd, the better I do. Each time I have done a presentation (and I have done thousands), it gets better. Each book is better. Each book idea is better.

Here are "Ralph's Tips": Autograph books at every bookstore you can. If they are autographed, it's a lot harder to return them to the publisher. Make sure your books are facing out when you see them. If the bookstore people can't find them, they aren't going to send them back and someone is going to buy them. I just learned this one: Cultivate a relationship with people in the stores, and say, "You only have two of my paperback, one of my hardback, and seven of my new books. Can you increase your inventory on my paperback and my hardback? When people buy my second book, they will want my first." They have the authority to increase inventory by about two to six, which helps. Also, anytime you go hear seminar speakers, give them a copy of your book. Many of the speakers I've seen have taught me a lot. So I will give them a book or just let them know I am in the room. Sometimes they announce me as the world's greatest salesperson or something.

I have a shadow program. If you want to be a great salesperson, I believe you have to shadow other salespeople. If you want to be a great speaker, shadow speakers. If you want to be a great writer, shadow other writers. I recently got people who want to write and who know I have done two books and have a couple Chicken Soup books, paying me to give them advice on writing. Advice is where it's at. We turned all the energy of people calling and writing us into a new book idea, *The 101 Greatest Sales People*. We keep track of everyone who writes to us. What industry are they in? What do they do? How can we use this information in the future? How do we keep them on our mailing list?

Also, any time you are on an airplane, give the pilot an autographed copy of your book. It's awesome to hear the pilot announce: "We have Ralph Roberts, the world's greatest salesperson, on board." I've taken the book to the counter and they've upgraded me to first class because I'm an author. Give a discount or give away as many books as you can. I went to Harper and said I had a PR person who wants to give away 1,000 books. I got the books free and another 1,000 at cost. Now I get interviewed every single business day—250 times a year. I recently went on a cruise ship, and when I told them I was an author, they said, "If you ever want to come back, we will let you and your wife cruise for free if you just do two or three programs for an hour or less each." I haven't even started to figure it all out yet.

My book tour is over, but I got an opportunity to do another interview. I called my publisher and asked them to cover the cost and they agreed. I was able to get them a bookstore that moves into a convention of 20,000 people. I sold 600 books at one convention.

The first time I saw someone carrying one of my books was totally unbelievable. I was on an airplane going to California. I asked the lady who had my book how it was. She said, "I don't know. My friend in sales gave it to me and said, 'You've got to read it!'" I said, "That's really interesting. I'm in sales." She had no idea, so I told her to look on the back. Then she said, "Oh, my God! This is you." Then she was telling people on the airplane.

When you do books, include other people. The success of the Chicken Soup books was because they included a lot of people. If you included 100 people in your book, you guarantee that 100 people are going to buy it. Don't be afraid to ask your publisher for stuff—not by mail or phone. Get out and meet your publisher and the public and sell yourself.

If you get published in the future, your success is virtually endless. Someone told me, with all my information that people want, I could actually be a small book mill, with books going out continually. That is my goal. Let people know what you look like. You can ultimately be a bestselling author if everyone in your field knows what you look like.

## ANN MARIE SABATH

*Ann Marie Sabath is the founder of At Ease Inc., a company specializing in business protocol and etiquette programs. Also a successful author, her first book was published in 1993 and is in its eighth printing. Her second book,* Business Etiquette: 101 Ways to Conduct Business with Charm and Savvy, *was released internationally in 1998 and is in its second printing. Her third book,* International Business Etiquette: Asia & The Pacific Rim, *was released internationally in 1998. Since 1987, Sabath and her staff have trained more than 40,000 individuals in the business, industry, government, and educational sectors on how to gain the competitive edge. In January 1992, At Ease Inc. became an international firm by licensing its concept in Taiwan. Sabath's At Ease Business Etiquette Hotline has been recognized by* The Wall Street Journal, Dun & Bradstreet Reports, The CBS Morning Program, 20/20, Oprah, *and more than 30 other sources, both nationally and internationally. Sabath has also served as Business Manners Columnist for several major publications. Her Web site is www2.eos.net/atease.*

I'm a teacher by profession, and I realized that if you can teach, you can do a lot of things. I got into publishing by writing a curriculum, then noticed that sometimes people need things explained to them. That's how my writing came about.

We have been very fortunate to have a lot of success with our books because they are written in a down-to-earth, crisp matter. We get right to the point, rather than include a lot of theory. We cater to the Miss

> **Research is half of it, and the rest is feeling the beat.**

Manners generation, people who have very short attention spans (like myself), so it's important to cut to the chase. All our books are in paperback, and the type is big so people over 40 don't need to put on their bifocals, and it's compact enough to throw into a carry-on bag.

Writing is a very good way to get your message out, and if you can do it succinctly, other doors will open. I, by nature, was not a writer; I was a Spanish major and minored in stage. When I began writing, I realized what I couldn't do and made sure I had an editor right off the bat. I knew my weakness and made sure I filled the gap by having someone who knew how to dot the i's and cross the t's. Eventually you learn what to do, what not to do.

> **When I began writing, I realized what I couldn't do, and made sure I had an editor right off the bat.**

One of the best for me is having great, tenacious parents—and grandparents. I never knew I couldn't do something. I always knew that if I believed in something, I could do it. My parents always encouraged me. Their belief in me helped me believe my dreams would come true. And I attribute some of my writing success to my grandparents. Anyone who visits Ellis Island will really have a kick in the tail, especially if their grandparents really did come over that way. None of us really know how to work hard, how to take risks.

The most important thing is to be careful what you ask for, because you will get it. Everything I visualized has been attained through nothing other than believing. My point is just as Deepak Chopra, my favorite author, says: Intention plus attention equals reality. For that reason, I would say believing is probably most important. Everything that has come to me is something I made happen, brought to the universe.

I always make sure I am available. We were in Hong Kong last May and *Cosmopolitan* called. My assistant faxed me, and at 11:00 that night, I called them. I take every opportunity—do lots of cross selling, give free books away, do book signings, and lots of radio interviews. Probably the biggest key for anyone who wants to make it big is to be responsive. When I am not in the mood to do something, I do it anyway. You can bet your sweet whatever that I will always be available, whether it's 6:00 in the morning or 3:00 in the morning. If someone needs our help, we do it. Probably the other thing that helped us is to send a thank you note to anyone who took more than fifteen minutes to do something for us.

I've been on *Oprah* twice, on *20/20*, on CNN and CNBC many times, on the CBS morning programs, and a lot of locals. The key is to know how to position your book, to be able to say, "My book is the best." One reason our book is very good is because we always list the best books in it. We just give one perspective; other people give other terrific perspectives.

Lots of people haven't gotten what they wanted because they haven't visualized. Number one, pick and choose very carefully where you expend your energy. You're not doing this for your health, but to sell books, so your publisher believes in you for the next book contract. Number two, visualize what you want. When my first book came out, I put it in our dining-room hutch with my china and tarnished silver. I had also bought Oprah's book and put it right next to mine, making sure they touched. I told my children, "Our books are exchanging energy." They said, "Mom, you are very weird," and I said "Thank you." And guess what? Three years later the phone rang, and my assistant said, "Call this number—it's Oprah's." I thought it was a joke. What the mind conceives, you will achieve.

Oprah found us when they were doing research on public manners and pulled an article we did for the *Dallas Times Herald*. What is meant to be will be. One reason the Oprah show is so successful is that they do what they say they are going to do. They have a passion about it, and it starts at the top.

I love radio hosts. Authors have to be receptive and available to them. The key is to always give them more than what they want. Be available at a moment's notice. If they have a cancellation, do it. Never be too proud; people remember that.

I write at home and only in certain directions, from a Feng Shui standpoint. I think better in a particular position, and everybody's position will be different. The most important thing is to figure out your direction for the desk you work on at home, whether the kitchen table or official office upstairs. I've written on cruise ships at 4:30 in the morning, in hotel lobbies. When I write I need to hear myself think clearly. Research is half of it, and the rest is feeling the beat.

I cherish my readers, every single one. Our readers respond very nicely because I give them a gift. Anyone who buys our books has an opportunity to stay in touch with us. When our first book came out, we gave them continual access to our At Ease business hot line. With our second book, they have continued access to our e-mail line. I genuinely do care about people, and at the same time we have some wonderful doors open, in terms of getting clients. The idea is to be accessible.

I take what I know, what I've researched and enjoy knowing, and stay focused on maintaining a professional attitude. I notice what the market will bear and what the interest levels are.

Everybody is born a writer, or whatever they want to be. That's number one. How do you make it big? By believing in yourself, never stopping, and always making sure you are helping other people, because you want people to owe you more than you owe them.

## WILLIE JOLLEY

*Willie Jolley is a speaker, singer, and author who focuses on leadership, empowerment, motivation, team building, and staff development. He is the host of* The Magnificent Motivational Minute *daily radio program, author of* It Only Takes a Minute to Change Your Life, *and co-author of* Only the Best on Success. *He was the 1995–1996 President of National Capital Speakers Association. According to Zig Ziglar, "Willie is a multi-talented speaker/singer who brings power and excitement to every audience and persuades them to be more and do more so they can have more." Jolley's Web site is www.getaheadpro.com/jolly.htm.*

All of this is funny to me. My former teacher told me, "I can't believe it! You wrote a book! I can remember when you couldn't even read a book." To transform and change my life so I am considered a bestselling author is funny to me. It gives encouragement to people who may not be great writers, who might not have been exceptional students.

I'm introduced as "Willie Jolley—America's leading motivational entertainer." I am a motivational speaker and singer who has gone on to having some success in the field of writing books. My first book, *It Only Takes a Minute to Change Your Life*, describes minutes that have changed people's lives. It includes short, one-minute stories that give you a powerful message. The new book, *A Setback Is Nothing But a Setup for a Comeback*, literally tells my story of how I got fired from my nightclub singing job and replaced by a karaoke machine to cut costs. After that setback, I started speaking to schools and colleges and corporations and trade associations, and that grew

> **My first book describes . . . minutes that have changed people's lives.**

from small groups to bigger groups to national groups to international groups, from radio to television to bestselling books to music albums to CDs to all sorts of things—all because I got fired. That's the gist of the book, which also tells stories of people I've interviewed who also turned setbacks into powerful comebacks.

What drew me into writing was that, as a member of the National Speakers Association, I got a letter from a small custom publisher who said, "Have you ever thought about writing a book?" I thought, "You know what? I never really have." I contacted the publisher, and he said, "Oh we've been hearing your radio show, and people in the office love it. Would you be interested in writing a book?" So I took the different scripts from the shows and started formulating *It Only Takes a Minute*. It seemed exciting and people kept asking for more scripts. That's how the concept started. I never thought I had the capacity to be an author, but once I did it, I realized that I have a way of writing that people enjoy.

*It Only Takes a Minute* is in its seventh printing here in America. It's also selling wonderfully in Australia, China, Germany, the Czech Republic, Great Britain, France, and is doing well on the Internet around the world. It was the book of the month for Amway of Australia in January of 1998 and then Amway of America, which sold a lot of copies on both continents. It was chosen as a top pick by *Selling Power* magazine and has been the subject of numerous articles because one-minute messages appeal to a wide demographic. Parents get it for their kids, teachers order it, school systems, hospitals, corporations . . . numerous people have bought copies. It's now considered a bestseller, and I am excited about that. And I've got a great agent, which helps a lot.

> **The struggle—rewriting and working to develop it—makes me better, in my estimation.**

My teachers never encouraged me. I was a good student, but did not have exceptional writing skills. The struggle—rewriting and working to develop it—makes me better, in my estimation.

One of the best things happened when I was riding down the street in Washington, D.C.—a guy pulled up next to me, bumping the horn like something's wrong. I rolled down the window, and he said, "I love your book. I ride with it in the car. Wow! It's you!" Isn't that something?

People just come up to me and say, "I saw your book in the airport bookstore. I love it." People have e-mailed me and said the book literally changed their lives. People from London, France, Germany, Australia, and all over America send e-mail notes, saying, "I was negative, on my way out, and somebody gave me your book" or "I saw your book in a K-mart and thought 'Maybe this book will change my life,' and it did." Those are the best things.

I am always surprised by people's responses. I was surprised when *The Rikki Lake Show* wanted to produce a show based on my book and had me fly in to do that. Also, I'm surprised the book continues to sell well after over a year out in the market. Stores call and say they can't keep it in stock.

I try to stick to a writing schedule when I have a book on deadline. I like to put an hour in every morning. Sometimes I end up going away for a few days to get it done. For my first book, I got up religiously every morning. After the book came out, I was traveling more, so it was hard to say where I'd be at any particular moment.

I've done book signings, television, radio. I promoted it via my radio show that moved to television, and now is seen in 500,000 homes every day on the success channel. I've actually done radio ads, commercials, and have a new CD called *It Only Takes a Minute to Change Your Life: The Music,* a companion piece to the book. It features me singing and speaking, and each chapter from the book has a corresponding song. We're distributing it across the country—getting it into stores as well as Web sites and direct sales. We also have the Motivational Minute Hotline, 1-888-2MOTIV8, sponsored by a long-distance telephone service. People get a free minute of motivation, an excerpt from the book that changes weekly.

Next up is to start doing more television, and not only speak, sing, and write, but develop the ability to communicate in a number of different modes to reach as many people in as many ways as I can.

## BARRY FARBER

*Barry J. Farber is president of Farber Training Systems, Inc., a sales motivational training company. He also is president of The Diamond Group, which produces radio and television programs and is a literary agency that represents authors in the business and entertainment fields. After several years on radio, he now hosts his own television show,* Diamonds in the Rough, *a program focused on personal achievement. He has published seven bestselling books and several audio programs, including* Diamonds Under Pressure, Diamonds in the Rough, State-of-the-Art Selling, Superstar Sales Secrets, *and* Dive Right In. *His Web site can be found at www.barryfarber.com.*

My first book got 26 rejections. My background is sales and marketing, and for the last ten years I've owned my own business, that deals with seminars, radio, television. As I'm working on my eighth book, I got a brainstorm for the ninth. My goal is to just keep going.

People have always asked me: What trait do you think is responsible for your achieving success? I don't attribute success to any talent. If I look back at everything, it's doing something that takes a lot of balls. Sometimes when you do unconventional things, people think you're crazy or taking a risk. I know some people say, what does courage have to do with writing a book? What about going to 50 companies with half a manuscript, sending it with a letter, knocking on their doors and asking them to read it? Then taking those letters and submitting them with the manuscript to the publisher, showing that you already have pre-sales of over 10,000 copies. Or walking into the publisher's office or leaving a phone message saying, "Look, if you don't feel that this is the most powerful marketing plan for a book—solid content backed up with letters from people who have the power to buy a lot of books—I'll walk home barefoot, backwards."

> **Once you're succeeding a lot and not experiencing failure, you should start to worry.**

Hunger is the most important trait for success in any business. Hunger and the tenacity to focus on your goal can offset a lot of deficiencies. Nobody's perfect. The great equalizer is the ability to be tenacious, to not give up, to have that passionate feeling that nobody is going to stop you. You've got to have a strong spirit; nobody can break it unless you let them. When you start achieving success, people get jealous, but success is the greatest revenge.

You are going to get a lot of rejection once you start submitting manuscripts to publishers or agents. You can handle rejection in three ways: 1) *Let it get to you.* That's what I used to do—get upset and take it. 2) *Learn from the rejection, then move on.* So you got some input, but I don't think it helps all that much. 3) *Let it motivate you.* Now, I take every single rejection as a powerful motivator to prove them wrong because success is the best revenge. People say they hate rejection, but if I'm not getting rejected, then I'm not working hard enough, not really taking chances. Rejection is a good measurement. Once you're succeeding a lot and not experiencing failure, you should start to worry.

Publishers today are hit by a lot of authors who don't deliver. After they are burned many times, they become very cautious about taking on new books. You have to come in with ammunition, show what you did with other publishers—documentation, numbers, facts. Once you have built credibility, you just need to build relationships, network, and sell.

I can tell writers that they can sit and think, but you know what? Put it down on paper! I remember somebody saying that you shouldn't do anything until you are 100 percent prepared. To me, part of the preparation is failing, not being prepared. I know that sounds crazy, but by going in and actually doing it, you find things you're missing that you could never have found by sitting back, and probably would miss the opportunity five years later. I jump out there. Yes, I have fear. You'd be crazy if you weren't afraid. But I know the fear is self-induced, that the mind creates its own fear. I start saying, "Wait a second, what am I fearing?" Look back at everything you've feared; nothing is what you expected.

## BARBARA BURNETT SMITH

*Barbara Burnett Smith is the author of a modern, traditional mystery series of four books set in a small fictional town called Purple*

*Sage. The first book was nominated for an Agatha for best first mystery. The second book,* Mistletoe from Purple Sage, *was selected by* Mostly Murder *as one of the top ten of the year. Smith spent 16 years in the broadcast field before becoming an author.*

My father-in-law was Thomas B. Dewey, a very well-known mystery novelist from the '40s and '50s. He and his wife, Doris, encouraged me like crazy. In fact, I wrote my very first book, which was before computers, on a little portable typewriter. He edited it for me and was going to send it back to his agent in New York. I was very young at the time and the book probably wasn't any good, but he was willing to do that for me. But I said, "Oh, no! I have to retype this?" and quit writing.

I was born a communicator, but didn't much like writing things out by hand, was fine with the typewriter, then really became a writer after the creation of computers.

I think the best things about writing are when I get to speak at schools. I don't have a writing degree, so when the kids say, "I can't do that because . . ." I say, "You know, you can do anything. It may take you longer to learn now, but you can still do it." I am a classic example. The other best thing is being on the Sisters in Crime board. I just love that. People who are involved in Sisters in Crime are wonderful, the best people in the world. The board is just phenomenal.

It surprises me how I have never been in a field before where you can do well and still not do well. In other words, you can write a book that will get some acclaim, something that people would love, but nobody notices it. I'm really surprised about how difficult it is even after you break in and start having a bit of success. I can't name all the mid-list authors who are in just terrible financial shape.

I've been humbled. I had just been in San Francisco on Union Square, where I signed my books and they were delighted. Then I went into this chain bookstore somewhere in California, and they had a lot of my books in hardcover and paperback. I went to the counter, plopped the books down, and said, "I am the author of these books and I would like to sign them for you." The young man at the counter said, "Don't you touch those books until I talk to the manager!"

I've done everything to promote books but blimp-flying. For the first one, *Writers of the Purple Sage,* I made note cards, then pressed about a million pieces of real purple sage and glued them on the front with the name of the book. The back told about the book, had quotes from other authors, and the ISBN. I left the inside blank, packaged it in an envelope, put it in cellophane wrapping, and sent it to every mystery bookstore I could think of in the United States. There are only about 100, but still . . . . I also gave them away at conferences when I spoke. For my second book, *Dust Devils,* I put purple sand in plastic test tubes (dormant dust devils) and tied them with raffia.

> # I think the best things about writing are when I get to speak at schools.

For the third book was another note card with glitter and musical notes across that said "Celebration." Every time the bookstores got them, they could mail them out to someone. Then for *Mistletoe* (I can't believe I did this), I saw these art note cards for about $12 apiece and copied the idea. In the center of the card is a green square, then red foil, and I put special confetti in these white glassine envelopes they use for stamps, with red reindeer, green Christmas trees, snowmen, and whatever. I glued the flaps down with a reindeer or something, and underneath it said, "Mistletoe from Purple Sage." A lot of handiwork went into every one of them. My husband said, "You know, somebody is going to make a fortune off those cards someday—more than you did with the books." I've done bookmarks, sent out postcards, and certainly toured. I speak at a lot of schools, and always donate a book for their library. Some schools don't have a lot of money, and sometimes they invite parents to come listen, which is great fun, so I'll sell some books as well. Sometimes they send me out to some book club, and I have a lot of fun speaking to a hundred women or so because that's what I like to do.

I mostly get a really warm reaction from readers. Readers tell me, "I wish I could go visit these people." They can actually see the streets of Purple Sage. My characters are that way for me too, like I could recognize them on the street, so it's gratifying. I think the nicest thing that has happened a couple of times is when people either stopped me at a conference or sent an e-mail saying they were going through a really hard time—one's grandmother was in the hospital, another's husband had a serious accident—and one of my books helped them get through it. When my own mom was dying of cancer, it was an author and her books that got us all through. So, to have someone actually thanking me is just overwhelming, a real feeling of success.

> **Just write; don't give up. Somebody has to get published, and it might as well be you.**

I was nominated for an Agatha Award for my first book. I was brand new as an author and got this e-mail from author Deborah Adams saying, "It feels terrific, doesn't it?" I sent her an e-mail saying, "Huh? I think I missed something." Then a little bit later, my agent called and said, "You were nominated for an Agatha." Then my editor called, and it was like "WOW." So I e-mailed Deborah, "Yes, it feels great." The funny part of the story is that Jeff Abbott, who is in my writers group, was nominated, too. I did the final edit on his book, and he did the final edit on mine. So who is the better writer? That's what I tell Jeff, and he says, "Well, that's your story."

Just write; don't give up. Somebody has to get published, and it might as well be you.

## BOB SHOOK

*Bob Shook sold insurance for 17 years. With his father, he started his own company and was chairman of the board of American Executive*

*Life Insurance Company. He has written 43 nonfiction books, mostly on sales and marketing. Two of his books have been* New York Times *bestsellers. He has ghostwritten books and written some company books—on IBM, Honda, and Ford. Two forthcoming books are* It Takes a Prophet to Make a Profit, *co-authored by Britt Beemer, and* The Business of America Is Business.

Life Insurance is a pretty boring business, and I loved writing, so I moved to full-time writing. But I am a salesman first and a writer second. Anybody can learn how to write (you learn in first grade), but very few are good professional salespeople. I find the combination has made me a better writer, or at least a more successful writer.

My biggest success was in ghostwriting (sorry, my contract stated that I wouldn't reveal that I had written the book to any media). The second book I ghostwrote was on the *New York Times* bestseller's list for ten weeks and the third made number one nonfiction book in the country. For the book with IBM, I collaborated with Buck Rogers, who was in charge of worldwide marketing. It was a worldwide bestseller, number one in Japan, number five in England. Those are my most successful books. I also wrote *The Greatest Sales Stories Ever Told*, *The Perfect Sales Presentation*, *The Ten Greatest Sales Persons*, *The Chief Executive Officer*, *The Entrepreneurs*, and *Honda: An American Success Story*.

When most writers write a nonfiction piece, they usually write the whole book, take it to the publisher, and say, "Here's my book." The publisher says, "We don't want to publish that book, not because it's not well-written, but because there isn't a market for it." I do things backwards, or maybe they do things backwards. I figure out the market first. I think of a book like any product you would sell, and ask, "Who has a need for this product?" When you find a need, you manufacture the product.

For some reason writers don't think like that; they don't put on their business cap and think like businesspeople. The first thing a writer should do is find other books written on the subject and find out how they did. The easiest way to do that is get *Books in Print;* go to the library; and, best of all, go to bookstores and talk to the managers to see what they think about your idea. These people know far more about how books sell than publishers do because they deal directly with customers. Just because one book has been successful doesn't mean five or ten books on the subject can't be just as successful. And if there are no books on the subject, don't assume you should write about it because there may be a good reason no one has written on it. There are 60,000 books published every year, so rarely will you come across a book idea no one ever thought of, but that doesn't mean you can't come up with an original idea.

When I talk to publishers or send in proposals, I always include a marketing plan describing who the market is for the book and why there is a need for it; I give them ideas about how they can promote and sell the book. I also think of ways to sell the book in nontraditional markets (outside bookstores). Sometimes book publishers tell you they have a special marketing department, but I have never met anyone who sold books for me that I didn't sell myself. They didn't know how to sell them or were working on too many other projects.

You have the most interest in the book, stand to make the most money, and thought the most about it, so you should understand your market better than anyone. If you want things to happen, you have to make them happen yourself. Books can be premiums, for example. My son and I wrote a book called *The Winner's Circle*, in which we interviewed ten of the top stockbrokers. We told the brokers, "You're in this book. What a great tool that is for marketing and promoting yourself." We sold about 20,000 books that way. I did a book on Honda, and Honda bought 10,000 copies. I did a book on Ford, and they bought 5,000 books.

After I wrote *The Healing Family,* a book on cancer, I called up an insurance company called AFLAC, which had 30 or 40 people who sell cancer policies. I called them cold, didn't know anyone there. I talked to the VP of marketing, explained the book, and said, "In the past, when insurance companies sell you a policy, you never hear from them again. I wrote this book that teaches people how to give support to family members who have cancer. I want you to buy

10,000 copies and have your agents give them to buyers. No one in the industry ever gives a gift like that; they hardly even return calls. You give these people a gift that will cost you about $4 or $5 apiece, and think of the goodwill you will create, of the referrals you will get. Give me five names—your president, the CEO, and others, I'll give you five autographed copies of the book, and I'll call you back in two weeks." I sold them 10,000 copies.

If I were writing a health book, I would go to health stores (there are more health stores than bookstores!). Everyone in those stores is interested in diet or health. So you are not competing with 80,000 other books. If I wrote a book about sports, I would contact sports distributors; on religion, I would contact churches; for a feel-good book, I would contact Hallmark. This is what I mean by creating a market outside the bookstores. I did a book on United Consumers Club, and they bought 100,000 copies. When I did one on the franchising industry, the National Association of Franchisers contacted me and helped me market the book. Century 21, which was in the book, bought 10,000 copies. Then ten salespeople in the *Ten Greatest Sales Persons* bought 10,000 copies total. I make a bigger profit there than at the bookstores, and made a lot of those books successful outside the bookstore. Once

> **The first thing a writer should do is find other books written on the subject, and find out how they did.**

I had this track record, I could tell publishers, "I'm going to sell a lot of books for you." I send them my track record so they see I'm not just talking, and they want to publish my book.

Most writers are very thin-skinned people. People in the arts are. When their art is rejected, they take it very personally. Writers think, "They rejected my thoughts." If you sell automobiles or real estate, it's "they rejected my product." If you change your mindset as a writer and say, "My book is just a product; they aren't rejecting me personally," that will make you a more effective salesperson. You can't put that artist's hat on and think you are too good to be a salesperson.

My daughter Carrie Coolidge is a reporter for *Forbes Magazine*. She has written six books, and I co-authored several with her. My son, R. J., who works for Prudential Securities, has written five books; he just sold the *Wall Street Dictionary*. He is going to try to sell them to Prudential, so the brokers can give it to their customers and will put "Prudential Securities, Wall Street Dictionary" on the cover. My son Michael is finishing his seventh book, *The Complete Idiot's Guide to Fly Fishing*. He is a professional fly-fisherman and has his own business publishing fly-fishing guides, so he has a built-in market. When he goes to the fishing stores to sell his guides, he will take his book and try to sell it.

> **You almost have to be an introvert to be a writer because it is so confining.**

You almost have to be an introvert to be a writer because it is so confining. I love to be around people, so it takes ten times more discipline for me to write than it does for an introvert. I can't wait until I can start selling my books. From the time you start with your idea until you finish your book, it's months and months before you get any gratification. I can call someone on the phone, sell 500 or 1,000 books, and get instant gratification.

I also have a contract on a book called *It Takes a Prophet to Make a Profit* with Britt Beemer, with whom I did *Predatory Marketing*. He uses this book on talk shows, and I can just sit back and write while he promotes my book for me. Then I have a contract with Big Brothers to write a book called *The Business of America Is Business*. The deal is Big Brothers will buy the books and give them to little brothers for good grades, good behavior, and stuff.

A writer should be willing to do book tours, book signings, whatever it takes to make the book really happen. He has a responsibility to help sell his book, just like they do.

Nearly 15 years ago, when my children were young, their mother died of cancer, and I told them that each of them had to write a book and dedicate it in her memory. First I wanted them to get over their grief; I also wanted them to be able to write because it's a good skill to have. When their resumes say they wrote a book, they will get some pretty good jobs. I'd tell them that writing is 98 percent discipline and 2 percent creativity. I've changed that; it's 99 percent discipline. Everybody is creative—whether a plumber or a dentist. The only difference is that writers have a vehicle for creativity and get credited for having creative thoughts. Other people talk to one or two people, but don't get the credit; writer's creativity is there on the page.

I always tell writers to carry a recorder with them. I keep one with me 24 hours a day, and I never have writer's block because I never run out of ideas. If I sit down to write cold, I would never remember 99 percent of the ideas. Also, most writers are not organized, and that is one reason they hate to start writing. I have such a good filing system that sitting down to write is painless; I know exactly what I have to do every day. I used to try to finish a chapter or a page or paragraph, but now I don't plan to finish a sentence, which makes it easier to get into writing the next day. I exercise every morning of my life. I hate it, but that is part of the discipline of being a writer. You have to be in good physical shape to sit and stare at that screen all day, and keep your mind sharp.

## EVELYN COLEMAN

*Evelyn Coleman is an award-winning children's picture book author, with titles such as* The Foot Warmer and the Crow, The Glass Bottle Tree, *and* White Socks Only. *She often writes her original stories in the language of folklore, but also writes in a more modern language as well. She's ghostwritten* Boxcar, *a children's book, and published educational books for primary children. Coleman has also written a suspense thriller for adults titled* What a Woman's Gotta Do, *which made the bestseller lists of Emerge Magazine, Chapter 11\*, and Waldenbooks (South De Kalb Mall). The novel was recommended reading in Ebony, Essence, Emerge, Direct Wire, and Black*

*Woman. A second suspense thriller,* Bloody Water, *comes out in the spring of 2000; and a third book deal is in the works to continue the story of the protagonist Patricia Conley of* What a Woman's Gotta Do. *Coleman has a background in psychology and was a psychotherapist for 33 years, as well as a hypnotherapist and stress management trainer.*

I am a very controversial children's book writer. I did not start out to be, but some people are concerned that I have only black heroes in my stories and no white heroes to balance them out. For that I have been criticized greatly. It's a wonderful experience because I am opening dialogue and doing things I say writers should do—make somebody cry, make somebody laugh, or piss somebody off. So as long as I am doing one of those three, I am happy.

> **I used to be the storyteller of the family and made a lot of money telling stories to my brother.**

I think I was born a writer. I used to be the storyteller of the family and made a lot of money telling stories to my brother. He used to give me his lunch money, his allowance, make my bed, do chores for me, as long as I would tell him a story at bedtime. My father loved to write poetry, so I think writing is just a part of me. When I was in college, my English teacher suggested I become a writer, but at that time I never knew a living black writer. Because it didn't seem to be a reasonable goal, I did not pursue it until I was thirty-seven years old.

My background in psychology—I was a psychotherapist for 33 years, and a hypnotherapist and stress management trainer—helped and continues to help me in my writing, to know people's motivations and innermost thoughts and desires. I know a lot about addictions, even though I've never been addicted to anything but chocolate and sex.

I went to the bookstore and I read about 200 children's books over the period of months. I would go every Saturday and Sunday, sit in there and actually dissect the sentences, count the number of paragraphs, and pay attention to the verbs. When I found something that had the style and rhythm of something I was writing, I called Macmillan and asked them who edited that particular book, and they gave me the gentleman's name, and then I sent my story to him.

I believe in spiritual guidance. I was getting ready to go live in a cave in Tibet when I had an accident that totally wrecked my car and injured my back so I couldn't go. While I was convalescing I had nothing to do but write, then I was encouraged to submit that writing to a North Carolina fellowship for published and non-published writers. I had no notion that I would win, but once I did, I decided to become a writer. So that is who I am now; there is nothing else for me to do.

The best thing that has happened to me was having one of my titles named the Smithsonian Most Outstanding Title for 1996. That's because, when I was a child, I loved *National Geographic* (which is a part of the Smithsonian) because it was the only place I could see black people in a book. The Smithsonian Institution has always been dear to my heart, so it was a great honor for me.

I only write about things I'm passionate about. If I am passionate about justice and fairness and love, that's what I write about.

I don't have a writing schedule per se. I just write all the time— every day, seven days a week, unless I'm traveling. I use a computer and I believe in my heart of hearts that if there were no computers, I wouldn't be a writer. I would become a storyteller because I hated to type on a typewriter and I hate writing in longhand. I absolutely adore computers. When my office becomes overwhelmingly junky, I have to stop and clean it up because my mind is also cluttered. And when I clean up, my mind clears.

I've done everything to promote my books—postcards, mailings, a lot of e-mailing. I would spend time reading in different areas of the Internet, then I would, with great apology, approach different people I'd seen posted on the Internet, and introduce them to my book. I've done touring—Simon & Schuster sent me on a tour for my first adult book—and I do conferences and teaching because that exposes you to new groups of people. And I do a lot of sharing because I think it's important to share with other authors and people who wish to be authors. I do have one caveat, though: I do not care for writers who are not extremely serious about what they are doing. If they haven't been to workshops and don't know what the writer's market is, but just sat down and wrote their book without any crafting kind of preparation, I'm not usually open to sharing. If the writer researched the market, knows the publishing industry, and is respectful enough of me that they've read or know something about my work, I will do anything for that person. I have introduced writers to my agent, given editors' names, and I even sat down and reshaped a writer's work (she actually got it published!). I am really in love with writers; we're all one step away from not being published.

I guess in my career I would like to win a national literary award. Right now I am seeking out places to improve my writing, to learn about literary writing, to move in that direction. I went to three writing schools for children's books before I tried selling children's books. I went to Vassar, to Rice, to Highlight's, and then to many Society of Children's Book Writers and Illustrators conferences. I believe it's important to have natural talent, but learning the craft you work in is even more important. Just as I, even though I know a lot about science and medicine, would not operate on my kids, I wouldn't just sit down, write a story, and try to publish it.

> ## I only write about things I'm passionate about.

Writers should take writing as seriously as attending medical school or law school. I don't know anyone in this country with natural talent who takes the final exam without having been to medical school, or at least reading a medical book. I hope people understand that writing is a craft people give their lives to, and it should be held in high esteem because writers are the people who can actually change the world. There aren't many mediums where you can change minds through debate rather than torture.

## JEFF SLUTSKY

*Jeff Slutsky is the president and founder of Street Fighter Marketing. He has a background in advertising and public relations, but it wasn't until he became part owner of a nightclub and a health club that the program known as Street Fighting was born. Slutsky began discovering and developing results-oriented, low-cost tactics to build sales, which became known as Street Fighting. He is the author of six books, including* Streetfighter Marketing, How to Get Clients, Street Smart Teleselling, *and* The Toastmasters International Guide to Successful Speaking. *He is also the author and producer of three audio albums and a video series, which are part of the Street Fighter's Profit Package, a complete video and audio training program with telephone consulting. His Street Fighting program has received much media attention, including* The Wall Street Journal, USA Today, Success, Inc. Magazine, Investor's Business Daily, CNN, Sally Jesse Raphael, *and is a regular on the PBS series,* Small Business Today, *and CNN's* Who's in Charge. *His Web site is www.streetfighter.com/jefff.html.*

I started this business in 1980. That includes 20 years—of mostly public speaking and seminars, which also sell the books and tapes and videos. More recently, we started doing public seminars in conjunction with a syndicated column we run in *The Columbus Dispatch* that then goes out to eight other markets over the Knight Ridder News Service. I've also expanded to writing musical parody shows for the cooperate market.

The main way we sell more books is to make them available in the back of the room when I speak. After a speech is when somebody wants a piece of you. We always price the books into $20 increments ($10 for paperbacks), and also sell three books in a package for $55.

So we make it easy to get the money, and probably three-quarters of the people who buy actually buy all three books right then. It is not uncommon to sell a couple cases of books at a seminar.

We also use the books as an add-sale if someone is booking us for a speech. Before the speech, we try to convince them to make one of the books available to everybody in the audience and offer them

> **The fact that I've published seven books makes me more in demand as a speaker, consultant, and trainer.**

at a really good price. That way 200 people each have a book, then we still sell the others in the back of the room—a pretty nice add-on sale. And the more books floating around, the more people call up wanting the new ones. We also sell online a little bit. Our Web page is just starting to get some interest, and we want to get books that way, or through Amazon.com. And we also promote it via our own weekly column, which is broadcast-faxed to 2,000 meeting planners a week.

I do book signings when I travel, but not quite as many now. I spoke, along with my co-author Michael On, at the Toastmasters annual convention last year in New Orleans to promote the *Toastmasters* book and sold 800 or 900, which is nice. We do radio interviews, print reviews, the typical things publishers set up. The last publisher, Career Press, has been pretty good lining up interviews and getting reviews done on the book.

Our success is more than the revenue generated directly from book sales (which is probably a minor amount for us); it's how it enhances our business related to the book topic. The fact that I've published seven books makes me more in demand as a speaker, consultant, and trainer. Once I picked up a client who just happened to read a one-paragraph review of *How to Get Clients* in a furniture trade magazine and called me up and booked me for their convention.

We make the most money on the books when we sell them ourselves, obviously, and sell probably 10,000 copies a year ourselves. Since we print the self-published ones ourselves, the markup is really good.

We are waiting to hear from our publishers. The last book was basically 52 of our columns as 52 book chapters. People seemed to like that a lot because each chapter is short, a couple pages. We can crank out a book a year like that. We're trying to find a publisher that's interested. We've actually signed a deal now with someone who's a hotshot in Internet marketing, but he can't write. This expands our marketing base to the Internet, which is hot. I'm also helping a few other writers get published in some of their areas, but most will be collaborative efforts. I have pretty much tapped out my area of marketing and sales so to expand my horizons, I have to find partners who have different expertise than I do, so I can bring something to the table there.

## BEATTY COHAN AND ELLIOT COHAN

*Beatty Cynthia Cohan, MSW, LICSW, and Elliot Cohan, M.Ed., are the married collaborative authors of* For Better, For Worse, Forever: Ten Steps for Building a Lasting Relationship with the Man You Love. *According to the Cohans, the book is the definitive guide for women who want to accurately assess their potential partner and make the right decisions about dating, commitment, and marriage. "Ten Key Ingredients" comprise the formula that is revolutionizing relationships in this country. Beatty Cohan is a psychotherapist and sex therapist in private practice, with 27 years of clinical experience. She is the resident psychotherapist for radio's Carolyn Fox Show and has hosted her own radio call-in counseling show. For years, she had her own segment, "Ask Beatty," on ABC-TV 6 Providence Noon News. Elliot Cohan, a counselor, teacher, and professional leader in human services for more than 35 years, is also a stage and film actor. The Cohans co-conduct Compatibility Consultants seminars.*

BEATTY: We feel we have something so important that everybody in the world needs to know about it. This is a gift we want to leave to the world. It may sound narcissistic and egotistical, but we truly feel our formula is going to change the world, at least the western world, and decrease the divorce statistics. Our book has done very well. We found a fabulous agent in Pat Snapp.

ELLIOT: We had had two agents before, neither of whom knew anything about self-help books, and we didn't know anything about agents. But it's like anything else. Unless this person knows the market, knows how to market your book, and will help you market it, forget it. What happened was, we'd agreed that if they didn't sell the book in six months, we would move on, which we did. I started to send out query letters to agents, and one out of 18 or 20 came back with a phrase saying "Interesting, not bad writing, let's see a proposal." We had a proposal at that point, but it was a poor version . . .

B: But we thought it was a good version . . .

E: So we sent it to Pat, and she sent it back with a primer on how to write a book proposal. From that moment on, she spent at least two weeks out of every month going back and forth with us, writing and rewriting the proposal.

B: And we had never met Pat and Michael Snow; this has all been done over the phone. Elliot needs to take about 99.9 percent of the credit for keeping this going during the day because I was in my office with clients.

E: Pat told us how to really make a proposal marketable—which requires that you be very interesting, very distinguished from others, with a cover that had a picture reflecting the content in an engaging way.

B: Yeah, so everything was written and rewritten so many times. We had maybe half a dozen different covers, many different titles, rewrites, lots and lots of discussion. If one of us got discouraged, the other would say, "Look, you are having a tough day. This is wonderful, terrific; we are going to sell it," and we would get back on track emotionally.

E: And after a year of having the first proposal rejected six times, our agent called back and said, "Just think about this as your first try and refocus." And that's what we did, refocused the proposal because we then saw that we had to work within the premarital counseling market; the trends were pointing towards that.

B: We really jumped on the trends. Before we signed the contract, I had a television series, and you couldn't ask for more. That was great to get people to come to Compatibility Consultants and helpful to get feedback, but the key to the success was just keeping our process going.

E: If you believe in something, no matter what anyone says, you must pursue it until it is done.

B: And people were not encouraging. My media group was encouraging, but my own patients knew we were up to something.

E: We certainly didn't get encouragement from agents and publishers.

B: We are very pragmatic people. I have often said that my skill base is very limited. I know what I'm great at and where I know nothing and have absolutely no talent. It kept coming back to the formula that this is going to be an absolutely great book, so we need to do the rewrites and stick to the program. There was never a question of stopping. Ever.

E: I wanted also to have a legacy for my daughters. I really feel good about being able to send each of them a copy of the book.

B: For promotion, we have two super publicists, and we have had fabulous print coverage, thirty national magazines from *Cosmo* to *Redbook*. I did an analysis of "Can This Marriage Be Saved" in the *LA Times*. And we did a wonderful

**From that moment on, she spent at least two weeks out of every month going back and forth with us, writing and rewriting the proposal.**

radio show in Washington, D.C. that was going to be aired over like 2,000 stations. We've done radio shows where they called us at home, constant local stuff, and *Christian Science Monitor, LA Times, LA News, Florida Times Union, The Sun, Men's Health Magazine, Seventeen* . . . .

But we haven't heard from *Oprah* or the national TV gang; Barbara Walters was very close last year, but that broke down. As far as this book goes, we want to make sure there isn't a stone un-turned. We are going to try to take this formula on the road, cer-tainly in North America, via speaking venues, engagements, so that even if we don't have the publicist, we will try to make sure every-body knows about this formula. And we very possibly might write another book.

## There was never a question of stopping. Ever.

E: The second book would en-capsulate the other end. The central problem with singles is that they don't really know who they are mar-rying, which is why there's a 50 per-cent divorce rate.

B: I was surprised that everything took such a long time. I thought the writing would go quicker, that there wouldn't be so many rewrites. I thought we would be a household name, on the *New York Times* bestseller list within the first few weeks.

E: The other surprise was that an author had to work so hard to market his own book. In addition to what the publicists are doing, thank God Beatty has all these local contacts because we have just about covered the local media, radio and TV, and are about to do the one newspaper in Rhode Island.

B: You have to be really comfortable and skilled to promote your book. I have spent a lot of time doing this media stuff, and it is so easy to mess up. I had to work really hard at getting it right. Now I'm as comfortable on radio and television as I am in my office, so for me promotion was a real perk. People who are out there promot-ing their books really need to take some lessons. I don't believe that many people would just be able to come across the way they want to without some background and training.

E: The training is easy to get. Just about every town has a community college or university where you can take classes—on-camera courses is what they call them.

B: Authors have to hone their media skills as well as their writing skills—even little things like getting your colors straight and knowing what to wear. And you don't want to be like non-media types who are so boring you think, "Get this segment over with."

E: You have to be very social to promote your book. How else is anyone going to read it? We want to influence people with this book.

## DR. HOWARD ROSENTHAL

*Dr. Howard Rosenthal is the author or editor/contributor of three counseling and therapy books.* The Encyclopedia of Counseling: Master Review and Tutorial *is used by therapists nationwide to become licensed or certified as a professional counselor/therapist. He was the editor/contributor of* Favorite Counseling and Therapy Techniques: 51 Therapists Share Their Most Creative Strategies. *Within one year the text became one of Accelerated Development/Taylor & Francis' top sellers. He co-authored* Help Yourself to Positive Mental Health *with Dr. Joseph Hollis, the former owner of Accelerated Development Publishers. The book was written in a "reader-friendly" style to make it easy to understand and to apply complex psychological principles. The book has been an Online Psych Cover Story for America Online on several occasions.*

I wrote my first book, *Not with My Life I Don't: Preventing Your Suicide and That of Others,* in 1988. I was lecturing to 10,000 people a year on suicide prevention. The audiences loved my speeches and kept asking, "Where can I buy your book?" The truth was there wasn't one. So I sat down at my kitchen table and wrote one. Passages from parts of my book were identical to my lectures so I knew people would like it.

I remember taking a college composition course and my professor marked one of my papers with an A+ and wrote: "Good enough to be published." For almost twenty years I sat on her sage advice.

After I completed my master's degree, I wrote a few technical articles, but deep down I always wanted to write a book. Books had had a tremendous impact on my life.

Everybody told me it was impossible to get a book published, and that made me want to do it even more! In fact an agent told me I would never sell my first book. Just for the record, I sold it to the first publisher I sent it to! Yes, success really is the best revenge.

I stayed motivated because I knew I had something to say and a better way to say it. You need a tad of arrogance if you are going to write because the field itself can humble you.

The best thing that happened in my writing was creating the *Encyclopedia of Counseling, Master Review, and Tutorial.* I saw an opening for a book and capitalized on it. I knew that studying for professional exams was tedious and boring (most study guides could and should double as sleep therapy!) and I insist that all my works are fun, lively, and easy to read. Readers loved it. I get thank-you cards, letters, and calls on a regular basis. Talk about fulfilling!

Once I was at a party and a woman asked my wife what I did for a living. She answered that I was a professor who ran a community college program and was also an author with a part-time therapy practice. The other lady said, "Oh my, that's very interesting. What type of books does your husband write?" My wife replied, "The type that don't make a lot of money."

> **If I can't add something to the existing literature (or say it better), I don't write anything.**

I only write about topics I know about and am interested in. If I can't add something to the existing literature (or say it better), I don't write anything.

I'd have a better chance of winning the lottery today (and I haven't purchased a ticket) than of sticking to a writing schedule. Sometimes I write at midnight; other times at 6:00 A.M. When you have a two-year-old and a five-year-old, you write when and where you get the chance. I currently write on my 400 MHZ computer, but wrote my first book with a 99-cent pen on my kitchen table, then had somebody type it. I often write with my 200-plus-watt stereo blasting music out of my studio monitor speakers or earphones.

My advice for aspiring authors is simple: Read as many books as you can on the topic of book publishing. Next, size up your competition. Most aspiring authors know about as much about the existing books in the field as monkeys know about building a nuclear ballistic missile. Ask yourself: Is there really a market for your book? (Hint: Unless you're Oprah, a famous movie star, politician, or athlete, the chances are excellent that nobody is interested in a book about your life!) I say this because whenever I've given seminars on how to get your book published, aspiring authors tell me about a book idea on their own life. How is your book different from the other books on the market? Spend time hanging out in bookstores and surfing Amazon.com. Also, why are you qualified to write the book? Lastly, write because you have something to say, not because you are trying to get rich. The great psychologist Andrew Salter once commented that "the author who fears he will prostitute his work usually can't give it away."

Success is an inner process. Once you have an idea, keep it for a book that will sell. Keep the image firmly implanted in your mind and go for it. See yourself in your mind writing it and later giving autographed copies to others. When you visualize the process, make it as real and enjoyable as possible. To hell with well-meaning friends and relatives who say it can't be done. Many bestsellers were rejected by numerous editors and agents.

## CHAPTER 5

# The Niche Authors

The Niche Authors have made a name for themselves in one particular arena. They are the experts in a subject area, like Judy Guggenheim, whose focus is after-death communication. They are the genre authors, like mystery author Kate Flora or romance author Joanna Wayne. Sure, they may have a book or two outside the genre or usual arena. But these authors know that one way to make it big is to establish yourself in your niche, and the fans will flock.

"I got started as a mystery addict," says Elaine Viets. "I was reading five a week and I decided, why don't I try writing one?"

"I got a big following in Europe," says Carol Adrienne. "Through an amazing synchronicity, there was this controversy about the Pope making a statement about the New Age. Because I was kind of a New Age author, I got to be the spokesperson for the New Age."

"After thirty years as a biomedical scientist I got the urge to write about the experience. And the murder mystery has been the best form," says Dirk Wyle.

"My book is the product of over seven years of research . . . it was the first research of its kind ever done," says Judy Guggenheim. "I really think I found my voice, my passion, the message that love and life are eternal."

Not everyone thinks the Niche Author is an expert on the topic. "My daughter told me I could never write a romance novel because 'those novels' have sex in them, and women my age (thirty-eight at the time) didn't know anything about sex," says Jeanette Baker.

"I look for anything going on with Indians in the West," says Margaret Coel, "typical issues that Native Americans deal with, Plains Indian ledger books, details about life on the plains, people who have recorded their lives and history all inspire me. I wanted to tell their story."

## CAROL ADRIENNE

*Carol Adrienne, Ph.D., is a bestselling author, artist, and numerologist, with a background in archetypal psychology. Carol's latest book is* The Purpose of Your Life. *Her other books include the* New York Times *bestseller* The Celestine Prophecy: An Experimental Guide *and* The Tenth Insight: Holding the Vision, *both co-authored with James Redfield. Her first book was* The Numerology Kit, *an easy, how-to guide for finding the blueprint in names and birthdays.* Your Child's Destiny, *a book for parents, is available in Australia. Since 1994, Adrienne has devoted her time to writing, lecturing, and facilitating workshops internationally on spiritual principles. She also writes a monthly column for* The Celestine Journal, *an international newsletter (see www.celestinevision.com). Her Web site is www.spiralpath.com.*

I write in the realm of personal and spiritual development. I've written the *Celestine Prophecy's Experiential Guide* with James Redfield, *The Purpose of Your Life Book,* and two books on numerology.

I have a knack for explaining ideas. I synthesize them and add stories to illustrate the principles. So helping people discover how to apply principles to their own lives in everyday life is sort of the niche I'm in. My books on numerology are very easy-to-use books, where you can figure it out for yourself and everybody in your life. I take an esoteric subject and make it more accessible by showing people how to apply it so they can live a more positive life, know themselves better, or be happier and connected to what matters to them.

*The Celestine Prophecy Experiential Guide* was on the *New York Times* bestseller's list. I've been on bestseller's lists in Canada, Italy, and here in the United States. The last time I heard, *The Purpose of Your Life* had sold over 65,000 copies. *The Experiential Guide* has probably sold over a million copies, but I don't have figures on that. It has really been fun and heartening to make a living at this. I love it! It is exactly what I was born to do.

**One day I woke up thinking that maybe I could help someone write a book.**

I got a $1,000 advance for my first book, which I thought was just terrific. The book came out the same year that my whole life fell apart. I got breast cancer and went into treatment, got a divorce, and had to quit working. And you know, a small book like that doesn't change your life very much. It isn't like, "Oh, now I have a book. My life is set." I'm sure you are very well aware that it's not common to start making a living off your first book. You have to really work this system.

It wasn't until 1990 that I started pursuing my writing career. Since all this chaos had happened, my life had shifted quite a bit. I was feeling the need to make more money to supplement my full-time metaphysical counseling. One day I woke up thinking that maybe I could help someone write a book. I don't know where that thought came from, but I had the intuition to call my friend Candace, the only one I knew in the literary arena, and said to her, "If you hear of anyone who needs help writing a book, give me a call." By the end of the day she called back and said, "There is a doctor who needs help ghostwriting a book on homeopathy and sports medicine." Of course, I thought, "No. I don't have knowledge of either of those fields." But the universe was saying, "Here is your opportunity to do what you wanted to do, what you asked for. It's like my angels heard me and gave me the opportunity, so I had to call him up. I found I knew more about writing than he did, so that was enough to get me going. He gave me a contract for about four months so I had money coming in, and I ghostwrote the book for him. The book was very successful, at least when it came out, so I wound up ghostwriting a similar project on financial recovery.

This gave me a feeling that I had talent for writing and making ideas clear. Then again, I didn't try to do any more writing for a while because my metaphysical practice was still growing, and I was teaching classes and keeping people on track—my life's purpose by this time.

Then I read *The Celestine Prophecy* in 1993. I got very excited about the ideas in there, especially that we choose our parents and that all experiences have a purpose, which I already believed. As I began to apply this to my own clients, Candace called, just to talk about social things. Then I had the intuition to tell her about the book, really an offhand remark at the end of the conversation. I said I'd read this new book called *The Celestine Prophecy* that really changed my practice. She said, "That was a self-published book." (James self-published it in the beginning.) "Let me call him and see if he'd like to have an agent." So she called him and he didn't need an agent. (The miracle was that she actually got through to him; you simply can't do that now!) Then she came up with the idea of a guidebook for it, but he said he didn't have time to write one. That's when she called me back and said, "Why don't you write a proposal for this thing?" At first I was taken aback and thought, "Oh, my God, can I do this?" Then I realized that everything I'd been working on led me to this.

> **This gave me a feeling that I had talent for writing and making ideas clear.**

So I bought a book about how to write book proposals, filled in the blanks for this project, and sent it off to James. I had to wait a few months before he agreed to work with me. That was the real beginning of my writing career. I wrote that book in four months, then he asked me to write the guide for *Tenth Insight*, which I again did in about four months. It sort of flowed.

My editor from Time-Warner (who actually went over to William Morrow) wanted me to write a book on my own. We decided to make it a book on life purpose, which is my passion. She asked me to write a workbook for one that just came out, which I did. I loved it so much I was thinking, "This is a stand-alone book." She read it, called me back, and said, "You know, this book is so good, I'm going to put it on the fall list instead of this summer. We'll give you more money and will turn it into a hardcover." When you are following what you love to do, and are not really attached to the outcome or how the results should look, things seem to flow. That's the end of my story, about writing anyway. My books are published in maybe twelve or twenty other countries now. I've got a big following in Italy through an amazing synchronicity last year. There was this controversy about the Pope making a statement about the New Age. Because I was in Italy and was kind of a New Age author, I became the spokesperson for New Age and got all over the newspapers, magazines, and on the biggest TV show in Italy. Again, it was something I didn't plan to do.

I now have a PR person and an agency. Last year the publisher was nice enough to do some PR on *The Purpose of Your Life,* and that's when I got on *Oprah.* They sent the galleys to Oprah before my book was in the stores. They were doing a segment on synchronicity and called me to be the expert on the show. Again, there was sort of an odd situation, because they called a couple of times, but hadn't formally invited me. In the meantime, I was doing some work with a friend about expanding my vision and looking at blockages I might have about reaching out, going further. After I did that work, they called to formally invite me on *Oprah.* So I flew to Amarillo when she was involved in that trial down there and did the show. Oprah raved about my book, even though it wasn't out. She had read the galleys, and said it was great and showed the cover. A lot of people remembered that and bought it when it came out. Plus there was a sticker on it that said "As Seen on Oprah," which helped a lot.

Oprah is wonderful. You can just sense her intelligence and her humor and her power. I think she is doing more to change people's belief systems than anyone else in America. Everyone who saw the show said I looked very relaxed. Of course, I wish I would have remembered certain points, but she made them so it worked out okay. I would love to do it again.

> **If you love to write, keep writing. Don't keep making excuses.**

The most surprising thing related to my writing was getting the opportunity to write the guidebook for *The Celestine Prophecy*. James certainly had his input, but I did the majority of the actual writing and organizing. What has also been great is that I'm well known for my own book now. I'm getting an enormous number of letters from people who feel they changed their lives because of stories and little exercises I put in the book. What surprises me now is that my work is known nationally. Like I said, writing wasn't something I started out to do; it just developed. My bachelor's is Art History and my master's is Archetypal Psychology. Now I have a Ph.D. based on the work I've done through writing, and that came to me effortlessly as well. What I love more than anything is teaching—it's so much fun and so rewarding. I love all of the facets of my life—sitting down to write, teaching people, exchanging ideas and information, and seeing how people actually make changes in their lives that mean something.

I do lectures and seminars all over the country, all over the world now. I have been to Istanbul, to South Africa, Cape Town, all over Canada and Nova Scotia, Italy, and Germany. I am going back to Italy for the third time and to Germany to visit my German publishers and to speak at a New Age conference.

I am really happy where I am—on the path and doing things that are making a difference for people. I just look forward to more opportunities to teach and write books.

If you love to write, keep writing. Don't keep making excuses. Write ten minutes a day if that is all you have—not because you think it is some good idea to be an author, to have some elevated position; do it because you enjoy it. Do you have something to say? Put yourself in your chair, turn on the computer, and start writing, or do it with your notebook. I teach people in all types of occupations to keep connecting to why you want to do this and how much fun it is. And look for ways to learn. Take classes on writing, talk to writers, join a writer's group—anything to amp up the energy. I was in Seattle on a tour and had a media escort, a wonderful, bright guy named Gary Macavoy. He said, "You know, I took this job as a part-time thing so I could meet authors and get into their energy. Now I know a lot of famous authors." He is writing a novel and has clear goals about wanting it to come out next year. He has put his energy into being around authors, which can only enhance the opportunities to get published.

## BURL BARER

*Burl Barer is an award-winning author of such books as* The Saint: A Complete History in Print, Radio, Film, and Television, *which was a 1994 Edgar Award Winner and Anthony Award nominee;* Maverick, *based on the feature film starring Mel Gibson and Jodie Foster; and* Man Overboard: The Counterfeit Resurrection of Phil Champagne, *nominated Best True Crime Book of the Year (Anthony Award) by the World Mystery Convention.* Man Overboard *will soon be either a made-for-TV movie or feature film. Barer's newest book,* Capture the Saint, *is the first all-new Simon Templar (The Saint) adventure approved by the estate of Leslie Charteris, creator of the character. Barer's novelization of* The Saint, *based on the screenplay of the feature film starring Val Kilmer, is still available. His Web site is bigjohn.bmi.net/burlb.*

My first authored book, *The Saint: A Complete History in Radio, Television, and Film,* came out in 1993 from MacFarlane and Company. I won the Edgar award for the critical biographical category, so

I figure that was a good start. It's kind of like Aldo Ray, who won the Academy Award for best supporting actor, and even at the end of his life when he was all burned out and making porno movies, he was still Academy Award–winner Aldo Ray. So no matter how low I go from here, I will always be an Edgar Award winner. The book was also nominated for an Anthony but didn't get it. Then I think after that was *Maverick: The Making of the Movie: The Official Guide to the Television Series.*

The book, which came out the same time as the movie, has all sorts of background stuff about the making of the movie. I went on the set and had lots of fun. Mel Gibson made me cappuccino in his trailer; James Garner is exactly like James Garner; and Jodie Foster looks a lot like Jodie Foster. And Richard Donner, who was directing, was great.

Then I wrote a brilliant . . . (laughter) humorous true crime. I like to do things in genres that are different, to do something different with it. I wanted *The Saint* to be a critical work that met all the standards, that you could actually use as a textbook for a class on popular culture. It's the history of how this one character was portrayed in various media over many decades and social and cultural conditions. But I wanted it in a fun style because the Saint books themselves are fun. The *Maverick* book, like the series, was very tongue in cheek. My commentary on the old TV shows and my plot descriptions are rather peculiar. I was having a good time.

I'm known as the king of BSP (Blatant Self-Promotion). I have irritated and offended more fellow authors, unintentionally. A lot of authors are shy; they hide out and pour themselves out in their books. Writing is such a solitary thing, except for the relationship between the editor and writer, which is sort of a dominatrix, sexual thing. But I really like the promotional aspect once the book is done.

Once, I set up at the Midatlantic Mystery Conference, in their "big dealer" (not drug dealers; book dealers). It was a circular room so you could come in one door and go out the other side. I positioned myself right by the going-out door so I could see the name tags of the people coming in. I would yell, "Julie, so nice to see you! I've got your book for you," and they would go, "Huh?" And I would say, "I'm Burl Barer and this is my new book *The Counterfeit Resurrection of Phil Champagne.*" They would say, "Is it fact or fiction?" and I would say "It's a true crime," and they would say "I don't read true crime. I only read fiction," and I would say, "You will be pleased to know that it's a pack of lies."

I had a whole pitch prepared—memorized the blurb on the inside of the jacket. I came in with two boxes, each with 52 hardback books, $29.95 a book, and sold them all in a day and a half. It's almost self-parody, me hocking books like a vegematic salesman, telling people, "Even if you're illiterate, it's one of the great bookends of the twentieth century. Think of the pride of ownership. Thin book, thick plot, right price." I run up and down the hallways, yelling "I'm a writer, I can prove it, I've got a pen."

> So the book didn't come out, and I didn't get paid, which really financially hurt me.

With *Man Overboard,* I took the criminal with me on the book signing tour. His crime was counterfeiting, not murder. So when you came to the Seattle book signing, you got the author's signature and the signatures of the two major perpetrators, the counterfeiter and his wife, who had both gone to prison. President Clinton has a copy.

There is nothing like having a reading and no one shows up except my mom and my brother. I do well in those mall settings and like doing independent stores, too. At the bookshops I try to be real supportive of anyone who will sell my books.

On *Man Overboard: The Counterfeit Resurrection of Phil Champagne*, I wanted to do a true crime book that wasn't about a psycho/sexual rapist serial killer. I thought it would be interesting to do bizarre stories of interesting characters, where the narrator (me) would sort of break the fourth wall and make little side comments. Instead of being the omniscient objective journalistic narrator, I made little bantering comments about the characters, which was fun. That book also was nominated for an Anthony for best true crime but lost out to Ann Rule, which is an interesting coincidence. Ann Rule appears as herself in my book because her daughter and Phil Champagne's daughter were best friends. Ann's book, *Dead by Sunset,* was about this woman who worked for a law firm who was murdered by her husband. The law firm was Garbry, Schubert, Adams, and Barer, my brother's firm. Neither of us made the connection when we were writing, then I said, "Well, your name is in my book, and my name is in yours, so that works out."

> **When we get a new house I will have a view, but I have been writing in the basement for years.**

*Man Overboard* was supposed to be made into a movie about three different times, but has always fallen through, so we never got rich off that. And the publisher went bankrupt; in fact the publisher is in prison, allegedly for embezzling ten million dollars from his own company, which he cashed at Checks R Us at the mini-mall and paid $250,000 in check-cashing charges.

They had paid me for *Man Overboard*, and were going to pay me even more for the next book, *Hidden Words*, about an Alaskan mail-bomb conspiracy/murder case. I had the complete cooperation of the U.S. government and the postal service, which cracked the case. The postal inspectors wanted to know how the book was coming, and I said, "We are behind schedule because the publisher has not paid me for our contract." Anyway, I went off and when I came back had a fax waiting from the postal inspector, saying: "Dear Mr. Barer: You will appreciate this press release. . . . Agents of the U.S. Postal service, raided the offices of . . . confiscated all their computers, business records. . . put them under investigation for mail fraud." (laughter)

So the book didn't come out, and I didn't get paid, which really financially hurt me. So that's how I made it big in writing—by living off my Visa cards, waiting for a bankrupt publisher to send me money.

I wrote *Capture the Saint*, the first new original Saint novel since 1980-something, approved by the estate of Leslie Charteris. It came out in a limited edition for charity—600 signed and numbered copies with all the money going to the Arbor Youth Center for Disadvantaged Children in Stepney, London. (Had I become one of those children, I could have gotten some money!) And now they're having 200 extra copies printed to give out at the test-drive of the new Volvo S40 and V40 in Seattle this spring.

Before that came out, I was contracted by Simon & Schuster Pocket Books to write the novelization of *The Saint*, which did very well. Of course, it's brilliant, witty, wise, wonderful. They did a two million–dollar reshoot, and I had to do a last-minute rewrite.

Elizabeth Shue was the main female character, and in the original movie she got killed halfway through. But the screening audiences didn't like that; they thought it was like having Princess Leia getting killed before the first droid lands. So they re-did the movie so she wasn't dead, which meant the entire second half of the movie about him going after her killer had to be redone. I had to rewrite and re-structure the novel over Christmas vacation when I was in Palm Springs visiting my mommy. I didn't have a fax machine and they didn't have e-mail, so I was reading my rewrites over the phone to the editor. But we got it done in time.

The best thing? Being published. No, winning the Edgar was beyond all expectations, a total rush. Now, they read the nominees at the Academy Awards and the people sit there like they aren't having a nervous breakdown. I'm not the kind of guy who gets nervous as a general rule, and almost didn't go to the Edgar awards because I didn't think I was going to win. But I went, and I sat next to some guy from CBS, then there was someone from ABC, and a famous author was on the other side getting sloshed. And they read the nominees, and all of a sudden I got really nervous, which is unlike me. And the woman next to me was just like, "Close your eyes. It will all be over in a minute." I said, "What, are they going to shoot me?" When they said my name, my head exploded.

When we get a new house I will have a view, but I have been writing in the basement for years. I sit hunched over my computer and make my eyes and my neck sore, and do a lot of cutting and pasting, and get upset at all my passive sentences.

This true crime I'm doing now is work. Writing is basically like doing the world's biggest term paper. It's highly structured, lots of research, not very creative . . . more like journalism.

How have my readers responded to my work? By buying it. I get fan mail, fan e-mail. I'll remember getting Val Kilmer's fan e-mail for a while.

> **I'm just the guy who's writing; I'm too close to it to see what's happening.**

When people ask me, "How do I find an agent who won't steal my idea and a publisher who won't change it?" my answer is "Go get a job." If words are that sacred to you, and you think you're that brilliant, then be a playwright; don't write books. My first experience with an editor was with a man who taught me many things. All my editors after that have been women. I prefer women, like a male submissive to a dominatrix. You say, "Was this good enough?" They say, "No, restructure it, redo it, do it again. I want more forward moving action, too many adjectives, not enough adverbs!" That's what it's like—working with a strong-willed female who knows what she wants. Just tell me what you want, I can change the words, move them around. You can't be married to the script, you have to be willing to change it, that's what you are being paid for. I'm just the guy who's writing; I'm too close to it to see what's happening.

Keith Snyder was being interviewed and someone asked, "What's the best advice you can give to an aspiring author?" He said two words: "Finish it!"

## JUDY GUGGENHEIM

*Judy and Bill Guggenheim are the founders of The ADC Project, the first in-depth research of After-Death Communications (ADC). They interviewed 2,000 people, all from 50 American cities and ten Canadian provinces, and collected more than 3,300 first-hand accounts of the experience of ADC. The Guggenheims have written the first book ever to document this field of research.* Hello from Heaven! *contains 353 accounts of After Death Communication. It is widely available in the United States and Canada, as well as in the United Kingdom and throughout the Commonwealth. It has also been printed in Dutch, German, and Italian editions. Their Web site is www.after-death.com.*

*Hello from Heaven!* is the product of over seven years of research on the phenomenon of after-death communication, which is a direct and spontaneous communication from a deceased loved one without the use of a psychic, a medium, or a ritualistic device. It is the first research of this kind ever done.

Bill had already done some vast searching, looking for books that may have already covered this subject. We couldn't find any, not a one. We already knew we were writing a book, and knew we would have to do the research in such a way that we could pull a book together with the results. Even though neither of us had been a published writer, we were clear thinkers and could put together our thoughts in such a way that they were very clear to readers.

I was brought into writing based on my research and my passion for sharing it. I was not a born writer. I found the writing experience arduous. It took about a year because we had to compile over 350 firsthand accounts and organize them in a way that would make sense to a reader. Considering the great variety; that was tedious!

There was some discouragement from others who felt that because I did it with a partner, we would never agree and never get it done. That *was* a trick—two people writing and collaborating—and we had to cooperate.

We self-published first. We turned down a book deal from HarperCollins because they wanted too much editorial license—change the title and kill off fifty pages. We were told that we were fools as first-time authors to turn down this deal, and did quite a bit of soul-searching. Would we ever get another shot? That was a difficult few weeks, but we held our ground and didn't look back. The publishers ended up coming to us. And Bantam never changed a word of our book. It's important not to skip steps, but don't be too eager to sign a contract. Even though they gave us an interesting deal, we self-published 5,000 copies in the trade edition, which is paperback size but hardbound with a soft, glossy cover. We sold that substantially by mail order. We sold the first case of those books to our literary agent in Washington, D.C. Each time she would go to New York to meet with another client, she distributed them informally. Then four publishers came to us, so it became a bidding war between four major publishers. That all happened within 60 days of self-publishing and continued until Bantam Books finally won our favor and released it. We continued to sell our self-published edition.

The reader response has been fabulous. We created a Web site to accommodate responses, and are still getting a major flow of letters and media. We answer all our mail, which has been a challenge.

Our Web site is called the ADC Project, which is sort of the umbrella for all our work. The address is www.after-death.com. It's a rather extensive Web site with links, a message board, and over 20 chat rooms that are well monitored by over 20 volunteers.

The fact that Bill and I could work so well together, and come to an agreement, was a surprise—a big surprise, since he and I are formerly married. We didn't try writing till the early '90s, and I assumed it would be terribly difficult, but it worked out really well. We would each write, then compare what we had written on the topic, then integrate the two. It surprised me that two formerly married people could get through that without committing homicide.

I really think I found my voice, my passion—the message that love and life are eternal. However I can bring credibility to that which has brought me the pleasure and knowledge that I do have a voice, a respected one, and can speak in public without butterflies, and can write with authority because I have broken through that writer's block.

I'm considered a good writer and a good speaker, which is really surprising because I was the kid who couldn't stand up to give an oral book report. Even as far along as high school, it terrified me. I tell people, you can always speak when you speak from your heart. You will never find it through your intellect.

> **Our Web site is called the ADC Project, which is sort of the umbrella for all our work.**

Early on we received a huge flurry of media attention and were immediately invited to participate in a *20/20* segment titled *Hello from Heaven!* that was aired nationally. I was on the *Leeza Show, Sightings,* and *Unsolved Mysteries.* I didn't get a chance to do *Oprah,* but that doesn't mean that I won't someday. And a whole lot of radio and print, of course, came our way. I was surprised so many traditional church groups were interested in our work—people speaking to their deceased loved ones.

Bantam provided some PR (six to eight weeks is the typical run on any book), then we picked up a publicist in New York for a short time to keep the momentum going. But we haven't used anybody in quite a while, because I'm known for workshops and lectures.

I tell authors to define what they're willing to do. Define who you are in relationship to your work and find your strengths. Are you good with radio, TV, submitting ideas for print media, or doing interviews? My strength is radio, so I focus on that. It's a way to reach a lot of people in a small amount of time, and can be done remotely so you don't have to travel.

Now don't be starry-eyed about that end of the business. Someone needs to represent you in the publishing arena because you will find your book has a minimal run or 10,000, minimal distribution, and you have nothing to say about it. They own your book until 18 months after they stop publishing. That is a long time. Don't be so concerned with an advance, which is just the publisher saying they believe in this book to this degree. If your advance is huge, be cautious how you use it because you aren't going to see any more for a long time, until that advance is met.

## MARGARET COEL

*Margaret Coel is the author of a series of mystery novels set on the Wind River Reservation with the Arapahos. Titles in the series are* The Eagle Catcher, The Ghost Walker, *and* The Dream Stalker. *She is also the author of four nonfiction books, including the award-winning* Chief Left Hand. *Coleman also contributes articles on the West to many publications, including the* New York Times, *the* Christian Science Monitor, American Heritage of Invention & Technology, *and* Creativity! *She is also a speaker, traveling around the country and even as far as Australia to talk about her subjects. Her Web site is www.margaretcole.com/dreamstalker.*

Getting published is a powerful motivator. When you're not getting published, you have to motivate yourself by telling yourself it's a very subjective business. You have to find the proper home for what you write, keep sending them out. You also have to keep working at the craft, to motivate yourself to keep getting better, more skilled. I've run into some people who were more talented, but they gave up. There is a reason that you are driven to be a writer; you have to believe in that, work at your craft, and develop it.

I would say that I was born a writer, I never had the sense to do anything else—or the ability. It's the only thing I ever wanted to do. I've been pretty active as a writer all my life. I think my most relevant educational experience was getting a really good liberal arts education at Marquette University. By that, I mean a lot of literature and philosophy, which helps everyone to develop an inquiring mind. You have to learn new things all the time. I most definitely think you have to be a reader, and you have to want to learn to be successful. I was lucky to get that background.

People around me have always encouraged me. I'm very lucky in that sense, as I know it isn't the case for many writers. To be surrounded by people who believe in you should really be an aid in developing talent you might have.

> I've run into some people who were more talented, but they gave up.

The best things that happened to me were when the editor at Berkley bought my novels, and when my articles were published. Getting a three-novel contract was pretty exciting. When people come up and say, "I read your book," it's like a high. The worst is when rejections come in. When you put a lot of work, your heart and soul, into your book, it's hard to have that dismissed. To get beyond that is tough.

The most embarrassing thing is having a mistake creep into one of your books, like The Morning Star Rose being in the wrong place. I heard from a lot astrologers on that one.

I definitely get ideas from newspapers and headlines that grow into plots. I read three newspapers daily, and very carefully. I look for anything going on with Indians in the West—typical issues that Native American peoples deal with, Plains Indian ledger books, details about life on the plains, people who have recorded their lives and history, all inspire me. I wanted to tell their story. And of course, a darn good book really inspires me to do as well as other authors.

I work under some pretty close deadlines. Every day at home, I write for about five to six hours. Research takes up two to three hours just reading. I don't write when I'm traveling and lecturing for my books. I'm not the kind who travels with a laptop on the plane. I use my computer, WordPerfect 5.1 in my home office. When

I go into my office I know I'm going to work. It's a place I can sit down and write.

I've done book tours, radio, TV, newspaper interviews, all kinds of things. Book festivals and trade fairs all give me the chance to make acquaintance with bookstore owners, the people who really sell the books. I do a lot of speaking as well. I've been invited to speak all over the country in regards to my book topics. Book signings have also proved to be helpful.

I have two pieces of advice for writers: Learn your craft and be persistent. Always work at mastering the craft. You can never know enough of it, and there is always room for improvement. Be persistent, keep writing, and keep selling.

## SHIRLEY KENNETT

*Shirley Kennett is the author of the P.J. Gray series of suspense novels that have been featured in the Doubleday Book Club, Literary Guild, and Mystery Guild. Titles in the series are* Gray Matter, Fire Cracker, Chameleon, *and* Cut Loose. *These popular novels feature female computer expert Dr. P.J. Gray and computer-phobic Detective Leo Schultz. As a member of the St. Louis Police Department, Gray uses Virtual Reality to solve crimes, a tool just recently showing up in crime scene analysis and in courtrooms. According to Kennett, "P.J. Gray and Detective Schultz are pioneers in the use of VR in fiction, but soon they will have plenty of real-life counterparts." Kennett has been involved with computers in many fields, as a corporate analyst, business systems programmer, independent consultant, and computer systems designer. She is a member of the Mystery Writers of America, Sisters in Crime, and the American Crime Writers League. Her e-mail address is SAKwriter@aol.com.*

I wrote my first short story, about a disillusioned character in a repressive society, at age eight. The reader learned in the last line that the character was an ant. I thought it was the height of sophistication at the time, and I didn't realize that kind of twist was already overused. What did I know anyway? I was in second grade. During high school, I wrote poetry and short fiction. In college my English instructor urged me to choose writing as a career, but I was swept off my feet by a new love: the computer. I built a life for myself as a computer consultant and floated down the river of complacency for years. Decades. From time to time, I'd get enthusiastic about writing, dash off a few short stories, and collect rejection slips. When I turned 40, I decided it was time to get serious. I'm glad I dusted off that dream. I've still got the ant story from second grade, but I doubt I can interest an editor in it.

Since I was in an engineering program in college, I didn't have much in the way of formal education in writing. I attended writer's workshops, read books about writing, and spent a lot of time just doing it. There are two experiences I consider valuable now: daily writing practice and dissecting books I enjoy to find out what gives them vibrancy, what makes them memorable.

When I finished my first novel-length manuscript, I got an agent right away. Any minute, the armored cars filled with cash were going to pull into my driveway. A year went by, and that manuscript didn't sell. I have since learned that many writers have one or more practice books under their belts by the time they get published, but I didn't know it then. It was a bleak time, during which I assumed my dream was dead and I'd never be an author. Then I pulled myself together and began to rethink my entire approach to writing. I tried new techniques and set higher goals. Instead of sitting around waiting for another rejection, I was actively involved in a new project, and hitting my stride in it. Now that I have gotten published, all I have to do to get motivated is look at what I've achieved so far and pick up and thumb through one of my books.

> **I attended writer's workshops, read books about writing, and spent a lot of time just doing it.**

The best thing that has happened to me with regard to my writing career is having one. I came close to letting my dream slip away.

The thing that seemed bad to me at the time was losing the editor who acquired my first two books. She moved to another publishing house. Objectively, I knew such things happened, but figured it would never happen to me. I felt lost, worried, and most of all, that I was starting my career all over again. I went through a lot of worry for nothing. After working with my new editor, I felt confident my career hadn't been derailed. I now realize my confidence comes from within. I can weather such things as losing an editor.

> They spotted my name tag, and right there in the elevator, I signed my first two copies ever.

I attended a major fan convention, Bouchercon, shortly after the publication of my first book. I didn't expect to be the center of attention, but was hoping I'd make some sort of splash—even a tiny one—in a very big pool. On the very first day, I rode in an elevator with a few other attendees, and two of them were carrying my book! They spotted my name tag, and right there in the elevator, I signed my first two copies ever.

I have started all my books with an interesting villain, and my villains reflect contemporary issues that are meaningful to me. The search for self is the basis for *Gray Matter,* as the villain tries to establish self-esteem and a sense of identity by sampling and then usurping that of others. In *Fire Cracker,* I started with my concern about whether hospitals are really the safe havens we'd like to think they are. In *Chameleon,* the issue of increasing violence by the young in our society is personified by a twelve-year-old boy who resorts to murder for reasons that seem trivial from an adult viewpoint. In my upcoming release, *Cut Loose,* I deal with a web of family connections, giving an intimate portrayal of denial, betrayal, and loyalty of family members under extreme stress.

Once I have a villain and a theme, I begin to see how that villain will interact with my series characters. The plot unfolds from letting their emotions and personalities guide them. Most of the time, my characters tell me what will happen next.

I write five days a week, from about 9:00 A.M. to 4:00 P.M. Not all of those hours are direct writing activity. A good part is taken up with the business of writing: correspondence, promotion, and classes I teach. On the weekends, I spend a couple of hours a day working. When I'm approaching a deadline and feel I haven't shown enough progress on a manuscript, I'll switch to a full seven-day work week and cut out as many other activities as I can. If I'm away from writing for more than a couple of days, I start to feel deprived. I genuinely miss the simple act of putting words together. If I don't write regularly, it takes me a long time to fully immerse myself in my work in progress when I do return to it. I have to put myself back into the situation again, find out where my characters are emotionally before I can continue. I strongly feel that a writer should make time to write on a daily basis, even if the time is short.

I write in a well-equipped office on the lower level of my home, away from the family activities. A large window gives me a view of the woods, and I have several bird feeders outside, so I can take a break and watch the wide variety of birds that visit. Just outside my office door is an indoor atrium flooded with natural light. It contains wonderful river rocks and a bubbling fountain. I can take a cup of coffee out to the atrium, sit in a rocking chair nearby, and watch the sunlight on the rocks and the moving water. For some people it might be too isolated, but I can't think of a better writing environment for me.

I'd advise aspiring authors to polish their writing, but don't get caught in a cycle of endless revisions. At some point, you've got to shove that manuscript out the door. When you do, start another project immediately. The period of time when you're trying to find a publisher for a manuscript can be demoralizing and can cause you to question your ability to make it as a writer. The best medicine is to fall in love all over again, with another story.

I hope to reach higher with each book, to tell fascinating stories in a compelling and memorable fashion, to provide deeper characterizations, and to move my readers in the same way I have been moved by books I've read. That's the best thing about a writing career—there's no limit to the opportunities for personal and professional growth, all of it triggered from within myself. I want to make each book better than the last, and I want to explore short fiction. I skipped that stage of writing that most authors go through—getting short stories published. I did it backwards. I had two books on the shelves before I got my first short story published, and even then only because I was invited to contribute ("A Warm Nest: Cat Crimes Through Time"). I want to study short fiction with the goal of getting stories published often and one day having my own anthology.

> **I work just as hard the fourth time around as the first.**

I try not to become complacent. I don't take for granted that getting my next book accepted is a shoo-in because I already have several published. I work just as hard the fourth time around as the first. There are plenty of highly talented writers out there waiting for a shot at my slot in the publisher's list. If I don't work hard to build readership and constantly strive to improve, I could find myself back in my day job. And that's as it should be. Publishers don't owe me a living because I managed to stay the course and get a few books published. On the contrary, I owe it to my readers to deliver not just a good book, but a book that shakes them up, makes them think, and leaves them breathless. Not an easy task!

## MARY DORIA RUSSELL

*Mary Doria Russell is the bestselling and award-winning author of two books,* The Sparrow *and* Children of God. *Both are complex, theologically based science fiction novels, have made bestseller lists around the country, and have won five literary awards. Both books are optioned by Universal Studios for a feature film starring Anto-*

*nio Banderas. Russell is currently working on* A Thread of Grace, *a historical thriller about the Jewish underground in Genoa during the Nazi occupation of Italy. Russell holds a B.A. in cultural anthropology, an M.A. in social anthropology, and a Ph.D. in biological anthropology. She has done extensive fieldwork, living overseas and studying a number of foreign languages, and credits that with the background she brings to her fiction.*

I have always enjoyed writing, but my apprenticeship was a fifteen-year correspondence with my Aunt Mary, back when people actually wrote letters. Every week, we sent one another seven to ten pages of prose, much of which amounted to short stories. I was born an anthropologist, I guess. In some sense, that is still my profession, but I'm applying the scholarship in a different medium.

When I started writing *The Sparrow,* I was 42. Nobody was in a position to give or deny me psychic permission to write, except me. My characters have kept me motivated. I routinely decided that fiction was just too hard. (Doing science is comparatively easy, believe me!) But I couldn't let my characters die. I had to keep going back to them until the books were finished.

The best thing with regard to my writing career was when Jane Dystel became my literary agent. It's been all joy since the day she called saying she would "love to represent *The Sparrow.*" She is absolutely the best—a consummate professional and a woman of integrity.

While it was happening, being turned down by 31 other agents was awful; in retrospect it was lucky, because Jane was number 32! I was so desperate toward the end that I actually gave my credit card number out and authorized a book doctor to edit my manuscript. This man was later indicted for defrauding hopeful authors of millions of dollars.

Most surprising is that the manuscript those 31 agents turned down has gone on to be called the best SF novel of the decade, and to win both critical and commercial success.

The funniest thing was when Jesuit priests told me that my portrayal of Jesuit everyday life and spirituality was so uncannily accurate, they were convinced that I was either a Jesuit writing under a pseudonym, or a Jesuit in a past life! Not bad for a nice Jewish girl!

> ## Nobody was in a position to give or deny me psychic permission to write, except me.

There has been a combination of theme, character, and ethical issues that fascinates me. It takes me two to three years to do the research and writing, so the topics have to be engaging enough to sustain obsession for a long time.

I stick to a writing schedule. I make yardage every single day rather than waiting to throw a long bomb into the end zone, even if all I do is untangle a paragraph or choose a better word or phrase. Most working days, I put in four to five hours.

My advice is to never pay an agent or publisher up front for anything, ever. Don't pay to have your book edited or represented or printed. Anyone who charges you for services like that is playing you for a patsy.

When I walk into a book signing and I'm treated like a rock star, I try not to inhale. There is a big difference between being an Author and being a writer. When I'm out on tour, I'm just talking about stuff I already did. I'm not writing; I'm not making a new story happen. I always remember that what makes people come to the signings is that I worked my guts out on my first two books. When I go back home, it's back to work—doing the research, the endless rewriting and editing, the slavish attention to detail, the relentless insistence on getting everything right. There are moments of grace, when the perfect combination of character, action, and word come together, but most of it is just very hard work.

I've had a grand ride so far.

## JOANNA WAYNE

*Joanna Wayne is the author of intrigue and romance novels. Her books in the popular Harlequin Intrigue series have won praise. Lone*

Star Lawman *and* All I Want for Christmas *received 4 stars and* Jodie's Little Secrets *received 4 stars from the* Romantic Times. Family Ties *won the 1998 Texas Gold Award in the Single Title/Long Contemporary Division. Other books by Wayne are* Extreme Heat, Behind the Mask, *and* Deep in the Bayou. *Her latest book is* Memories at Midnight, *part of the Countdown 2000 Series. Wayne teaches writing classes at a local university and is active in several writing groups. Her Web site is ww.eclectics.com/authorsgalore/joannawayne/indexhtml.*

I always loved reading. I always thought I'd be a writer, but kept putting it off. I finally made up my mind that I was going to do it and get it published—give it my best shot.

What really got me started was a class at a University called "Writing a Romance Novel." I realized I would never be happy until I saw my book in print. It kind of gets in your blood. Of course, people said it was going to be a lot of hard work, which it has been. My family and my husband were so supportive and believed in me. I'm a very determined person. You just have to keep at it, when rewards are few.

When I first started, I joined up with a critique group, three of us who had never been published before. Now all three have been published. We would not let each other slide, but kept on each other all the time. It made us be the best we could. The best thing that happened in my writing career was hooking up with my agent, who had a feel for the marketing of my book and sold my second book almost immediately.

I start with coffee in the morning with my husband, walk ten miles because it gets the blood flowing, then I spend from 10:00 A.M. to 3:00 P.M. at the computer. That's my primary creative time. As my book nears the end, I may write all night. Sometimes, I just can't quite pull away.

My best writing is done in my own space, the work environment I'm used to. I always write on a computer (I can't read my own writing!).

Ideas come to me from news and things that happen to me. I think to myself, "What's the most suspenseful?" Little things trigger my mind, such as the idea I got from a book called *Behind the*

*Mask,* where I was looking in a window from a Mardi Gras float and noticed that I could see things other people can't.

Once I start writing the story, I get so involved that I lose myself. Knowing that someone else will read this and get out of it what I do, that it will become real for others and warm their hearts. I love to write. Even if I won the lottery, writing would be the one thing I'd still do.

> **It's important to align with other writers, so you don't feel by yourself in this.**

Most surprising is when you get "the call" that your book is going to get published. People heard me shouting blocks away. Secondly, the way you feel when your book is in print is like giving birth.

In New York City, I was meeting my agent for the second time and we were talking at this deli. My agent asked me how I felt about sex (in romance novels), and I said, "I like it hot." A guy behind me, who was leaning forward to hear what I was saying, fell off his stool and right onto me. We still laugh about that.

Learn all you can about marketing, techniques, writing, skills. It's important to believe in yourself and your ability to write, and believe in yourself when you get rejected. It's important to align with other writers, so you don't feel by yourself in this.

I would like to have continued success and write something someday that makes the *Times* bestseller list. I would like to keep writing and have other people read the books.

I get numerous letters and e-mails from fans, many people who feel like they know me and have been so warm. When they write and say I've touched their lives, it's amazing. I have happy endings in my books, and hope the books make their lives happier.

## AUDREY SCHULMAN

*Audrey Schulman is the bestselling and award-winning author of three books:* The Cage, Swimming with Jonah, *and* A House Named

Brazil, *due out in 2000. The Cage was reviewed positively in* The New Yorker, *received many accolades, and was translated into nine languages. It has also been optioned for a movie by Wes Craven. She started writing at the age of twelve, and it has been a profession "that has given me meaning, sanity, and a vast love of life and people." Her Web site is www.audreyschulman.com/audrey.html.*

People told me writing was a difficult profession, but they underestimated how difficult by a lot. Still, I would never give it up. Without writing, life is flat. When I go through a difficult time in my life, the pain is just pain if I am not writing. If I am writing, then at least I am learning about life.

I wrote my first "novel" when I was 12 in English class. Although handwritten and only 57 pages long (probably just a short story), I got so much attention from the teacher and the students that I decided writing would become my career. I never got into an MFA writing program. It made me discover what I believed about writing rather than what I was supposed to believe. I created my own style, rather than monkeying the style of the teacher.

The best thing I did was to start a writing group with three other intensely motivated writers. We all became great friends, taught each other about writing, and helped each other through the tough times

The most painful was not getting published until I had written nine novels. Only then was my fifth novel accepted for publication. The biggest surprise was getting that call saying I was published. It took me a full year to really believe I was an author—until I held the actual book in my hands

My topics have chosen me. They fascinate me. I start reading about them, thinking about them, and have to write about them. If the idea of reading for a year about the subject of your book doesn't thrill you, pick a new topic.

I write first thing every morning for three to five hours. I try not to answer the phone during that time, talk to other people, or even clean up the house. If you do that every day for a while, it becomes habit and you do it automatically and peacefully.

I am always nervous about public appearances. Once I went down to North Carolina to do a radio show that my publicist kept saying had 600,000 listeners. I got more and more nervous, and couldn't eat for a full two days before the event. Then a few hours before the interview I got hungry and had three Taco Bell black bean tortillas. Not a good idea!

> **Don't worry if you are a bad writer. You will get better.**

At this point I realize that no one will take my books' success as seriously as I will. I do my own publicity, send out letters for readings, call up talk shows, create Web sites, contact friends. I work so hard writing the books, I figure I have to follow it up with selling the book.

If you know that writing is all you want to do, then do it. You only live once. Don't worry if you are a bad writer. You will get better.

## KATE FLORA

*Kate Flora is the author of two series of mysteries.* Chosen for Death *is the first book in the* Thea Kozak *series, and she followed that with* Silent Buddy, *with biology teacher Ross McIntyre as the main character. She alternates between the two series, although the Ross McIntyre books haven't made it to print. She is President of the New England chapter of Sisters in Crime. She teaches mystery writing at the Cambridge Center for Adult Education and does the mystery segment of a local radio show,* Pages to People. *She was a practicing lawyer for a number of years before starting her writing career. Her Web site is www.kateflora.com/katebio.htm.*

I'm one of the lucky ones. My mother was a writer, so I always had the writing life modeled for me. I knew both the hardships and the joys, the difficulties and the benefits, from childhood. Instead, I discouraged myself, knowing how hard it was to make a living at writing, and also how much I dislike rejection.

I think writers are made, not born. By that I mean many are born with the longing and the passion, but converting it into a productive writing life takes discipline and determination. I always wanted to be a writer, but I was afraid of the risks, both emotional and financial, for a long time.

I think the most relevant thing for most writers is being a reader. It is the experience of loving books, of being enchanted by story and by the love of words and written language. That said, I found both my background as an English major and my training as a lawyer to be very helpful.

What kept me motivated? I think that once I gave into the passion, I gradually became a storyteller instead of a lawyer. I got hooked on the incredible endorphin highs that come from being deeply engaged in the writing process. I also learned, early on, that no one is going to support a writer more than the writer herself. As I tell my students, no one will ever ring your doorbell and ask for the privilege of publishing your work; you have to be your own cheerleader. In a way, stubbornness keeps me motivated. I refused to accept other people's rejections as the measure of my worth; I was not willing to let someone else say that I wasn't a writer and a storyteller.

There are several surprises: First, discovering that, because I write a series character, I now share my character with my readers and have certain obligations that arise from that contract. Discovering how loyal and generous fans can be. Discovering how much I like to talk about writing to readers. Discovering how much I know about writing, and how little. How wonderful other writers are, and also how generous.

Perhaps the biggest surprise, though, was doing a book with Ballantine and finding that after years of unreturned phone calls and an information void, I was being treated like a valued person, the way I had always imagined authors were treated—a delightful experience for which I am profoundly grateful.

Most excruciating, for all of us, are book signing and speaking events where nobody comes. Or speaking to the homeless, who come in to get out of the cold, or watching the three or four people who really want to buy your book give up while you're monopolized by a slobbering lunatic telling you, at top volume, why he's going to let you have his great book idea (described at great length) for only half the profits. As most of us frequently ask . . . what profits were those exactly?

I always think my topics chose me. I'm a character-driven writer and a storyteller. Stories come, or characters come who want me to tell their stories, and I do it. It all comes from reading stories in the paper, or hearing something, and thinking, "I wonder what the story behind that story is" or "I wonder how that feels, when you're in the middle of it" or "How does anyone handle something that awful or *do* something that awful?"

I write every day. I believe that writing is like exercise. You have to use your writing muscles regularly to keep them strong and toned. Also, of course, I'm a compulsive writer. I can't stop.

> **Believe in yourself because no one else may, especially at first.**

I use a word processor, one printer, one chair (glue to stick me to the chair!), my college Shakespeare, *American Heritage Dictionary*, *Rodale's Synonym Finder*, books about forensics, causes of death, police procedures, and the *Bible.* I write on a small balcony over my living room—very open, yet very private. All the wood is a warm, red cherry, the carpet blue, and there are stacks and stacks of papers everywhere. I could be buried under them. (If I'm missing, look there first!)

Do I have any advice for aspiring writers? Three things: Believe in yourself because no one else may, especially at first. Honor your writing: Don't place it below the laundry and errands. Do it and keep doing it until it owns you. Be more aggressive than you can imagine: Use every tool and every person at your disposal if you really want to get published. Don't hang your head and be shy and hopeful. You can't afford to be. Unfortunately for all of us, publishing is as much a world of chance and contacts as a world of writing and talent. So maximize your chances.

I look forward, every day, to learning something new about the writing process. I look forward to a "career" from which I'll never want to retire. I look forward to becoming better, to trying harder, to the new discoveries that wait around the corner.

I've been writing steadily for fifteen years. I've published six books, but I was in the unpublished writer's corner for ten years. The only security in this business comes from your faith in yourself. So I maintain my success through attitude, through believing in myself, through having the luxury of believing that the writing comes first.

## LINDA MEEKS

*Linda Meeks is the co-author of more than 200 health books and multimedia programs that are used by millions of students, pre-school through college. She is an Associate Professor Emeritus in the College of Education at Ohio State University. She teamed up with Philip Heit to form Meeks Heit Publishing Company. They are America's most widely published health education authors.*

I had a passion for writing and teaching as a child. I would line up my dolls and lecture to them, which required that I organize my thoughts in a succinct manner. As early as in elementary school, I would write volumes instead of the two or three pages required for a report. I never saw report writing as work; instead I became energized when one was assigned. I began writing my first book as an undergraduate. It was published in five languages by the time I was 25.

I learned and continue to learn a great deal from my father, who had an advertising agency. He demonstrated creativity in writing copy for ads and precision in his accompanying illustration, and taught me the value of detail and deadlines. My many years of education, including graduate school, could not compare to what I learned from him.

Has anyone tried to discourage me from writing? In the musical *Chorus Line*, there is a scene where those auditioning relate their personal experiences. Each one says in his or her own way that there really was no choice; each had to express himself or herself. I, too, believe I must express myself. My parents, siblings, and daughter all are creative, and I choose creative and passionate friends. These choices eliminate the distraction of being discouraged.

Psychologist and author Hugh Prather once wrote: "If you tell me the way you see it, rather than the way it is, it helps me to more fully discover the way I see it." Being published, I have been blessed with the opportunity to share "how I see it" with others, to make a difference by writing books that help others achieve optimal health. I have been blessed with the opportunity to speak to many audiences which, in turn, allows me to connect with a broad range of people who enrich my life.

The worst thing that happened to me was when another publisher copied a model my co-author and I had developed without my permission. I was so disappointed and hurt (I knew the people involved) that I was quiet for days.

A teacher once told me that a robber had stolen her television, jewelry, other valuables, and a sex education book Philip Heit and I had written. The robber, her neighbor, might not have been caught, except the police saw the book when they questioned him at his apartment. Later, the teacher went to the police station to get her valuables and inquired about the book. The investigating officer told her it was in the back of the station. She found several police officers with their noses buried in the book!

I choose topics for which I have a passion, based upon the pressing health issues facing different segments of the population. When I write for teens, I think of how I might empower them to have an optimal lifestyle—through choosing healthful relationships, preventing violence, and making responsible decisions. When I write for women, I might choose topics such as stress management, physical fitness, and healthful aging. My gut tells me I will emphasize women's health. I'm interested in helping younger women clarify what they believe "to have it all" means.

I begin a book by scheduling blocks of time for writing in order to benefit from what I describe as a "writer's high," when the beta-endorphins kick in and words and ideas flow. It's comparable to the "runner's high," about which most people know.

> My parents, siblings, and daughter all are creative, and I choose creative and passionate friends.

I write in a well-organized office furnished with a long L-shaped desk, bookshelves, and storage cabinets I had custom-designed. My office is tastefully decorated and has a fireplace. I have the 200 or so books I have written on bookshelves above my computer. They remind me of where I have been and empower me to move into another book or creative effort. I am looking for a second office overlooking the ocean.

I have promoted my books through speaking engagements, television and radio programs, Congressional hearings, catalogues, and brochures.

My advice to aspiring authors: Proverbs 16:1 "Ask the Lord to bless your plans and you will be successful carrying them out."

Have faith. "Wonderful things happen when you live expectantly, believe confidently, and pray affirmatively."

## ELAINE VIETS

*Elaine Viets is the popular murder mystery author of a series of books titled* Backstab, Rubout, *and* The Pink Flamingo Murders. *The books, with a six-foot-tall newspaper columnist as the main character, have gotten good reviews in Amazon.com and* The Washington Post. *She also has written* How to Commit Monogamy: A

Lighthearted Look at Long-Term Love, *and writes a column in the* St. Louis Dispatch. *Her Web site is www.e-pages.net/elaine.html.*

I write murder mysteries for Dell. *Backstab* was the first, *Rubout* the second, and the third, which is coming out in July, is called *The Pink Flamingo Murders.* All are in paperback. Andrews and MacNeil published *How to Commit Monogamy* in hardcover. My mystery series features a six-foot-tall newspaper columnist who writes for the mythical *St. Louis City Gazette.* The books have gotten nice reviews on Amazon.com and was one of an Internet reviewer's top six picks of the year and a reader's pick of *The Washington Post Bookworld.*

> **I could never work a real job; I just don't have the temperament.**

I could never work a real job; I just don't have the temperament. I've always wanted to do something romantic, probably because I grew up in the suburbs. For a while I was going to be an artist and live in a cold-water flat in New York, but then I discovered I couldn't draw . . . .

I always liked to write, and I was encouraged to write so I decided to do that for a living.

My teacher in high school, in particular, encouraged me, for which I am really grateful. I was in high school in the 60s, when there weren't many careers for girls. They were still teaching us home "ec" and how to be good wives and mothers so I greatly appreciated the teachers who encouraged me to write.

My degree was in Journalism, and I spent 25 years at a newspaper. I did have one college teacher who told me I couldn't write, but he was hitting on me at the time. I worked for the *St. Louis Post Dispatch* as a columnist. I'm now writing a column for the United Features Syndicate in New York. I like the newspaper business, but after a while it isn't a job for a grown-up. My character in my novels is a newspaper columnist, and what I really tried to convey is the *Dilbert* world of newspapers. A friend told me a great story, which I used in the book. He had worked for a paper where management decided to use "African-American" instead of "black," so they got some computer whiz to rig the spell checker so that it automatically changed black to African-American. Within a week, there was an African-American hole in space and Nelson Mandela was referred to as an African-American leader. What finally got the entire system to unfold was that someone was struck by an African-American Cadillac. I had a good deal of fun making fun of newspaper consultants.

My husband is a very good, encouraging spouse. I really think harmony at home helps a writer. He's a writer himself, and one writer tends to understand another. I don't think it's fair to inflict yourself on someone who isn't a writer.

I have a good agent, which I think is absolutely essential to a writing career. Nowadays an agent really works as a first line-editor, particularly when you send a proposal. You know he will tell you the plot needs some tightening here, or this character needs some tweaking. He obviously does it from the standpoint of making it saleable. My agent is also really good with career advice. He keeps a handle on things, and keeps me from writing letters and doing things I shouldn't do.

I laugh when I remember how I got my agent. I was living in Washington, D.C., and had told my editor, who worked for one of the wire services, that I was looking for an agent. He said, "Well, there is this guy who's working for Miss Manners right now, but I'll give you his name." So I sent him this really groveling letter, and it turned out he was this guy I sat next to in college. You just don't expect someone from the University of Missouri to become a New York agent.

It surprised me how fun it is, what a great way to make a living. I would hate to sit in an office all day; I marvel at people who do it for a living.

I tend to choose topics I have researched for the newspapers because I like to write on offbeat subjects. *Rubout* is about an event that actually takes place every year in St. Louis, the annual biker's ball where 1,000 Harley riders get together and dance at the Cassoloma

Ballroom. Outsiders are not invited, but somehow I got an invitation. And I saw some of the wildest outfits ever: the queen of the ball was a natural blond wearing cowboy boots and a lace body stocking. That's all. The king was wearing only leather chaps, a g-string, and a vest, which was really impressive. And his girlfriend, who drove a Caterpillar tractor, was pretty impressive herself. I wound up being one of the first female judges of the vest and lace contest. I used that event as the background for cross-dressers in St. Louis. I saw incredibly gorgeous women who were really men, which was extremely humiliating. These guys were wearing $10,000 Bob Mackie gowns and bringing in hair stylists from Elizabeth Arden. You could pick out the real women; we were just sort of drab. None of us wore the stuff that really drove the guys crazy—spike heels and long, dangly earrings. None of the women could understand why the men would want to torture themselves. But they looked absolutely gorgeous. So in my first book, a female impersonator is found dead in a dumpster, and I managed to get in all the things about the ball.

I've had a lot of help with promoting my books. Dell has been very kind to me. I do the usual rounds, make all the book tours. I call it the Willy Loman tour—sometimes you sell a lot, sometimes you're lucky to sell five books and end up looking like a puppy at the pound. But you have to go around to the stores. You need to know your bookstores, particularly your local mystery bookstore, because they hand-sell your books. Also, go to the conferences. You really, really need to know your profession, and to read the hot new mysteries, the award winners. Join groups just for networking and to know the issues. I belong to the Mystery Writers of America and Sisters in Crime, and have found that both groups are very helpful.

People often portray writers as bitchy, but I have to say that the mystery writers are wonderful. They welcome you into the ranks; they really help the young writers who are, technically, competition.

I live on the beach, and get up and go for a long walk on the water, and think about ways to kill people. Then I usually come back. I write on my book until I have about 1,500 words, which takes about two or three hours, then I work on my column.

I like working at home. My office looks out over the water so I can see all the people having fun while I'm working. It allows me to feel sorry for myself, which goes with the territory.

I like to write humor, but I seem to have a mind for murder. It's very satisfying to work off your frustrations thinking about ways to kill people . . . .

I have long conversations with a pathologist friend. I'll call her up and, without identifying myself, say,

> Join groups just for networking and to know the issues.

"Hi. Can you kill someone with a wine bottle?" She'll go, "Empty or full?" and I'll say, "Full. It's Elaine," and she'll say, "Of course it's Elaine. Who else would call me with this?" I was on the Sally Jesse Raphael show, in the green room with Don Fetterstone, the inventor of the pink plastic lawn flamingo, who brought poor taste to the poor people. He said, "You really ought to find a way to kill people with a pink flamingo," and I said, "Would you mind?" He said, "Not if it's a genuine Fetterstone flamingo." I called my pathologist friend and asked, "Can you kill someone with a pink flamingo?" She showed me how to do it.

If you really want to write, do it. A lot of people say they would like to write and have half a book in the drawer somewhere; but if you really want to do it, do it. I got started as a mystery addict. I was reading five a week and finally decided why don't I try writing one? So just do it! You might be surprised at the results.

## JEANETTE BAKER

*Jeanette Baker is the author of Celtic historical romances, as well as a literature and writing teacher and a member of Romance Writer's of America. Her books have been nominated for the Reviewer's*

*Choice Award. She graduated from the University of California at Irvine and later earned her master's degree in education. Baker says, "I became an anglophile in 1971 on my first trip to Europe. To pass long hours on the train, I picked up a copy of Georgette Heyer's* These Old Shades. *At the end of three months, I had consumed every Regency I could find, a few Jane Austen novels, and the poetry of Yeats, Burns, Byron, and Milton. My 18-year-old mind knew that whatever my future plans held, they would include English literature. I spent the following years visiting the most remote and historical corners of Ireland, Wales, and Scotland and teaching what I loved. Because of my penchant for the underdog, England's 'conquered tribes' became my passion."*

I was definitely born a reader and a lover of words with a great imagination. As a child I fabricated regularly and believably. Some of my teachers were horrified, others amused, but it didn't stop me. I created elaborate tales of how I wanted life to be, which is what genre fiction really is. Writing was a natural evolution. I was always recognized for writing at a level above everyone else.

> **Usually an incident in history triggers an emotional response, and I create a character and go from there.**

My senior high school English teacher, Sister Mary Columba, an Irish nun, was responsible for developing my social consciousness and my empathy for oppressed populations.

My daughter told me I could never write a romance novel because "those novels" had sex in them and women my age (38 at the time) didn't know anything about sex.

The best thing that happened to me as a writer was that Kate Collins, my editor at Pocket Books, said that my book, *Legacy*, transcended the genre. The worst thing was the amount of my first advance.

Usually an incident in history triggers an emotional response, and I create a character and go from there. My novels usually revolve around Britain's conquered colonies. After a proposal is accepted, I sit down with a calendar and figure out how much I have to write every week. I like to give myself a month or so at the end in case something goes wrong or to just let the manuscript sit. Looking at it much later gives me an entirely new perspective.

I write on my laptop in my family room on the couch in front of the fireplace. My favorite time is early afternoon through evening.

I look forward to traveling more. The best part of writing is researching on location. There is a level of authenticity in a book that an author has researched on site. The novel I'm working on now, *Irish Fire*, a story about thoroughbred racing in Ireland, had to be revised considerably after my last visit.

In my case, a great deal of success was based on luck and instinct, finding an editor and an agent who appreciated my work, writing in a genre that became very popular, knowing when to move on when it was time, keeping in touch with people who understand the industry, striving to improve with every book, and writing about subjects I love. Each book is an adventure and each one is better than the one before. Never forget that writing is a business and take advantage of promotional activities.

## PATTY SLEEM

*Patty Sleem is the author of* What The Bible Says About . . . Words That Can Lead to Success and Happiness, *and mystery novels* Second Time Around *and* Back in Time. *Foreign rights to* Second Time Around *were sold in Chinese.* Back in Time *introduces a new character, Maggie Dilitz, "whose career change from the business world into ministry leads to murderous surprises." The sequel is due out in 2000. Sleem's writings have appeared in a number of publications, including the* Wall Street Journal.

You have very intense feelings with a first book you write, and you learn a lot. It can be your messiest book; you look back and see things you would change. By the time you get to your second book, you've learned some valuable lessons, such as which characters not to kill off. Someone told me once, don't kill off good characters; it's true. I won't give away too much of the plot a second time around. I think a first book is like a first love, which is a unique relationship.

When I did the second book I was already thinking more long range, about what she's going to do in the third and fourth novels. The first book, for me at least, was a more free-wheeling, creative experience. I really didn't know what the protagonist was going to do next. Whereas I have tried to plot, somewhat, the protagonist's future action in the sequel. I don't know whether that will work or not, because you sit down to the computer and—I know it sounds very cliché—then all of a sudden you go into a different plot direction. You realize that she or he wouldn't do that. So, I think you might be more professional about writing the second book and future books. But the first book is like that tender little first-love experience you always hold close to your heart. The mere act of finishing it is something you don't know you can do until you do it.

On the fiction side, I basically do mysteries. I've been the books-in-print editor for Sisters in Crime. My most recent mystery, *Back in Time,* introduces Maggie Dilitz, who changes her career from business to ministry. I'm working on a sequel to that book now and basically have my hands in a lot of different pies. I have four books in the Anne McKinney career series coming out this year.

I made sure, during my teenage years, then as I went off to get a degree in English, that I learned the tricks of the trade and the techniques of my craft. Everything you can learn to a high degree of competence certainly is a time-saver and gives you confidence as a writer. The creative part of writing is very difficult and may not even lend itself to being explained in words. I always encourage young people when I do workshops to learn all they can. I remember looking up words and writing definitions down in the back of books when I was in sixth, seventh, eighth grade, maybe a little older. That probably helped me become a very good speller.

Anything that gets to be a crutch is not good because eventually you have to throw yourself naked into the creative process. Nobody can hold your hand while you create the manuscript, or tell you who to kill if you're a mystery writer. It can certainly boost your confidence to keep going when a manuscript seems like it'll never get finished. In general, I think a book is like a pregnancy; it takes about nine months to write. That's a long time. Now if some people have elephant pregnancies, and some have little rodent pregnancies, fine. I know people that can kick out a book in a month, but not me. And I have respect for all the different styles. Some people can take years to create a sequel. The more you know craft and technique, the more persistence you have to just push on with an interminable thing that you don't know if anyone's going to read anyway.

I read fairly recently in *Publisher's Weekly* about a writer who said that she pays a lot more attention to how she writes her books now that she's been published and knows people are reading her work. In business, you can't go wrong if you put yourself in your customer's shoes, understand their problem, or help them achieve whatever they're doing; the more reader-oriented one is in writing a book could be helpful too.

> **I think authors struggle with promotions, not only because they conflict with day jobs, but certainly eat into writing time.**

I think authors struggle with promotions, not only because they conflict with day jobs, but they also certainly eat into writing time. If we took this calendar out and figured how many working days there are . . . well, promotions add up. Writers jealously protect their writing time. For example, I am on the brink of deciding whether to go to SEBA (Southeastern Booksellers Association) or do a group author face-to-face reading. It'll take a day of my time with three hours of travel.

I could be on the road a lot more than I am now, but I just can't fly all over the place. Traveling is certainly fun and can pump you up, keep you from being too remote and losing the sense that anyone is going to read anything you're writing.

> **Starting a book is easy, but finishing is what writing a book is all about.**

People can make a comment, and all of a sudden you know you handled something a little precariously in a book. For example, for the *Second Time Around* I took out a map and selected Macon, Georgia, as the place the protagonist lives. I've never lived in Macon. At a recent signing, a librarian asked, "Have you ever been to Macon?" I think she realized I didn't get Macon exactly right. If I had it to do over again, would I call it Mason and make up the town totally so I wouldn't have to get all the little technical details right? Those are things you learn on a first book. When you connect with your readers, you learn a lot about what you might do next, or (oops!) what you might not have done on that last one.

The old advice about simply persisting is really true. In general, if a book is worth starting, it's probably worth finishing. It's much easier to start a business than it is to keep it going. Starting a book is easy, but finishing is what writing a book is all about. Believe in the concept when you start and just push on through to the end. Once you get the final line written, things can be edited or refined. Don't be too much of a perfectionist. I've lived with a perfectionist, bless his little heart; perfectionists have a hard time finishing things. Don't try to perfect everything as you go along, and don't go off on too many detours.

If you're writing a scene about Russia and feel like you've got to know Russian, figure out Russia later. Lots of writers finish the research after the book. In general, that could be a helpful strategy, especially for novices who also have day jobs. And don't let the tail wag the dog. Of course, there's research and facts to check, but write the book then go back and check things out. Besides, you may change a story line and wipe out half the scene for which you were doing the research. Finishing the book is a wonderful feeling—even if it never gets published, even if nobody reads it. Of course, it has to be edited, marketed, promoted. But first, carry the book to term.

## DIRK WYLE

*Dirk Wyle is the author of mystery and suspense novels involving professionals working in biomedical science. Wyle is a thirty-year veteran of biomedical science. The first novel in his series is* Pharmacology Is Murder, *with main character Ben Candidi. It was judged Best First Detective Novel of 1998 by Joe Lofgreen's Detective Pages and has received numerous positive reviews from many publications. He is hard at work on two more books for the series. His Web site is www.dirk-wyle.com.*

My dad was a journalist. He would have liked me to follow in his footsteps, but I opted for science. After thirty years as a biomedical scientist, I got the urge to write about the experience, and the murder mystery has proven the best form. I conduct research during the day and write at night. Science has taught me to be methodical; a life-long hobby interest in literature furnished me with examples; my interest in psychology and aesthetics has melded the two.

The desire to tell a story that nobody has ever conceived and which few are capable of emulating has kept me motivated.

The best thing that happens is someone telling me he's read my book, understood exactly what was going on, and couldn't put it down to the last page. Or when a graduate student wrote that my book gave him the encouragement to keep working on his dissertation research. Or the woman who wrote that my last chapter brought tears to her eyes. The most surprising was when a whistle-blowing biomedical scientist wrote, proposing that I cast his story in the form of a novel.

My books' background are from my direct experience (science) and locale (South Florida). My characters come from experience and

imagination. My plots arise from imaginable conflicts of my characters, motivated by lust for fame, money, power (the usual stuff). I
use only serious people (scumballs need not apply).

I write three hours of outlining, writing, revising, reviewing, or
meditating (or any combination of the above) *every* evening.

I once used a tape recorder, forcing myself to make rapid-fire
descriptions during walk-throughs or run-throughs of my scenes or
scenarios. Now, I just hold the memory of the sights, stimuli, and
feelings until I get them typed into my computer.

> My advice for aspiring authors is compile a checklist of 15 to 20 most important attributes of an excellent novel.

My advice for aspiring authors
is compile a checklist of 15 to 20
most important attributes of an excellent novel. Make sure you include all the tactical issues of style
and the strategic issues of plot and
resolution. Then check *every* aspect
of your novel against *every* item on
your checklist. Then run down
every item through the length of
your novel. If anything is out of line, fix it, and make sure you didn't
mess up anything else in the process. When you have finished the
process, you should have a good novel.

I look forward to seeing a Dirk Wyle section on the mystery
shelves, twenty novels long. I've promised to maintain the same
standards as in my other professional life—to not let any damn
committee dictate the content of my finished product.

## JO BEVERLEY

*Jo Beverley is the popular and prolific writer of romance novels. She
published her first Regency Romance,* Lord Wrayborne's *Betrothed,
in 1988. She has since published such titles as* My Lady Notorious,
Something Wicked, *and* Lord of Midnight. *She has written tradi-*

*tional regencies, medieval-era romance, books about Georgian England, the Rogue and the Malloren series, and a science fiction story. Beverley collaborated with three other authors on* Faery Magic, *Georgian and regency stories involving humans and the world of faeries, as well as published 11 novellas. Beverley has received numerous awards, including four RITA awards, a Romantic Times award, three Golden Lead awards, and two reader's choice awards. Her Web site is www.theromancereader.com/beverley.html.*

I am the author of 19 published regency and historical romances, all set in my native England. I write in three periods: the Middle Ages (around 1100), the Georgian (the 1760s), and the regency (1811 to 1820). I started out writing the short traditional regency romance, the "comedy of manners" style, but wrote a historical in Middle Ages, my first love, when I was a teenager. Historical romance is, of course, longer and sexier than traditional regency, and I found I liked both forms. Now, because of the limited market for traditional regency, I write exclusively historical romance.

I think I was born a writer but took a long time to take it seriously. I had the feeling that ordinary people didn't become published authors.

A string of "best things" have happened to me, but what got me out of lethargy and on the way was a two-weekend course at a local library on how to write romance, taught by Janet Adams. The next was probably getting a rave review on my first book and it making the finals of the Romance Writers of America Golden Medallion for Best Regency. Definitely encouragement to keep at it and aim high.

The worst thing was when a book of mine was set adrift by a publisher's change of heart about it and me.

Most surprising was when publishers first offered me big money. I naively hadn't realized that some romance writers were making a serious income. It was rather frightening; however, it helped when I realized my "big money" was not extraordinarily large. I think it's very important to keep informed both through professional organizations and a network of fellow authors.

My topic is always the same—the human mating dance. And I choose the periods because they interest me and give me different sorts of stories. The early Middle Ages in England were more sophisticated than many people think, but were still in many ways a subsistence economy. If the crops failed, you died. If you were weak, you were oppressed. It gives a strong background for love stories, but doesn't allow much space for playing games. The high Georgian period, by contrast, is one of philosophy, arts, science, and mental exploration, where game-playing was all. The Regency is the cusp between this brilliance and decadence and the dark formality of the high Victorian.

I like good people, so my characters are usually good people placed in difficult situations, and since honor is important to me, they usually have to face moral dilemmas. Through these struggles, they prove themselves worthy of each other and forge the invincible bond.

I usually write from 9:00 A.M. to 4:00 P.M. on weekdays, but that includes research, thinking, and administrative stuff. I think most people do better with a regular schedule. One of the biggest problems women writers face (I think it is a bit different for men) is claiming time for themselves. Children, spouses, parents, extended family, friends, neighbors, and community often think they have a right to a woman's time, and many women feel it is selfish to demand some time for themselves. In some cases, they're so used to feeling validated by their usefulness that they are afraid of saying no.

> **My advice for aspiring authors is to write the book you want to read but can't find.**

My advice for aspiring authors is to write the book you want to read but can't find.

I hope to keep selling books so I can keep writing them. These days that seems to mean doing better and better, so I suppose I'd better look forward to making the full *New York Times* list.

I think it's important to hold onto the magic that got us started, to not let the writing become just a job. If I'm not excited as I write, I doubt the reader will be excited as she reads. If I detect any signs of strain or drudgery in myself, I look at everything to see how I can fix it. I've learned to control my schedule, so I'm not trying to write too much for my situation at any time. I'm not a machine. I find it's better to undercommit than overcommit. If I have extra time, I can always write a fun project that will probably sell one day. To have something on the go for which there is no prior commitment, no expectation, and no deadline keeps me in touch with the magic.

## VERLA KAY

*Verla Kay is the author of children's books, written in her own style that she calls cryptic rhyme. Her first published book was* Gold Fever, *the historical fiction story of a farmer rushing to the gold fields of California in 1849 to make his fortune and returning home without one. Her second book was* Iron Horses, *a nonfiction account of the building of the transcontinental railroad. Upcoming books include* Covered Wagons/Bumpy Trails, *the story of a family crossing America in a covered wagon;* Tattered Sails, *about a family sailing from England to the colonies in the 1600s; and* Homespun Sarah, *the account of a colonial girl living in the 1700s. She is on contract for a picture book biography called* Rough, Tough Charley, *about the life of Charley Darkey Parhurst, a stagecoach driver in the 1850s and '60s who was discovered to be a woman at "his" death. Kay's Web site is www.mlode.com/~verlakay/index22.html.*

I was definitely drawn into writing. I'd always hated to write and thought I was the world's worst writer. I'm not heavily educated; a high school diploma and one semester of college English and Psychology comprise the formal schooling in my past. Taking a correspondence course through the Institute of Children's Literature (ICL) was the absolute best thing I ever did to further my career as a writer. Not only did that course give me the basic instruction I needed to write well for children, but it also taught me how to market what I wrote. I'm positive that this course enabled me to become published at least ten years before I could have done it on my own.

I had to constantly listen to comments like: You just aren't cut out to be a writer. Don't feel bad about the rejections, there are lots of other things you can do. Only people with contacts and connections ever get published. Why waste your time? Why don't you just give up this silly idea?

Determination and stubbornness kept me motivated—the deep-down desire to be published and see books I had written in print, a firm belief that I had the talent to get published and that, if I just kept trying long enough, it would happen.

The best thing was the absolutely sensational response to *Gold Fever*—the starred reviews, the dozens of e-mails from people all over the country and even some from outside telling me how much they loved it. After two years and marketing for three more years before *Gold Fever* sold, then waiting four more years to see it in print, it was an absolutely euphoric feeling when it was accepted so quickly by the public-at-large in such a dramatic and positive way.

The worst thing was coping with all the rejections before I made a sale, wondering if I would *ever* sell a book or was just fooling myself that I had what it takes to "make it."

The most surprising was getting starred reviews from *Publisher's Weekly, School Library Journal,* and *Kirkus Reviews.* Of course, I hoped and dreamed for that, but never really believed it would happen.

One of my first school visits took place in an empty classroom of the newly built wing of a school. After the first presentation, which included a live gold-panning demonstration for the children, I found myself alone in the room, cleaning up for a different presentation. Imagine my shock and dismay as I dumped the five gallons of water from the panning bucket into the sink, only to have the water instantly gush out from under the sink! I dove under the sink, trying to stop the flow of water with my right hand while I stretched and grabbed desperately for the bucket with my left hand. I managed to get about half the water back into the bucket, but both the carpet and the hem of my floor-length skirt were absolutely soaked. It's one school visit I will *never* forget!

I'm not a "schedule" person, but have to admit that most days I do follow a fairly steady routine. As soon as I wake up in the morning, I grab my current story and a pencil and revise some of the verses. Then I go down to my computer and respond to e-mails and type in the revised verses. I take breaks from the computer by working on research for both new stories and for ones "in production." Putnam comes up with tricky research questions that constantly send me back to my bookshelves and research materials to find answers.

> **I'd always hated to write and thought I was the world's worst writer.**

After lunch, I usually spend some time with my husband (who is retired and is home all day) or run errands. About five o'clock, I'm back at my computer, answering new e-mails, then joining the #Kidlit chat room. This room is connected to my Web site, and I try to be there most evenings for at least an hour or two, my "sharing time" with other children's writers. We cheer and hooray over our successes and moan and groan over our rejections (I still get lots of rejections, too). If one of us is stuck in a story, the chat group will help brainstorm the problem. It's our social time and it's greatly valued.

I write most anywhere and everywhere—in bed, in the hot tub, on a swing on my deck, at my computer, in the car with my laptop (only when my husband is driving!). There are few times I'm not "writing in my head," although I've learned the hard way to immediately write down an especially good phrase or word, otherwise it's often lost forever.

I love history and love the idea of writing it in a really fun way so that even young children can be exposed to it and learn to enjoy it, too.

I tell aspiring authors to learn their craft. Study the new books that are being published today. Join or start a critique group. Join an online critique group if you can't find people near you that can meet on a regular basis. Join SCBWI (Society of Children's Book Writers & Illustrators) if you're writing a children's book, and get involved in your Region. Attend every local conference you can afford. Get to know and listen to other writers and share information with them. Check out my Web site, which is filled with information and links to other sites for writers of children's literature.

If you're serious about your writing, treat it as a budding career, *not* as a hobby. Make it an important commitment in your life. Set goals for yourself, goals you can reach. Don't set "publishing" goals because you can't control that. Instead, commit to submitting your book to at least ten publishers during the next year. Write your goals down and post them next to your computer or workstation so you see them every day.

Keep your sense of humor; try to see rejections as a natural part of your chosen career, not as "rejections of you and your work." And never, *never* stop believing in yourself and your work. Don't stop learning and striving to be better, and most of all, don't give up and stop submitting.

## JOYCE CHRISTMAS

*Joyce Christmas has two series,* The Lady Margaret Priam *series and the Betty Trenka "senior sleuth" series about a retired office manager living in a small Connecticut town. There are nine Lady Margaret books, the best known of which is probably the first,* Suddenly in Her Sorbet, *and three Betty books, with the fourth,* Mood to Murder, *published in June 1999. Joyce is an executive with a consulting firm and has written everything from magazine articles to advertising copy, book reviews, and children's plays.*

I was born a reader, which is more than halfway to becoming a writer. I don't think anyone can be a writer if he or she doesn't read widely. That and writing itself, and rewriting until you get it right, are the equivalent of a pianist practicing scales. Once you have the skills, you don't need to think about every single word you put on paper. I spent a good many years ghostwriting books for others; that's how I learned what makes a book. I've always been writing something, and also spent a number of years as an editor, working with other people's writing, so I guess it was inevitable that I ended up writing what I wanted to write: mysteries. I think if you're meant to write, "better judgment" has nothing to do with it. You just do it.

Although I suspect that my father never thought of writing as a "real job," nobody ever tried to discourage me. Writing *is* a real job, and I was brought up to regard a job as something you do to the best of your ability. Motivation doesn't come into it, although getting paid is certainly a plus—that and the satisfaction of saying what one wants to say.

The best thing is seeing my books in print, meeting strangers who say how much they like my books, becoming friends with some truly exceptional colleagues—a lot of pluses.

I'm always surprised how unimpressed Americans are to meet writers, while Europeans treat them as worthy of great honor. Maybe it's because Americans think that anyone who can put down a sentence is a writer, so what's so special about this one?

For the Lady Margaret books, I keep close watch on the *Daily News* and the *New York Post,* which report some extraordinary and strange things people do. Often they give me a story idea. For Betty, I choose subjects that relate to her stage in life—the problems of loneliness and aging, illness, applying what she's learned in a long life to the immediate situation.

> **I think if you're meant to write, "better judgment" has nothing to do with it. You just do it.**

Computers have made life simpler for writers, but I find that the pages look so perfect that one doesn't revise as carefully as one should. For that reason, I often type first drafts on an old-fashioned typewriter.

Read in the field you want to write in, and everything else. Learn from what others have done. I do think that the ability to write is a talent, like being able to draw a horse. Everyone has something to say, but not everyone can say it so that others want to read it. The only way to find out is to try. Also, be aware of what the market is drawn to. Any creative person needs an audience to complete the equation: creative work plus an audience equals art (more or less).

Once you get hooked on writing, you can't stop. I'd like to write more short stories, which I find a challenge. Maybe I'd like to be very, very rich for a couple of weeks, but the sad truth about this business is that most of us will never get rich. However, there are other compensations—that stranger who appreciates my work, and my father's approval (he almost agreed that writing was a real job when he held my first book).

## TROY SOOS

*Troy Soos is the author of the Mickey Rawlings historical baseball series. The first in the series,* Murder at Fenway Park, *was lauded by* Publisher's Weekly: *"Soo's delightful debut is a four-bagger that will leave readers eager for subsequent innings." He followed with* Murder at Ebbets Field, Murder at Wrigley Field, Hunting a Detroit Tiger, *and* The Cincinnati Red Stalkings, *set in 1921. He is at work writing his sixth Mickey Rawlings novel, titled* Hanging Curve. *He also wrote a nonfiction work,* Before the Curse, *an illustrated history of early New England baseball. "Decision of the Umpire," his first short story, appears in the historical mystery anthology,* Crime Through Time. *Soos is a member of the Society for American Baseball Research (SABR) and Mystery Writers of America. He has taught mystery writing classes, and has been a panelist at mystery conventions. As a speaker, Soos frequently visits libraries and bookstores, and has made a number of television and radio appearances. His Web site is members.aol.com/TroySoos/bio.html.*

I was a born reader, not a writer. In school, I never wanted to write book reports because I wanted to read the next book instead. I didn't begin writing until I was in my thirties and had enough experiences and ideas that I thought would make a good story. Reading is probably the best preparation that I could have had for writing. I always suggest to beginning writers that they *read*, and read a variety of authors and genres, "bad" writing as well as good. "Bad" books can be analyzed for where they went wrong and what should have been done differently to make them better.

When I wrote *Murder at Fenway Park*, I had never written a short story or kept a journal, so part of what kept me going was the excitement of writing fiction for the first time. It was an act of discovery as much as creation, and the characters would always lead me to some unexpected twist of the plot. Since I was writing the book for "fun," with no intention of getting it published, I felt very free to change things, explore, and experiment. After I'd finished the book and rewritten it a couple of times, I decided to send it out to see if it was publishable. I found an agent, Meredith Bernstein (through the *Writer's Guide to Book Editors, Publishers, and Literary Agents*), who got me a three-book contract. My reaction was, "Great! What are the other two books?"

**I strongly suggest that beginning writers not worry yet if there will be a publisher for their work.**

A contract and deadlines for additional books was a terrific motivator for continuing the series. Another was curiosity: I wanted to see what these characters would do in certain situations and how they could grow as the series progressed. Once the books reached the public and I started to receive letters and e-mail from people who'd read and enjoyed them, that provided the greatest motivation.

The two best things that happened as a result of my writing career were totally unanticipated. I thought the biggest kick would be seeing my books on a bookstore shelf (which certainly was a thrill), but I hadn't expected they'd be put on school reading lists (apparently because of the history in them), so most of my mail is from younger readers. It's tremendously rewarding to hear a boy or girl say you're their "favorite author"! The second best thing has been meeting with former baseball players like Ted Willliams and Monte Irvin, and getting their perspectives on baseball history.

When I wrote *Murder at Fenway Park,* I used a pad and pencil. A pad seems far more patient than a computer, which hums and blinks and keeps reminding you that you need to reach a certain word count to meet your deadline. I do use a computer now and have a fairly regular writing schedule, in which I split up the workday into research, writing, and editing sessions.

I think the best way to keep the series successful, both for me and for readers, is to keep it fresh. My characters age and grow, face new conflicts and challenges, and I set the series during a rich and rapidly evolving period of American history. I also have a terrific editor, Kate Duffy, who encourages me to try new things, especially with *Hanging Curve,* which is very different in scope and tone from the others.

I was fortunate to write about topics that interested me and turned out to have a market. To paraphrase the old saw, "Write what you enjoy." I strongly suggest that beginning writers not worry yet if there will be a publisher for their work. The market changes so rapidly that it's impossible to predict what will sell a few years from now.

# HOW YOU CAN
# MAKE IT BIG

★

## SECTION TWO

## CHAPTER 6

# Reality Check

Some of the most talented writers become disheartened when they go out into the world to sell their work. They have dreamed of the day when they will see their name on the cover of a book. They define themselves as writers and know that what they have is as good or better than what they see on the shelves. They know without a doubt that when they are ready, they will be welcomed with open arms and a publisher's open checkbook.

Not!!! There is no greater illusion for writers than thinking talent is what takes a book from manuscript to store shelf. You may write like Papa Hemingway, spin a yarn like Mark Twain, or tell a tale of two cities like the dickens. But in this day of conglomerates, mergers, imprints, and bottom lines, even the masters would have to learn the rules of the game.

There is no way that you as artist, writer, and consumer could be expected to know the rules or even what the game really is. That is why we are going to give it to you straight.

The only interaction most people have with the book-publishing industry is perusing their selection while sipping latte in a superstore. For those who still have access to the independents, all they know is what they see, books on every subject imaginable—cookbooks, self-help books, books to help you understand the self-help books, inspiration, cogitation, religion, fantasy, and wellness. There is photography, philosophy, history, mystery, art, and even children's books on farts.

Every year more books are written and more are published. It is no wonder that unsuspecting neophyte writers are left with the impression that if these books can sell, theirs can too. We, of course, believe this is the case for the many writers who know what they are doing. If you know how to write a book or to package a good proposal (see chapter 8), that is part of the process. But that is only the beginning of your job. Doesn't it make sense that a lot more goes on between manuscript and the bestseller's list? Believe in fairy tales if you wish, but even Cinderella had to show up at the ball to marry the prince.

And don't wait for an engraved invitation. Until you have some status somewhere, no matter how much talent everyone says you have, you are nothing more than a peasant. The best way to gain status is to know your business. If you understand the inner workings of the industry that holds your future success, you have a better chance of reaching your goals. You need a strategy, which requires knowledge of the enemy. And right now, at your stage of the game, the industry is the enemy that stands between you and your dream.

Like anything else, the publishing industry has a structure. Although there are innumerable publishing houses, approximately six major conglomerates publish about 80 percent of the books. By the time you read this sentence, their names may be different and the players onto something else entirely. You can keep up to date by checking the *Literary Market Place (LMP)* found in the reference section of most libraries or our book *Writer's Guide to Book Editors, Publishers, and Literary Agents* (Prima). You can also hook up to our Web site at www.JeffHerman.com for the latest happenings.

For your purposes, you need to know that big companies control the major publishing houses and the major publishing houses have the clout for certain types of projects. This does not mean that the largest houses are the only game in town. They have certain advantages, but in actuality have more limitations on the types of projects they choose because more people are involved in the decisions.

In fact, your greatest opportunities will be with houses still willing to take some risks. There are independent houses and niche publishers that may be just right for your work.

Keep this in mind, and we will return to it time and again. Large houses have promotion budgets but rarely commit large sums of money to books they do not feel are a pretty sure bet. Most books are given minimal promotion through publishing houses, which means

> **Like anything else, the publishing industry has a structure.**

that books published by smaller houses with less up-front dollar commitment can have as much chance to become bestsellers, if the authors are savvy enough to promote them into prominence. In chapter 9 you will hear from the experts what you can do to promote your own book.

Before you develop your strategy to find a publisher, get to know who is out there. Develop a macrocosmic picture of who publishes books, then you will be ready to learn the inner workings of the publishing house. If you are not the database or reference book type, go to the bookstores and check who publishes the most popular books. You will see for yourself who has the most action and can visualize your own publishing family tree.

The typical publishing house is a bureaucracy. You have the publisher, who is above the editor-in-chief. The publisher has to coordinate the editorial issues with the sales and marketing issues. He or she is given the responsibility of bringing editorial matters into sync with the demands of the bottom line.

Then you have the editor-in-chief who is primarily the top editor. This person is the one to whom all editors report. Depending on the politics within the house, the editor-in-chief can either have direct autonomy in making decisions or can be a person who occupies the job but whose authority can be overridden by aggressive editors on various levels of the book-buying chain.

Then you have the editors. You will have a managing editor, who is like a traffic director. This editor will not directly acquire books but will be in charge of making sure each project has an editor-in-charge and is moving along according to schedule. This editor has no interaction with author or agent but will breathe down the neck of whoever is in charge of your project if you miss a deadline or hand in an inadequate manuscript.

> **Editors acquire the books you eventually see on your local bookstore shelves.**

The remaining titles are more arbitrary and relate more to seniority and prestige than to responsibilities. First you have the editorial assistant, who is usually someone right out of college. This person responds to the request for "coffee please."

The assistant editor has survived Coffee 101 and now may actually be called by name when asked for coffee.

The editor is someone who has his or her own desk, his or her own submissions, and his or her own headaches. Editors acquire the books you eventually see on your local bookstore shelves.

The senior editor is someone who has probably been around for about five years and is very much a part of the inner workings of the house. Agents know this person, and this person can make things happen.

The senior editor may have the privilege of having his or her own editorial assistant.

The editorial director is the person who has the bigger office and can pass off things he or she doesn't want to do to underlings. Also, the higher your rank, the better your expense account. Many editors spend lunch or dinner meetings with agents and their signed authors. Unfortunately for you, editors rarely will spend time or money on unsigned authors who want to give them a pitch.

In general the job of the editor is not what you might picture. Editors do not spend all day poring over manuscripts with a red pencil, lovingly turning an average book into a masterpiece. They do not spend great deals of time sipping wine with the writers whose books they may be publishing (although I wouldn't blame them for taking a belt or two from a bottle in their desk drawer).

The main job of editors in today's publishing houses is acquisitions. Editors are responsible for weeding through submissions and query letters from agents or from writers who have learned to bypass the gate, to find those few projects that can make it into print. Picture the marginally literate population of the world. At least one out of two people, literate or not, want to write a book. Now imagine how much mail a typical publishing house receives on a daily basis. It is enough to give your brain a hernia.

As you will learn in chapter 7, the best first contact to a publishing house is through an agent, if you are fortunate to have one, or through a well-crafted query letter. If your manuscript is selected as worthy of review, you now have the status necessary to be considered by an editor.

Every established publishing house has what is called their backlist. This includes all the books the house has published in the past that they still publish on an ongoing basis. These books continue to have a market and to generate profit. In making acquisition selections, some editors may look at a project in terms of its backlist potential, but more than likely they are looking for something that can be featured in the front-list. The front-list, those books that make up the future of the house, is the true domain of the editors. Editors are always on the lookout for projects that will bring in the most extensive future returns.

The editor's career hinges on his or her ability to recruit new front-list projects. A more accurate term for an editor might be "product acquisitions director." Like it or not, this aspect of their job is the backbone of how things get done. The editors who have the more successful careers are those who procure products that make more profit. Editors are not in it for the glamour of the job. They are typically well overworked. They know that if they consistently bring in mediocre or losing propositions, they can expect their careers to have the life span of a fruit fly.

Editors want to build the kind of reputation that will allow them to climb up the ladder. Even if they move from one house to another, a good track record with kudos and bestsellers will mean the difference between winning at the game or having to return to "go" without collecting the $200.

Editors have to have a good eye but do not wield unilateral decision-making power. Their acquisition requests must usually go to a board that consists of their colleagues at various levels. In other words, they have to lobby on behalf of a project they like and they can be shot down and humiliated or held as the hero of the day according to variables that are not easily controlled.

Editors need to gain support for their projects from other members of the editorial staff, but they must also garner support from other divisions within the publishing company. Each book produced uses company resources, both financial and physical, and each book must ultimately feed a lot of mouths when the returns are in.

At a typical editorial meeting concerning new acquisitions, you will also find members of the sales, marketing, and publicity staffs. A book may gain the support of an editor but lose that support at the level of the sales department. If sales does not support the acquisition, they will not devote energy to selling it to the booksellers. The editor may as well plan for the books to stay in the warehouse. Many books have been voted down by the sales staff even though editorial is in favor of them.

The marketing department, usually under the wing of sales, has the job of supporting sales as much as possible. Marketing is responsible for the creation of any promotional materials. If sales is not convinced they can move the book, that there will not be a perceived market strong enough to reach, the book again will be voted out. If marketing sees its potential, it can persuade sales to take another look.

If the house has a publicity department, it is in charge of getting to key media outlets to give exposure to the books and to create word of mouth. If the publicity department believes the book would lend itself to good promotion, this could influence the vote in favor. But if the publicity department feels the media is saturated with similar material, the book receives the thumbs down.

The publicity department may not be a major factor in many publishing houses. With the exception of major books, the publicity staff is typically understaffed, underpaid, and often undertrained. This is not where a great allocation of resources is made. For this reason, publicity can influence a decision if the success of the book hinges on the aggressiveness of a publicity campaign. Publishing houses more and more rely on authors to carry the ball into the public eye. The sales staff will gain distribution of the book through their contact with the booksellers, but the publicity may be minimal at best.

Essentially, no matter how many types of high-tech, electronic media exist for publicizing a book, what will make it sell is positive word of mouth. The old adage, "Any publicity is good publicity," does not apply to books.

**At least one out of two people, literate or not, want to write a book.**

In most situations no one person or department has the say of which projects are chosen. There is debate until the different factions reach a consensus that the project is a good calculated risk.

Editors have a lot of potential products from which to choose, but will choose only ten to 20 in a typical season. Among the potential books are at least hundreds of submissions directly from agents. These submissions always take precedence if the agent is respected by the editors as having an eye for good commercial books. If editors feel they can rely on the agent to conduct preliminary screening, they will bypass other material to look for the gold among the agent submissions.

So all submissions that are unagented yet still find their way to the publishing houses are given the status of *slush pile*. Or they are what we call the "uns"—unagented, unrequested submissions that will likely languish until someone feels ambitious enough to read them. Many larger houses hire outside readers to screen slush. But more than likely the material is returned with a form letter stating that the house does not accept unagented unsolicited submissions.

> **Editors have to have a good eye but do not wield unilateral decision-making power.**

So, as you can see, the writer is not the center of the publishing industry. Publishing is actually about acquiring a product, turning the product into a book, getting it into the pipeline, and getting it sold. It seems, especially to a writer, that the primary relationship is between a publisher and a writer. And in many ways this relationship is very consuming because those are the human factors. But as far as the publishing entity is concerned, probably the more important relationship is between the sales force and the retailer, including the in-between wholesaler and book jobbers. That determines the bottom line more than anything else—the relationship between the people who get the books into the stores and the public.

Indirectly, the relationship between the Jane Q Bookbuyer and the publisher is important, but many layers separate the book buyer from the publisher. Most book buyers have not heard of many book publishers. Oh, they may have heard of Simon & Schuster or Random House, but these names are not important to them. Book buyers are not faithful to any particular publisher. They may be faithful to certain authors or themes or bookstores but could not care less who publishes a particular book. If Stephen King were to jump publishers each time he published a book, the consumers would not say, "I am going to stay loyal to Putnam and never buy a Stephen King book again, since he jilted them." That doesn't happen with respect for the public, except perhaps for relatives of people who work for the publishing company.

In some ways the writer becomes one of the functionaries within the scheme of things. If you want to be cynical about it, the writer plays a similar role to the photocopy machine or the computer equipment or the modem lines. The writer becomes another means of production to the end result, a published book. Of course, it is an element of production that requires a great deal of nurturing. Photocopy machines can be replaced rather quickly; a talented writer does not lend himself or herself to that kind of replacement. Many writers in the mid-list can be seen as a dime a dozen, can be considered easily replaceable, if they are seen as being more trouble than the bottom line dictates they are worth.

Let's look at the financial aspects of the book-publishing industry. Where does the money go? Often writers will measure their own success by how much money they make, and a writer might be surprised at how many other mouths there are to feed in the process. Say for example, a hardcover book costs $20 (most hardcover books cost more than that today, but we'll use this number because the math is easy). First of all, the publisher is probably going to have to sell the book for 40 to 44 percent off the list price. That discount becomes the bookstore's part of the action. For simplicity purposes, let's say that we have a 50 percent discount. The book is listing at $30, but the publisher will only collect $10 for it. The other $10 is going to the bookstore or the wholesaler or the book jobber.

Out of the $10 the publisher gets to keep, it will have to pay about $3 to the author. In most cases, the author will max out at receiving 15 percent of the list price of the book, which leaves the publisher $7. Out of this $7 the publisher needs to produce the book, maintain its own overhead—and remember, they're not publishing just one book. If we're talking about a huge publisher, we're talking about hundreds of books in a season. All those books cumulatively have to support the publisher's overhead—the cost of the manufacturing, shipping, warehousing, moving the books around (the touch costs), paying the salaries of everyone involved, and the paying the various expenses. That's what the publisher has to do with its $7. Thus, you can understand why most publishers find their profit margins are generally below 10 percent and maybe even below 5 percent. It's hard to make a big profit in that kind of business with that kind of margin.

Where are the publishers' revenues being generated? And where do their profits come from? A couple of years ago, the then publisher of Random House, Harry Evans, made a public statement that people found surprising—not because of the factual content, but because he confessed to it in public. Basically he said Random House generally runs a big deficit on its front-list, which means its front-list is a big loss leader.

You might be aware that Random House is one of the larger publishing companies, along with Simon & Schuster and Time Warner. Random House is an umbrella for smaller companies, like a General Motors is. Over the last generation, Random House acquired other publishers. Within Random House you have many divisions that were once privately held mom-and-pop companies and are now part of this one big public company. And actually, Random House is owned by the largest German communications conglomerate, Bertelsmann, which, by the way, also happens to own Bantam Doubleday Dell, which in turn is a large company that owns smaller, at one time, privately owned mom-and-pop enterprises. Within Random House you have Knopf, Schocken Books, Pantheon, Times, Villard Books, and many others including, of course, the Random House imprint itself, which is the largest.

Well, over the years Random House, like the other large companies and many smaller ones, has acquired a huge backlist that consists of books that do not require any significant marketing, publicity, sales . . . it is a passive sell. All they have to do is produce the backlist book and they know it will sell within time. Backlist books would include the classics—books by George Orwell, Mark Twain, James Michener, and Joseph Heller. These are books that had an initial front-list life in hardcover of maybe one to two years, then usually go into mass-market paperback, which is an inexpensive production of about a $5 book. Or, they might be published as a more high-quality paperback known as a trade or quality paperback listed from $10 to $20.

The point of the front-list is to generate potential materials for the backlist. The backlist is really what generates the revenue. It can be very profitable to publish the backlist. A publisher who does not have a profitable backlist is a publisher who is on a very slippery slope because it is wholly dependent upon its front-list. And the front-list is very, very speculative—really where publishers go to Las Vegas. They're gambling that the book will be a success, especially if they've paid a very large advance for it. The *advance* is the money fronted to the author. Or, they might have put a lot of money into production.

You never know what is going to happen with the front-list; the majority of front-list books will not live to go to the backlist. Depending on the publisher, perhaps only 10 to 20 percent of the books from the front-list will survive more than three years in print in any format. And looking down the road another five to ten years, only about 5 percent of the books will go on to have any significant life. Now, that doesn't mean because a book didn't go to the backlist it didn't make money. It can still have made a lot of money, especially if the advance was modest. But, for the publisher to really have an ongoing cash flow, it will have to keep building the

> The old adage, "Any publicity is good publicity," does not apply to books.

backlist. The only way to do this is to keep gambling on the front-list, where about 90 percent of all editorial and marketing and publicity energy goes to reach the goal—to harvest a front-list that sizzles and will make money in and of itself, and will create product that will live a very long life on the backlist.

Now that you understand what you are dealing with, you should move onto making your product one that will make it to the top. If your product has what it takes, it can become an integral part of this loop that eventually makes it a big selling book.

## CHAPTER 7

# Creating Product
# That Sizzles

It seems like everyone wants to write a book. So many good ideas are available that the goal of writing a book and getting it published is not so out of reach. If you know the right things to do and are willing to stick with it long enough, you can find your name on the cover of the book of your dreams.

Fiction and nonfiction are entirely different animals. Fiction is the goal of most aspiring writers, as it is considered "high art." If your goal is to sip wine in a café at Martha's Vineyard while talking to writer friends about the wonderful novel you have been writing for the past 20 years, go ahead and have your fun. If you are interested in writing for a living, you may want to consider mixing in some commercial projects along the way to hone your craft, build your reputation, and learn the discipline it takes to write books.

If your love is fiction and nothing but getting your work published will do, then you can take some strategic steps to reach that goal. But first we will start with the path of the nonfiction writer, which does not require a completed manuscript to close a deal. You need a well thought-out idea, a marketing scheme, and a good book proposal.

## THE IDEA

When you know nothing about the publishing industry, you think there is a good idea for a book in everything. In fact, not everything is a good book idea. Certain criteria will help you determine whether your book is worth pursuing:

◆ Does your idea have a theme or a hook that can be expressed in one or two sentences?

◆ Does your idea have enough depth to sustain a book rather than a magazine article?

◆ Is anyone besides you interested in the topic?

◆ Does your idea reach a particular market of people who would be motivated to read it?

◆ Do you have the credentials or experience to be some kind of authority on the subject?

◆ Are there people who would plunk down cold cash to buy a book on your great idea?

◆ Are there people who would invest hours of their time reading your book?

◆ If your potential reader asked the question, "What is in it for me if I read this book?" could the book speak for itself?

If you are satisfied with your objective answers to these questions, you may just have an idea worthy of pursuing into the next phase, the book proposal.

Before you begin your proposal, consider this important adage for nonfiction writers: "Great minds think alike." If you think of an idea, count on the fact that someone else has thought about it as well. Don't panic. Just because a person has thought about an idea does not mean he or she has the will or the know-how to carry it out.

The next thing you must do with your idea (after you have run it through your handy-dandy list of criteria) is to look for the competition. This is no time for denial. Investigating your competition is one of the most important steps you can take in developing your book proposal. You are not looking for reasons you shouldn't write your book; you are looking for support that you should write and sell your book.

With the introduction of the Internet, investigating current books on similar topics should be fairly easy. Just go to one of the online booksellers and look for similar books on your subject. You can then read an annotated version or a review on the book to see how similar it is to your idea. If you do not have access to the Internet or are not yet proficient with it, use the *Books in Print* reference to research the area.

If you find books on your topic, determine whether or not any titles directly reflect your idea. If you find competitive titles, don't cry yet. Dig more deeply. Some titles may seem to be the same as your idea, but are entirely different in execution. Some books are too old to present any real competition for your treatment of the subject. Or maybe when you see what is already out there, you can think of a way to maneuver your idea to fill a new space in the field. If the subject matter is your passion, find a way to make your idea work.

> **The best nonfiction is readable and often enjoyable in its simplicity.**

If you see a tremendous number of books on a particular topic, the industry may be saturated. The book industry is at least a year behind itself in terms of what subjects are hot. If you see a lot of something, it may mean the industry has already moved on and you're seeing last year's trend. This is a good reason to move on to something else or to change your approach to hit the new wave of information demand.

You are going to confront the issue of competition in a section of your nonfiction book proposal. At this juncture you are just trying to determine if what you have is worth pursuing in a serious way.

Finding an idea that can sustain a book is not as simple as it seems. I recommend the tenacious writer read everything possible to be on top of what is now available. Then put that aside to see where things are heading. Now is too late; tomorrow is where you should be looking.

## DETERMINING YOUR MARKET

The second thing you want to determine after you have ruled out direct competition is whether a market for your book really exists. Maybe there is a very good reason there are no books on your subject. Maybe no one wants a book on your subject. Keep in mind who will actually go and buy your book. You may find a provocative topic but have to aim your hook toward the person who is going to want to read it, not necessarily the person who would benefit the most from your insights.

A good title is important to your book, but is not necessarily the one that makes you look the most intelligent and clever. When you are in the stage of trying to sell your idea to an agent or publisher, it is very important that she or he have some idea what your book is about just by looking at the title. So choose something that is descriptive but recognizable. *Think and Grow Rich* is an example of a good title.

We often receive book proposals with titles that are like works of art, but have no connection to the book being proposed. If you like a short title using perhaps three to five words, you can still use a subtitle consisting of a short explanatory sentence to further describe the book.

Although this is not always the case, it is usually best that your title is not too negative. Remember that consumers often choose nonfiction books by the title and the information on the cover. If it appears to have the information they want, they will choose it over another book on the same subject. The reaction is visceral, so if your title makes a person immediately feel defensive or humiliated, you will be losing a potential sale.

For example, do not use a title that says *The Stupidest Mistakes Only Truly Neurotic People Make* or *The Complete Scuzzball's Guide to Getting a Date*. When you have found a title that does justice to your great idea, be aware that it is a working title. This means that you may be asked to change it at some point along the line. Do not hang on to a title if someone who is either offering to represent you or pay you for your book has a better idea. You may be far more intelligent, but there are times to defer to the experts. Remember, if something is clever to you but no one else is smart enough to "get it," you do not "get" the workings of the commercial book business.

> **You are selling yourself and your book. Choose what will make the best impression.**

A nonfiction book proposal is a sales document. It is your opportunity to have some minimal undivided attention on the part of a prospective agent or editor. Imagine that you are in a meeting and have exactly one minute (or less) to entice your audience into wanting to know more. First impressions are highly important.

Begin your book proposal with a strong overview. Make sure you state your thesis within the first few lines. If someone does not know what your proposed book is about after the first few paragraphs, it is likely you will lose their interest. You want to set your hook and reel them in. You may never get another chance.

Every editor or agent has a different approach to reading and evaluating a book proposal. Some jump right to the outline to see what the book will look like. Some start with the overview, jump to the table of contents, then look at the author's qualifications. You will never know how your proposal will be received. You want to make sure that each element of your proposal is as strong and informative as the others.

When you write a proposal, write in a voice appropriate to the topic, but make sure the voice is natural for you. There is no greater turnoff than someone who writes above his own head. Use clear language that conveys information. Nonfiction does not need to be flowery or overwritten. The best nonfiction is readable and often enjoyable in its simplicity. This is not the same as writing for the uneducated; it is more a commercial approach that is inclusive rather than elitist in its use of language.

The elements of a nonfiction book proposal are:

◆ Overview

◆ Competition

◆ Markets

◆ Promotions

◆ Chapter-by-chapter outline

◆ Author biography

◆ Sample chapters

Not all the elements are relevant to each topic. The more complicated the topic, the more detailed the proposal. If you have nothing unique to add to the sections, it is best to move on. This is not a boilerplate form for every book proposal. Each proposal has a life of its own. For further examples of book proposals that sold and why, see *Write the Perfect Book Proposal* by Jeff and Deborah Herman (Wiley).

The best book proposals are interesting to read and provide a road map to your book. Never forget what you are trying to accomplish. You are trying to convince a publishing house to pay out money on the chance that your book will bring them some kind of return. Not all books need to be blockbusters, but no publishing house wants to waste its resources on something that appears too much of a gamble.

You have many strikes against you going into the fray. You want to eliminate as many of the little things as possible so your book proposal is given the best consideration.

◆ Make it readable and interesting.

◆ Support your thesis with research or credentials.

◆ Have a solid outline so your prospective agent or editor can be confident you can carry out the job.

- Package your proposal as professionally as possible.

- Do not rely on hype, hyperbole, or gimmicks. Editors and agents have seen it all.

- Check your spelling.

- Send clean copy, not dog-eared copies that look like they have been touched by everyone.

- Do not smoke around your proposal. Aside from the risk of fire, cigarette smoke practically wafts out of some boxes. The smell can be offensive.

- On the other hand, do not try to make your proposal smell too good. We almost lost one of our interns to an out-of-control dryer sheet that was placed in a submission. It turned out she was allergic to it.

- Use good quality paper and a decent typewriter or word processor.

- Always double-space.

- Always put your name and phone number on every proposal.

If you have unique attributes or viable contacts, put them in your marketing and promotions section. If you can translate memberships or affiliations into possible book sales, this can go a long way toward pushing your submission over the fence.

In your marketing and promotions section, do not make claims that can be met with the statement, "They all say that." Everyone wants to be on television and radio, in Oprah's Book Club. If you have some indication that these things will transpire (short of a miracle), by all means put the information in your book proposal. If you merely state that your book would be good in these venues, you appear amateurish.

The about-the-author section of your book proposal should be relevant to the book you are proposing. This is not a resume to show what a wonderful person you are or how much potential you have. This is your opportunity to carefully taper your credentials to show you are the person to write the book you are proposing. If you are a Ph.D., that always helps. But if you are proposing a book where your expertise or experience puts you in a position of knowledge and authority, this is as important as any formal education and should figure prominently in your description of yourself.

Find the balance between accessible and arrogant. You do not want someone to feel you are an ego with feet because this is a people business. No one wants to knowingly become involved with a potential project where they feel the client will be high maintenance. You also do not want to be so self-deprecating that they want to send you to a shrink for lessons in self-esteem. Be professional. This is the business aspect of writing. Do not take anything personally. Your objective is to compete .against the many submissions vying for the same few spots.

> **Keep in mind how many manuscripts the average agent or editor is exposed to each day.**

Past publishing credits are a plus. But do not be discouraged if you are not widely published. The beauty of the nonfiction proposal is that its viability is weighed heavily on the strength and marketability of the idea.

Your chapter-by-chapter outline should be annotated. This means your descriptions of your chapters will be like mini magazine articles. Each chapter description should read well and be thoroughly thought-out. As you write the book, you may have an entirely different approach. Books tend to take on lives of their own. But at this stage you want to show you have a clear vision of how to transform your idea into a book.

The length of your nonfiction proposal will depend on your topic. Some require 30 pages, some only five. If your elements are met, do not stretch out the length to some arbitrary number.

You should always have strong sample material. Writers tend to want to send the proposal out as is. You will be wasting your opportunity because anyone who is interested will want to see sample material before making a decision. The only people who can get out of writing sample chapters are those with long-standing relationships in the industry. Even then, sample materials are important to project development.

If you already have your manuscript finished, pick at least three representative chapters and include them in your package. If you are writing sample material, we recommend working chronologically (chapters 1 and 2 are good). This is your choice, however. If something highly dramatic will be covered in a later chapter of the book, send it along. You are selling yourself and your book. Choose what will make the best impression.

Your nonfiction proposal is probably the most important tool you can give to an agent, who will assist you in finding a publishing house. If you have an agent, the agent will get you the access you need, but the proposal will close the deal. Even the best of agents can't make up for a flawed project.

If you are a fiction writer, you can't rely on a book proposal in lieu of a completed manuscript. You must have the manuscript, and it is wise to also have what is called a fiction synopsis. There is a consensus among novelists that the synopsis is often more difficult to write than the book itself.

Think of the synopsis as a movie trailer. Although you may not want to think of your work in such commercial terms, this is really the function the synopsis serves. You want to whet the appetite of your potential editor or agent so they will want to make the commitment to read your book.

A synopsis is not a plot summary. That is where most authors make the mistake. You are really showing off some of your best writing style with a paraphrased condensed version of what is to come. You should not leave out a surprise ending. You want the editor or agent to see how clever you are. You want them to know how things turn out.

Keep in mind how many manuscripts the average agent or editor is exposed to each day. You want yours to be among the select few to at least make the first cut. You want someone to want to read the main manuscript. Your synopsis can do this for you.

**Fiction and nonfiction are entirely different animals.**

This is a difficult stage for the writer. When you finish a novel or a book proposal, you want to be finished with it. But, in a way, this is when the real work begins. Many talented writers who can write wonderful material will never be read except by close friends and relatives. If you want to be published, you need to learn to jump through the hoops that separate the amateur from the professional.

Think like a businessperson or a consumer. If you view your book from either perspective, you will be more objective about how well you are meeting the expectations of those who would either sponsor or buy your book. Give yourself that extra push to go beyond mediocrity. You may still not be published, but some common sense and writer's savvy can go a long way toward helping you realize your goal.

In the next chapter we will show you how to break down some walls and follow industry protocol.

**CHAPTER 8**

# Gaining Access to the Mysterious World of Publishing

When you have a good idea for a book and have prepared a sharp professional package, you have to crack the code, break into the vault of book publishing. You have to bypass the intricate security system designed to let the good stuff in and keep the perceived "bad stuff" out. And until you are out of the slush status, you are considered bad, a potential waste of time at a minimum.

Now don't be insulted. The sooner you realize that before you have status you are merely a pile of paper, the better you will feel about the process. Writing with the goal of being published is not for the faint of heart. You have to at least have enough moxie and confidence to follow the steps that will put you directly in the right person's face. You need a good product to carry you, but most importantly, you need access.

## WHY HAVE A LITERARY AGENT?

Unless you have total confidence, very thick skin, and a family history of longevity, you might want to skip the direct route to the publishing houses. Many people have the opinion that their work is so good they do not need to share the wealth with anyone, least of all a middle person. Keep this in mind: A qualified and legitimate literary agent has something you do not have. A literary agent has access to the right people at the publishing houses who might be interested in your work.

If you are fortunate enough to gain representation with a literary agent, you can be pretty well guaranteed that at minimum someone in authority will actually read your submission. Many publishing houses will not even considered unagented, unsolicited manuscripts. You will carefully send your beautiful manuscript to publishing houses, only to receive a form letter saying that no one will even look at it unless you have a middle person to vouch for the quality of your work.

Literary agents perform an important function in the publishing world. Agents who have developed the reputation and contacts among editors and others in the industry have a role as a prescreener of all the projects submitted over the transom. The literary agent presumably reviews the query letters and manuscripts and weeds out the projects unworthy of consideration. An editor can rely on a good agent to only send projects appropriate to the needs of that publishing house and only those of publishable quality.

Publishing is a hard-copy business. It can't rely on hype. A legitimate agent will typically not risk his or her reputation on questionable projects, because his or her greatest asset is access. An agent who constantly sends mediocre or inappropriate projects will become a pariah in the publishing industry and will certainly not have a thriving business. The contacts will dry up and the agent's submission will have no more status than that of anyone else.

## FINDING AN AGENT

So when you begin your efforts at gaining access, begin with the literary agent. It is not unusual to hear the writer's lament: "It is more difficult to get an agent than to get a publishing contract." This may be true, but it should not dissuade you. As we stated earlier, the business is so overloaded with submissions that your best avenue is with an agent. Agents also serve many other beneficial functions, but at this stage his or her most important function is to open the door, so you can put your foot through it.

So how do you go about getting an agent? Well first of all, make sure your product is impeccable. If you query an agent and the agent requests your manuscript or proposal, you will not win any points if you say, "Well, I'm not really ready. I was just seeing if anyone would be interested in my idea." And agents never forget! Have your project ready to go so that, if you are contacted, you can have it in the mail ASAP.

Then you have to determine who the agents are. You can't just call your Uncle Pete and ask if he would act as your agent. And do not ask your lawyer to be your agent, unless your lawyer actually happens to be in the literary agent business in book publishing. Nothing will set you back more than putting the wrong person in charge of negotiating your book deal. Lawyers outside the publishing industry are trained to tear apart a contract to make sure you get a good deal. Deals fall apart because of lawyers who do not understand the standards of the industry and who try to negotiate terms that are not negotiable. We are not talking about legitimate concerns, like signing a contract that gives away rights to all your books until you die and even in your afterlife. We are talking about clauses unique to the publishing industry that are just not understood by people out of the loop.

> **It is hard to tell a prophet that his proposed book is bad.**

You are really better off finding a lawyer familiar with publishing contracts or sticking to a search for a good agent. You need to find out who the agents are by looking in resources that list agents.

Of course, we recommend you look in the *Writer's Guide to Book Editors, Publishers, and Literary Agents,* because it was intended to make gaining access to this mysterious world of publishing as easy as possible for writers like you. We designed our agents survey to give you as much information as we could about each agent, so you could see where there might be a good match.

You want to find out what an agent represents or likes to represent. In the *Writer's Guide,* you can even learn about their hobbies and personal interests. It is always effective to add something personal in a query letter, as long as you are not too much of a syco-phant, such as I went to the same school or share the same unusual hobby. You want to develop an immediate rapport if possible.

You also can go to the library and look in the *Literary Market Place (LMP)* or contact the AAR (Association of Authors Representa-tives) for a listing of its members. Not all agents are members of the Association and agenting is not a field that needs licensing. How-ever, it does have a self-policing role for its members, which can give you some assurance of the agent's legitimacy.

If you are writing a certain type of book and have been influ-enced by other writers, look in the acknowledgment section at the front of their books. It is highly likely that they have acknowledged their literary agent. You might determine what agents might be good for you by seeing who is representing what. The only danger here is an agent would probably not want to represent something that closely competes. If it is the same type of book or in the same genre, by all means put this person on your list.

## THE QUERY LETTER

The way you approach an agent is simple. Write an effective query letter, making it clear what is in it for them. The letter will have to do the initial selling for you. A phone call to pitch an idea is not going to get you anywhere. The book business is not like Hollywood. You do not see power lunches with prospective writers verbally pitching ideas. The protocol is to start with the query, which takes the place of your face-to-face pitch. You want to appear professional and moti-vated, and if you have good connections, that doesn't hurt either. The elements of the query letter are:

- ◆ *Thesis statement or hook:* What your book is about.
- ◆ *Supporting material:* Why this book should exist, why any-one would want to read it.
- ◆ *Unique qualifications or education:* Why you are the person to write it.

◆ *Promotions:* How you could sell books, through unique marketing methods.

◆ *The close:* Asks for the sale, or in this case, to send the proposal or manuscript.

A query letter should be limited to one to two easily readable pages (one page is preferable). This means you need to choose your words very wisely and frugally. Your objective is to communicate an idea as quickly as possible, in as short a space as possible, and as intelligently as possible. Intelligence is not marked by flowery language. In fact, your academic vocabulary can work against you if it takes too much brain power for an agent to understand immediately what you are offering.

Think of it this way: When we evaluate query letters, we look at probably one hundred at a time. We rip through them quickly to single out the projects that appear to have some potential. One of our agents likes to bring a carry-on suitcase of query letters whenever she flies. She brings her own trash bag and whips through those letters between the time the cabin door closes until it opens again at her destination. If people give her strange stares, she tells them it is the only opportunity she has to answer her fan mail.

Your letter needs to get to the point immediately and to capture the interest of an agent so she or he wants to see more. In fact, the letter should be so good that the agent wants to call you from the airplane—or at least when she lands. Our agency rejects at least 90 to 95 percent of the query submissions we receive. Although the odds are against you, a good query will keep you in the running.

## THINGS NOT TO PUT IN A QUERY

People make common errors in writing a query. For example, you may want to use a friendly tone, especially if you find common interests as you research the agent; however, do not fool yourself into thinking the agent is your friend. Don't start your letter by unburdening your soul. We have actually received letters that begin, "My book has been rejected by every agent I have sent it to, but I know you will see what a good book it will be."

What agent wants to take a project that she knows has been rejected by all her peers? It may even be a good project (although it probably isn't); it is just bad psychology.

We also have had query letters that reflect a bit too much horn-blowing. You want to be confident about your importance to the project, but there is a limit. We have had people claim to be prophets, or to have the answers to all humanity's problems. This would not necessarily be a deterrent, but in these situations, the queries were just plain bad.

It is hard to tell a prophet that his proposed book is bad. We had a new intern who on his first day answered a call from such a prospective author. The man said, "I am a prophet of the Lord; you can't reject my book!" The intern simply wrote down the message as given and figured we would know what to do from there. We had told him we had some pretty important clients, so he didn't want to take any chances.

> **Remember that a query letter is still considered slush.**

If your query letter is for a novel, you want to entice the prospective agent into wanting to read more. Include some plot summary and maybe a quote. It is acceptable to send a short synopsis with a query letter. Make sure the letter is interesting. If your query is dull, readers will assume your novel will be dull as well.

If your query letter is for a nonfiction book, you may want to include your book's table of contents. Otherwise, it is best not to include a lot of additional material. If the agent is interested, you can send supporting materials with your proposal package.

If you have any unique news clippings related to the book or want to include a biography or curriculum vitae, that is fine. Just do not overload this initial contact.

When you are ready to send out your queries, make multiple submissions and always include a self-addressed stamped envelope.

The SASE increases your chances of hearing back from the agency at least a million-fold. A literary agency has no obligation to you, unless you become a client. You may get lost in the shuffle if you do not take certain steps to assure correspondence.

Multiple submissions (when you send the same letter to several agents at the same time) increase your chances of finding someone to represent your project. What you don't want to do is send a form letter (agents are not impressed with a "Dear Agent" letter). Take time to personalize each letter and indicate that the project has been sent to other agents at the same time.

If an agent shows interest but you have a different favorite you are hoping to hear from, use the opportunity to contact the agency of choice. Tell them you have an interested agent, but give your preference an opportunity to move you to the head of their stack. Although some agents advise against multiple submissions, it gives you the advantage of increasing your chances of at least one positive response. You know the odds.

## SCAMS AND READING FEES: AVOIDING THE VULTURES

Writers are at a vulnerable stage after the query letters hit the mail. You hope in doing your homework that you have only contacted legitimate agencies. But charlatans can find their way into even the most highly scrutinized databases. In the *Writer's Guide,* we rely on reports from our readers if agents are not operating within the parameters of ethical business practices. We have only had one or two situations where complaints, which proved valid, forced us to remove an agent from our directory.

However, proceed with caution when searching for an agent. Under no circumstances should an agent request a fee to read your manuscript based on your query letter. If you think about it, it is a nice little scam to take the number of queries that arrive at the typical agency in any given week and turn a percentage of them into fees for doing nothing but claiming to consider and read the manuscript.

Legitimate agents earn their living by selling books. Agents receive a commission of anywhere from 10 to 15 percent of the sale, often including subsidiary rights, such as audio, video, and film. Reviewing query letters and requested manuscripts is how we find our products. The time we invest in evaluating potential manuscripts is a cost of doing business.

> **A literary agency has no obligation to you, unless you become a client.**

There also are agencies that straddle a dangerous line when they offer editorial services. If an agency offers editorial services in conjunction with a promise of consideration of representation, there is an unfair advantage. There is no guarantee of representation, yet the author is willing to spend money on the possibility of consideration. It is a carrot-and-stick approach, but there isn't really a carrot. Not all agency editorial services are scams, but an author should see this blurring of the agent role as a red flag.

We do not consider it ethical for an agent to ask for a retainer for expenses. If all parties agree, often expenses such as printing or phone calls are charged back to the client. However, these expenses are a cost of doing business and should be either recouped out of the first proceeds or invoiced at such time as the writer and agent part ways. Sometimes writers are expected, if possible, to supply copies of projects for circulation to publishers, which eliminates the need for any expenses.

We don't want you to be paranoid about literary agents, especially since you really need one if you want the most direct route to getting published. However, be aware that this is an unregulated industry and a lot of people want to write books. Therefore, there is a lot of room for the bottom feeders of the world to try to take advantage of people's dreams and wallets. There are enough legitimate agents out there that you do not need to be a victim.

If you can't find an agent with your query submissions, either keep on trying or go back through the book to see whether you can do more to push yourself over the top.

You might get lucky and have several legitimate agents interested in your project. You'll want to choose the person you feel is most enthusiastic, someone who is either really into the project or someone who knows how to sell it. Either is fine. Just trust your gut instincts and go for it.

If you have a lot of agents interested in your project, you are fortunate. You can be more choosy about who represents you. Ask questions and be open with each interested agency as to your status with the others. Agents are competitive and will like a project they feel they finagled away from someone else. But if you put the agents too much on the defensive, you might just find yourself with no one. Agents have egos like anyone else. Maybe more so.

## HAVING STATUS

If the agent likes your query and sees potential for your project in terms of what he represents or feels he can sell, you will be invited to send a full proposal or manuscript, sometimes both. If you have a completed nonfiction manuscript, you should still have a proposal available because it will be needed to sell your work. Agents and editors prefer to work with proposals, even if there is a full manuscript, as they are easier to pitch at the editorial meetings.

After you send a query letter, be patient. Go on with your life. Do not wait by the phone or the mailbox. Do not quit your job. Do not take out two new credit cards and go on a shopping spree, anticipating a big advance any day. Forget about your book. You may hear from agents right away, which can mean instant rejection, or you may not hear for some time. If you want to assure response, whether good or bad, don't forget your SASE. It is good to keep track of rejections because outstanding queries can still mean prospects, and you want that information available as you continue your efforts.

Remember that a query letter is still considered slush. It is a tool that follows protocol but has not been invited into the game. It is acceptable to follow up after a while, but is best to simply send the letter again if you have not received an answer. Do not pester the agency with calls saying, "I sent you a query back in so-and-so year." Some agencies are more efficient than others are, and some agents are wonderful about keeping current on queries. But many agencies are so busy that they get to queries when they can but spend most of their time selling books. If you send your letter again, you might put yourself back at the front of the pile. It certainly can't hurt. If you call and are annoying, your project may be rejected simply because of the annoyance factor. The perceived advantage is outweighed by the perceived aggravation.

Remember: agents are human. Also, agents are not paid unless they sell a book, which means they do not work for you unless you are under contract with them. It is to your advantage to be professional and to treat the agent with the kind of respect owed to someone who potentially has your future in his or her hands. Like it or not, they are a necessary part of the process. If you have to be more patient and are treated with a little less attention than you are used to, remember that this is an entirely different process. You may be a successful person in your industry, but in the agent's office you're nuttin' until you are somethin'.

## SIGNING ON

When you sign up with an agent, do not let it go to your head. Don't call ten times a day to chat or to check on your manuscript. You want your agent to be out there hustling, not appeasing your ego. If you want to brag to friends, that's fine. Just don't make yourself a nuisance.

It will take several months to know whether the typical submission is going to sell or not. You will usually receive rejections at first. Do not drink away your sorrows, but realize there is nothing personal about rejections. If you remember the structure of the industry described in Chapter 5, you know that a lot has to go into the decision to produce a book.

Look at each rejection as information you can use any time you have to go back to the drawing board. It is crucial that you be open-minded enough to use the feedback you get through rejections as insights into what the market is looking for. This is how you crack the code so you can make your wonderful book proposal fit into what people want to read and what publishers want to sell.

Some books sell right away and some seemingly take forever. Some start at an advance-against-royalties range of $5,000 to $10,000, and some can be instant phenomena in six figures. Don't get too excited; first writers rarely see the figures go over four or five figures.

You want to get published. Do not focus all your energy on the size of the advance. Your agent wants the most for you because it will also be the most for him. But there are realities. You want to shoot for the stars but also want to have the mentality that no matter what the level of your advance, you are going to make your book a success. As you will see in the next section of this book, there are many ways for you to do that.

## IF YOU CAN'T GET AN AGENT

If you are unable to get an agent, you should not give up. You have several options. First, decide how much you believe in what you're doing. This is a vital question to consider. You are going to have to put your blood and guts into a project that is unagented and unsolicited. But if you have the tenacity, you can overcome the obstacles.

Remember, the most important thing you need is access. You need to contact publishing houses in ways that make you stand out from the slush pile. One way to do this is to go directly to the people who publish what it is that you write. We have designed the *Writer's Guide* to give you updated information on which editors acquire which kinds of books. You can gain even more up-to-the-minute information on our Web site.

You also can contact publishing houses and ask which editors acquire certain types of books. You may have some difficulty getting past the gate, but if you ask in a professional manner without unnecessary conversation, you can usually find the information you need.

It is important that you send your query letter to the right place. If you send your book proposal "To whom it may concern," you will find no one concerned enough to take your letter out of the slush pile. If you send your letter to an actual name of the bona fide acquisitions editor for the type of book you are proposing, at least the person screening the letter will see its relevance. If your letter is sizzling enough, you might find yourself slipping past the gate with a request for more.

If your material is requested, you have the status you need to be considered against the submissions made by the agents or those recruited by the editors. The editor needs a good reason to spend time looking at your manuscript. If the editor requests it himself, he has already made some kind of commitment to at least scan it for possible acquisition.

If you cannot get past the gate at the large publishing houses, do not rule out smaller houses. Many niche publishers or independents are clamoring for good material, and many prefer not to work with agents because they do not pay high advances. There is no advantage for either the agent or the publisher to work together. You will want someone to help you look over your publishing contract if one is offered, but for the most part many good alternatives are available for you.

**Do not focus all your energy on the size of the advance.**

If you are unable to make any headway with the publishing houses, whether big or small, and believe there is a market for your book, you have another option: self-publish. This is not the same thing as vanity publishing, some glorified company to which you pay money to provide you with a book of whatever you want to give your relatives to show them you are a published author. You pay the money, and they will publish anything you want them to.

There is nothing wrong with vanity publishing if you realize it does not have anything to do with the actual publishing industry. It can be great to turn up at your family reunion with a box of pretty hardbacks with your name on the front. Just do not expect your local bookstore to pay you to sell them. You are strictly on your own.

Self-publishing is like self-printing. You become a publisher and work hard to sell your book and distribute it to as many outlets as possible. If you are a public speaker, it often makes a lot of sense to self-publish because you can sell your book to people who attend your lectures or workshops. You can even build the price of the book into the cost of the program.

Some self-published books become so popular that they can be distributed in standard outlets. If a self-published book shows it can sell a certain number of copies, it lends tremendous credibility that the book would do well in the general marketplace. Once a market has been proven, you can take your self-published book back to the agents who didn't give you the time of day or to the publishing houses that love projects with little or no risk, and offer it to them for the big bucks. But do not be too greedy. When you self-publish, you have a greater profit margin, and some can do very well. But what you do not have is distribution in bookstores and popular outlets.

If your book is purchased by a mainstream book publisher, you will reach so many more people that your book has a chance of being a big seller. If you remain in a small distribution scheme without the bookstores behind you, you will never bring in the numbers that will enable you to compete in the marketplace.

There are many ways to get a book published. You need to be creative and flexible. If you can't go in the front door, try the side or the back. If you believe enough in the viability of your subject, keep at it until you become what is perceived as the "overnight success."

Authors who make it big do not do it by sitting at home with the remote. They usually are an integral part of their own book's success. In the next section you are going to learn the secrets of some of the most successful publicists who are behind the scenes orchestrating the visibility of the books you see on the bestseller lists—secrets you can use for your own bestseller-in-the-making.

## CHAPTER 9

# Promoting Your Book
# to the Big Time

If you have jumped through all the hoops, packaged yourself well, obtained an agent who sold your book for you—or you sold your book directly—you still can't sit back and wait for your book to hit the top. Very few books are sold for sizable advances, and few are given a promotion or publicity budget to speak of.

Nothing is more disappointing for a newly published author than to go to a bookstore with the idea that his or her book will be prominently displayed, only to find it is not even in stock. Many books sit lifelessly in the distribution warehouse, never to see the light of day. If the sales department of the particular publishing house does not give the book a push onto the shelves, there is no telling what the outcome will be. It isn't that the publishing house does not want to see all its books succeed; it simply has to prioritize its allocation of promotion resources.

So it is up to you to make your book big, to develop a strategy that will remove your book from the boxes and put them in the hands of the consumer. You didn't realize you have to be a businessperson to be a successful writer, did you? But don't worry. You have many options. If you are not the type who can market a book on your own, you can find a publicist, a person who will promote your book for you. You will need to spend some money, but the return will far outweigh the investment in terms of exposure and ultimate book sales.

## THE MAGIC MAKING OF A BESTSELLER

"There is no magic formula to creating a bestselling book," says Christopher Coates, National Accounts Manager of Prima Publishing. "Author reputation, public interest, and awareness of subject matter, marketing, and publicity all contribute to making a book a hit."

## HOW THE SALES STAFF SETS THE FOUNDATION

The sales staff at the publishing house will be instrumental in getting the book to the stores and giving it a great start. "Ideally, right from initial editorial concept the sales department should be closely collaborating with the editorial on shaping the book," Coates adds. "Is the price right? Is the title correct? Is the format suitable (paperback vs. hardcover)? Is the market warm or cool to the subject?" This is a vital part of the book development because it structures its ultimate marketing scheme."

Coates continues, "Once the project has been fine-tuned and adopted, a publishing season selected, marketing plans and budgets discussed, sales kits produced, and the title catalogued, the rep takes the title information to the buyer. At this point the relationship between the buyer and the rep is paramount. In any given month in the United States, 4,000 new books are being published. How successful a book ultimately becomes now rests entirely on this part of the process. The rep's knowledge of the title, buyer's likes and dislikes, publisher's promotional plans, customer marketing devices, and industry trends can all figure in how well the book is bought or if it's bought at all. Post-presentation is also critical.

"A sales rep's role is varied. He or she needs to use any excitement or potential marketing plans available to make the sale. If the books are not in the bookstores, the process may as well die here. The sales rep will share late-breaking news and publicity with the buyer.

"Intimate knowledge of internal promotional opportunities will drive a larger buy and a higher sell," says Coates. A rep's ability to sign off on things like endcap and front table displays, advertising or author interviews in customer marketing pieces (for example, *Walden Book Report, Inside Borders*) all contribute to the successful placing of a book.

Ideally, right from the initial editorial concept, every solid bit of promotion helps.

## WHAT CAN A PUBLICIST DO FOR YOU?

Help you achieve your goal of a big book, or even a bestseller.

Almost every one of today's bestselling authors have one thing in common: a publicist. Publicity is free advertising. Publicity includes book reviews and book signings. It includes author appearances on television, radio, in print, and on the Internet. Although publicity is gained through the media, the true goal of publicity is not to draw media attention to authors, but to result in sales.

There are two types of publicists: in-house and freelance. An in-house publicist works for a publishing company in its publicity or marketing department. And as you would surmise, a freelance publicist obtains clients on a freelance basis outside the confines of the publishing house.

**In any given month in the United States, 4,000 new books are being published.**

A first-time author must be prepared for minimal publicity effort on the part of the in-house publicity staff. Of course, the publisher wants the book to sell. However, in-house publicists are notoriously overworked and underpaid. A publicity department has to divide a small budget among all the books being launched in a season. And almost all that money will go toward publishing the big names who have the most chance of recovering the money spent.

Margaret Durante, Director of Publicity for Pearson, an imprint of Macmillan, USA, explains: "Access to company-owned publicists can be difficult due to downsizing and publisher's priorities. Every book cannot be an A title, nor can a publisher economically support individual publicity for books that just don't generate that type of interest in the media. It's a fact of life that there is just so much competition and only so much need for more books in certain subject areas."

**Publicity is free advertising.**

"Unfortunately, most authors walk away from their publishing experience unhappy," says Pat Eisemann, publicity director of Scribner who has worked with has worked with Patricia Cornwell, Barbara Bush, Annie Proulx, and Stephen King. It isn't only because they do not feel they got the exposure they wanted. Some people have very unrealistic expectations of what an in-house publicist's role is. "And that's because they haven't thought about their agenda clearly," says Eisemann. "You can't take a publicity department and expect them to manage your life dream. They can only promote your book. They can't, for the most part, take you from obscurity to fame. People look at *Angela's Ashes* and say Frank McCourt did it! But he wrote the perfect book. Every now and then lightning strikes. But it doesn't happen every day."

## THE FREELANCE PUBLICIST

Because of the limits placed on the in-house publicists, authors often choose to hire freelance publicists. Writers who think only the "A-list" of authors retain publicists are mistaken. Self-published authors who do not have an in-house publicist, and any authors who want additional publicity, are encouraged to use freelance publicists to achieve success.

Rick Frishman, President of Planned Television Arts, has represented such heavyweights as John Gray, Bill Moyers, Mark Victor Hansen, Harvey Mackay, Sophia Loren, and Jimmy Carter. However, he says, "While we work with a million stars at my company, unknowns can be a good challenge. For example, no one knew who the hell Mark Victor Hansen was, with a book on chicken soup, so at first it was a hard sell. But look what happened. Another unknown was Charles Gibbons, who wrote *Wealth without Risk.* He sold a million of his first, second, and third books, and was always number one on the *New York Times* list."

"Writers can potentially gain tremendous access with a free-lance publicist," says Phyllis Heller of PR with a Purpose. "I think it is quite difficult for an author to try to handle his or her own publicity. First of all, it becomes a situation where they could feel personally rejected. I don't care what an author says—when they call a pitch and the pitch is not interested, it's got to hurt. But I can get a 'no' and continue pitching without taking it personally."

Susan Schwartzman, of Susan Schwartzman Public Relations, agrees. "I'd discourage authors from doing all of their own publicity. Producers don't want to talk to authors. By doing your own publicity, the messages you send are a) The house doesn't want to spend money on this book, and b) I'm too cheap to hire a publicist. It's an investment with a great return. Of course this advice comes from a publicist . . ."

## THE COST OF A PUBLICIST

One reason authors are loathe to hire a freelance publicist is because of the expense. But are publicists expensive?

"If one were to calculate the money spent on publicity, it would pale in comparison to the advertising dollars normally spent on newspaper, magazine, and broadcast. Publicists are paid for their time and their ideas," says Margaret Durante.

"There are a lot of big PR agencies who charge a lot and are great if you can afford it," says Susan Schwartzman, "However, an author who has limited funds available can find a publicist such as myself. If I really believe in the project and think I can get publicity for them, it isn't always necessary to spend a lot of money."

"The money spent depends on the publicist," notes Phyllis Heller. "For example, if you hire someone to get nationals for your book—even if they charge you what you think is a lot of money—you should realize that two or three bookings makes that money back. It's not taking from you, it's giving you the opportunity to make more money and get more exposure."

## WHAT A PUBLICIST DOES

Early in the publishing process, an author will fill out an author questionnaire for the marketing department of the publishing house, which is the primary tool for writing promotional and catalog copy.

If the publishing house devotes resources to the promotion of your book a few months before the book is published, the publicist will send out advance copies, bound galleys, or the manuscript for review. These copies will be sent to periodicals like *Publishers Weekly, New York Times Book Review, Kirkus Review, Library Journal,* and *Booklist* for review.

The publicist will prepare a press kit, which contains a press release announcing the publication of your book, the author's bio, other promotional material, and possibly a copy of the book.

The publicist will evaluate the media for promotion opportunities. While television, radio, and print are obvious venues, not all books are appropriate for each of these media. A publicist will determine which are appropriate and tailor the publicity to the media that fits the author and book best. According to Justin Loeber, publicity director for Running Press, an in-house publicist will have databases of between five and 25 names that she or he regularly contacts for each author. A freelance publicist will have an enormous database to use.

Many authors have their first taste of making author appearance at a book signing, one of the most exciting events for bookstores. Some bookstores carefully plan signings in advance and promote them in the local media. The store may feature a blowup of the book cover and generate word-of-mouth among customers.

"Book signings are important," says Arielle Ford of The Ford Group, who has worked with Deepak Chopra, Marianne Williamson, and Neale Donald Walsch, as well as handling publicity for the legendary *Chicken Soup for the Soul* books.

"You need to get out and let people see you. For a lot of people, getting an autograph is a big deal. If you want to get the word out, you've got to do book signings and meet the people and the booksellers who decide which books go on the back table and which go on the front shelf.

For publishers, however, book signings are not often cost-effective. They do not sell large quantities of books for the average author. Authors often are disappointed with the turnout. If you are working with a publicist, you can work together to try to make the event into a success. Local book signings often bring out local fans and can be especially effective in an author's hometown. The publicist may work with the bookstore to do extra promotions before the signing takes place.

Another event in which authors may participate is a pre-publication party, although these are relatively rare. "Some authors do get publication parties thrown for them, which the press can attend, and it will get publicity. But publication parties are mostly a vanity thing. I had one thrown for *Hot Chocolate for the Mystical Soul*—and it was fun," says Arielle Ford.

> **One reason authors are loathe to hire a freelance publicist is because of the expense.**

## FINDING THE RIGHT PUBLICIST

As Margaret Durante puts it, "Where do you easily find someone who is a good writer, part psychological counselor, part media fanatic, an aerobically agile person with great sociological radar, and a good mouth who is willing to be a star's personal shiner and convince them to change it just a little bit to make it work in the public's eyes?"

Your in-house publicist can provide referrals to an appropriate freelance publicist. You also can check the listings in the *Literary Market Place* for names and contact information.

You will need to talk to the publicist to determine the working arrangement. Some publicists charge by the type of market—television, radio, or print. Some charge a flat fee, and others work on retainer with a time limit.

"You want to make sure that you are working with someone for at least three months," says Phyllis Heller. "It's very disappointing when I am hired by an author who expects everything right away. You certainly can get great bookings in a short amount of time, but often it can take three months to get the ball rolling."

"The best publicist you can hire is one who believes his or her gift to the world is to bring enlightenment, inspiration, and education to people everywhere. When your publicist has a personal mission to make a difference in this world, you can be assured you are in good hands," says Annie Jennings of Annie Jennings PR.

"Ask publicists what clients they've handled in the past," suggests Justin Loeber. "If you've heard of an author, the publicist did the job well!"

## PROMOTING YOUR OWN BOOK

The publicist will ask you how much publicity you are willing to do. It is important for an author to take some responsibility for promoting his or her book. And an author who does not hire a publicist can promote his or her own book with some success.

"I encourage authors to do as much as they can for their books," says Paul Bogaards, Publicity Director of Knopf, who has worked with Toni Morrison, Anne Rice, Carl Hiasson, Michael Crichton, and Richard North Patterson. "An author has to recognize that no one is closer to the work than they are; no one knows the work more than they do. An author should always come to a publisher (or freelance publicist) with ideas. An author and a publisher (publicist) are partners in the process. They have to work together to push the message out. I always welcome the ideas an author brings to the table during the first meeting. The job of both parties is to bring awareness of the book to the marketplace.

"Hey, you wrote a book," says Eric Yaverbaum, President of Jericho Communications. "You can certainly write a press release and your bibliography. And, if you didn't write the book, get your ghostwriter to do it!"

"If you want to help with your own publicity," suggests Rick Frishman, "start by reading Dan Poynter's books and other books about getting publicity."

Another popular book for authors who wish to promote their books is *1001 Ways to Market Your Books* by John Kremer. "The key thing to promoting your books yourself is persistence," says Kremer. "If you believe that your book belongs in a certain market or a certain media, just keep knocking on the doors until they say yes. You're really doing a disservice if you don't, because every good market or good media is looking for a good book to sell or a good story to tell. And book authors have the best stories to tell."

Beyond that, the one thing I've been hammering to authors more and more recently is to develop a database of about 100 key contacts that you want to do some sort of action on your book. These could be wholesalers or distributors, bookstore chains or catalogues, or media. Then really work that list, spending about 80 to 90 percent of your time on it, getting them to say yes.

Lisa Johnson, publicity director for Dutton, offers additional ideas: "There are resources you can purchase or get at the library that tell you television shows and markets contacts. You can do your own campaign. One thing I've seen authors be really successful with is to run an ad in a publication called *Radio and TV Reports.* I've seen self-published authors get on major television shows like Sally Jesse Raphael from spending a few hundred dollars there. Placing an ad in it is much less labor-intensive than calling and mailing to the media. And authors who are published by

> **You can do your own campaign.**

a small house or are self-published can do their own campaign to bookstores, whether it's sending a postcard letting people know about the book or a handwritten note with a copy of the book."

"Without a publicist, writers have to step out of the book writer's role, which is no easy feat. But once they accept that role, they can make lists of local media, author's forums, reader's groups, and book clubs, and try to meet with local booksellers to generate some reading and then some writing about the book," says Margaret Durante.

> ## "The biggest mistake is not having a hook . . ."

"Writers should do grass roots promotions," says Justin Loeber. "Nonfiction authors should support their books by doing speaker's tours and gathering quotes from authorities to support their claims. We have actually had some writers who freak out when their book is published. Authors should accept that they wrote a book, which means being prepared to promote it."

What are some common mistakes authors make when trying to publicize their books? "The biggest mistake is that they leave all the promotion to their publisher," says Paul Bogaards.

"The worst mistake I have seen authors and publishers make is that they don't follow up," says John Kremer. "By developing a database of key contacts, you are more likely to make the sales to that top 100. I would guess that if you actually do the follow-up over a period of time, you will get about 60 to 80 percent to respond, which would be significant in terms of the book sales.

"Another mistake some authors make," says Kremer, "is thinking that they should only go national in their promotional efforts, when it might make more sense to focus on their region. They should identify their nearest major metropolitan area where they can, at very low cost, penetrate the media and cover all the bookstores, as well as contact groups that take on speakers."

"The biggest mistake is not having a hook," notes Christen Brown, a media trainer from On Camera and author of *Star Quality.* "Authors do not know how to sell their book by conveying the key message. They're gone in 30 seconds. So whether you are on radio, TV, or print, you need to give a headline that represents your book, say something about your book on radio that will really grab their attention, give the host something to talk about or argue about, and have clear key points.

"For nonfiction authors, this can be really difficult. They have to call out their message and come up with an interesting story that will fit into a four-minute interview. Fiction writers need to learn to tease. They need to know how to sizzle. The key is to add the sizzle, the sex appeal, the hook that will talk people into wanting to find out more about this story and these characters."

## Work with Bookstores to Promote Your Book

"One of the best ways to work is to do some sort of presentation, whether it's a reading or a workshop based on your book," suggests John Kremer. "But you've got to work with the bookstore to promote that workshop, or it's not going to have much impact. I've done bookstore appearances where they did nothing to promote it other than put my picture in the window, and maybe six people showed up. Then another bookstore spent a lot of time and 60 people showed up. There are a couple of benefits to a local book signing. First of all, the bookstore becomes aware of your book in a very big way if they start selling a lot of copies. They also will buy a bunch of copies if you're going to do a workshop and so on. Plus they will ask you to sign copies of the book, so they can put it on their autograph shelf where books can sell very well.

"And you start to develop a relationship with the bookstore, so maybe you can come back another time, or maybe they'll just start to hand-sell your book. A bookstore that really likes a book can sell 300 to 1,000 copies. If you get a bookstore to champion you, that makes a lot of difference. A couple of books done by small publishers had this kind of success. *When I Am an Old Woman, I Shall Wear Purple* was voted favorite hand-sell of the year by bookstores and went on to sell 4 million copies plus." The *One Minute Manager* was originally self-published and 30,000 copies were sold in the San Diego area alone before a major publisher picked up the book. It then went on to be a bestseller nationally.

"Joanna Lund really worked the media in Iowa. She promoted the heck out her Middle America healthy cookbook for about six months to a year in Iowa and sold 30,000 copies. Then she sold the rights to Putnam, and now she is the bestselling author on QVC."

"There are many resources for authors to learn how to do their own publicity. If people can't afford my services, they can buy my tape series," points out Arielle Ford. "Absolutely everything we know is on these tapes—they are affordable at $195—and we have a workbook. There's nothing hard about publicity, but it requires perseverance, time, energy, and creativity."

> **There are a couple of benefits to a local book signing.**

Authors should be creative and brainstorm markets for their book sales. A premium sale is a sale to a buyer, usually a business, who purchases a large number of books to distribute or sell to its employees or consumers.

## CREATE A CORPORATE BUY

Some authors gain large quantity sales by convincing companies to purchase their books. The companies will then sell or distribute the books to their employees or customers. "This kind of sale," says John Kremer, "usually is going to take a lot footwork, and may take up to a year, year and a half to actually happen. For example, Diane Pfeiffer had a premium sell with a book that she had on grits. She figured Quaker Oats, one of the major grit marketers in the country, would be a natural for this book. It took a year and a half before they said yes, but she ended up selling 60,000 copies to them to sell with their product. It took work, a lot of persistence, her knocking on doors, and, when one of her contacts disappeared, finding another contact and starting all over again."

## NETWORKING FOR SUCCESS

Publicists recommend you network as much as possible with people in the book-publishing industry. You can learn from each other's successes and failures, while making valuable contacts. Join a national association, such as The Publisher's Marketing Association, or a regional one, such as the Rocky Mountain Book Publishers Association. Find an association in your genre, such as Sisters in Crime. Many of these associations are now available on the Internet and are listed in our *Writer's Guide to Book Editors, Publishers, and Literary Agents.*

Attend national writer's conferences if you can afford to do so, such as the American Library Association and the Book Expo, sponsored by the American Booksellers Association. Or, attend local and regional writer's conferences where you might meet editors, agents, and other authors. Talk to the speakers as well as the other attendees. Take advantage when agents offer times to meet with them.

## PUBLICITY SUCCESS STORIES

Everyone wants his or her book to be a bestseller. Here are some ideas of how some publicists have helped writers reach this lofty goal.

"To make a book into a bestseller takes 1) divine intervention, 2) Oprah, and 3) massive amounts of publicity. One or all three of those make it work," says Arielle Ford.

"Creating publicity for a potential bestseller is about finding the right mesh," adds Lisa Johnson. "You need to determine what segment of the population is going to respond to the book and figure out the right outlets to reach them—the right newspapers, the right magazines, the right television shows. It's like putting a puzzle together and getting all of the various little pieces in line."

Margaret Durante says, "Bestsellers are made by creating a buzz. Widespread distribution is necessary, but if you build awareness, readers will come running and create more channels than you can imagine."

Success stories of publicity helping to create bestsellers abound. All publicists agree that positive word of mouth is what really launches a book into the big leagues. The word of mouth may come after the author makes a media appearance in national radio or television. Or, it may come from an award the book wins, or a book tour. It can come very quickly or can build up over time.

"One of the great success stories was Dr. Andrew Weil's book *Spontaneous Healing*," says Paul Bogaards. "It was recognizing that American culture had reached a moment when they were ready to embrace the ideas that Dr. Weil had been espousing for three decades. And it was taking this book over to a news magazine called *Primetime Live* and saying, 'This is Andy's moment; the world is ready for him. Can you bring him to one of your correspondents?' So *Primetime* aired the piece on him and it effectively launched, or re-launched, his career.

"A long shot was getting Dr. Sherwin Nuland, the author of *How We Die,* on the *Oprah Winfrey Show.* It is a terrific book but was very tough to present on television because it's not, at least when you are talking to television folks, a terrifically upbeat message. But Oprah, who has a great instinct for stories, knew what was going to work on her show and she knew it was an important message to push out.

**Make yourself aware of how people on the shows come across.**

"One of the things you have to recognize as a publicist is when a book is starting to push through the noise of our culture and make a name for itself. You have to recognize when a book has momentum. And we did that with Arthur Golden and *Memoirs of a Geisha.* We knew when to send him out on the road, not once but four times. Four times! And the book was on the bestseller list for over a year."

Pat Eisemann says, "Frank McCourt was a teacher at Stuyvesant. Every appearance, his former students would turn out to see him and it was unbelievable to watch. This was great built-in publicity.

"We also love Charles Johnson, who wrote *Dreamer*. And I'll tell you what the secret hidden trick of Charles Johnson is. It's almost the same thing in Frank. They're teachers, and they know how to talk in front of people. With Charles, when he speaks, the books just come alive.

"I've had so much fun with Stephen King. I love working with him because he likes to think out of the box. For publicity, when you are at his level, you don't need the straight and narrow. The consumer is so trained to him. It's like the bride at the wedding; wherever the bride goes, people watch. Patricia Cornwell's secret of success is her drive. She was clear from day one what she wanted because she writes a genre book that people love to read."

"I started working with bestselling author Deepak Chopra eight years ago," says Arielle Ford. "I went to him and said he was the best-kept secret in America and he should hire me—he said yes. And the first couple of years it was really hard. It's hard to imagine now, but it was really hard to talk to the media about mind-body medicine. But we persevered and it paid off—in a really big way."

"One of our major success stories," says Lisa Johnson, "was Eric Jerome Dickey. Dickey is an African-American novelist who writes commercial fiction with smart women characters. He's just reeling on everyone's radar. Watching him start and grow has been a major success.

"Diane Johnson's book, *Le Divorce*, was just an absolutely delicious novel about an American in Paris. She ended up being nominated for prizes and it was just such a great project to work on. Her book is an example of a traditional publicity route, working with bookstores, working with reviewers, sending out lots of copies to get as many people as we could reading it. That was more of a kind of traditional, working-the-phones, wearing-out-the-mailroom kind of campaign."

One success for us as a publisher was a book that Phyllis Heller worked on, James Van Praagh's *Talking to Heaven*. It went out with a small first printing, a small tour, and nothing was really happening. But James had a connection with Larry King, through a producer he had crossed paths with at one point. He actually called her himself and ended up doing a reading over the phone. He got on the show and it skyrocketed the book to the bestseller list—from under 10,000 copies in print!"

Phyllis Heller, Van Praagh's freelance publicist, recalls why she thought he would be a good client. "He told me he communicated with the dead and that he was from Bayside, Queens. I was from Queens. And he wasn't from any frou-frou area; he was from a blue-collar area. If he could communicate with the dead, then anyone could relate to him. He had the ability to appear like your next-door neighbor because he was. It brought the 'whoo-whoo' factor down."

Margaret Durante's greatest triumph against the odds was the "bestsellerization" of *Politically Correct Bedtime Stories,* a first book by James Finn Garner, who was without an agent. "He personally sent his book to more than 30 publishers before it was accepted for publication. His book was given to a junior editor because the company who originally held the contract was just sold, and budgets, editorial staffs, and sales staffs were not in place to properly promote. Not one chain store would buy the book, so we started arranging book signings with the independent stores, primarily in the Midwest, from whence the author hailed. His book went on to stay on the *New York Times* bestseller list for nearly two years and at the end of the first year he successfully copied the format into two additional bestselling titles.

"People really liked *Politically Correct Bedtime Stories* because it was a fun and poignant read. But for the most part, we hawked the enthusiastic local media coverage to force the nationals to take notice. One day a staffer noticed President Clinton pointing to the book during local television coverage of his visit to a local bookstore. We marketed that tape and promoted a letter we received confirming Clinton's enthusiasm for the book from the White House. While I'm sure these instances are not unique, we were all stunned at how interest mushroomed in a short period of time (about six months) and just in time for the holiday buying season. Just as the title was creeping up the bestseller list, author interviews went from shy to cocky to comfortable chats where he was invited back again and again by major media. It was amazing."

One amazing success story for Eric Yaverbaum was the success of Matthew Lesko, whose books include *Information USA* and *Getting Yours: The Complete Guide to Government Money.* "His first book was nothing more than a compilation of government information, yet Matthew managed to not only get it on the *New York Times* bestseller list but have it stay there, and he got on all the talk shows.

> **You have to recognize when a book has momentum.**

"Another huge success was Naura Hayden's *How to Satisfy a Woman Every Time and Have Her Beg for More.* She had a great title and is really a great promoter. Her book was on the bestseller list forever."

A book that might have been relegated to gathering dust on university bookshelves was propelled into the mainstream through our publicity efforts. *The War in Bosnia-Herzegovina* by scholars Steven L. Burg and Paul S. Shoup was featured on Cable News Network, Fox News Channel, CBC, WOR Radio Network, National Public Radio, and other major networks and shows throughout the U.S. and Canada, and internationally. By tying the book into a breaking news story and carefully targeting our media selection, we were able to procure major media exposure for a scholarly book.

Besides the traditional means of getting publicity, publicists are looking for ways to get the attention of reviewers and their media contacts.

Running Press won a Best of 1998 Award from *Entertainment Weekly* for Best Marketing Gimmick. "We wrapped the unauthorized biography of Howard Stern in a g-string and sent it out," says Justin Loeber.

Loeber sent the authors of a book on twins out on a book tour that was financed in part through a co-sponsorship by Planet Hollywood and Wrigley's Doublemint Gum.

"You should look for a unique angle," notes Loeber. "Find three to five hooks about your book. Come up with a message that is one minute or less to leave on an answering machine. I launched Diane McKinney Whetstone's novel *Tumbling* even though first-time novelists are hard to place. We pitched it as, 'Writer by early morning, and mother by day.' Within a week she gets a $100,000 deal. People wanted to know how she did it and read the book."

"Jack Canfield and Mark Victor Hansen are two examples of authors who understand promotions," notes John Kremer. "They've picked up on the one thing in my book, where I say do five promotions a day. You know, if you do five promotions every day—or sometimes I say, if you just spend ten minutes a day marketing your book—you'll start to sell books. Because even 10 minutes a day means three contacts a day or 1,000 contacts a year. If you're making 1,000 contacts a year, you're going to sell books. So that's what they did. They said we're going to do a radio interview every day come rain or shine. It doesn't matter with radio because you can sit in your house and do the radio interview. They try to do other interviews as they go along, and, you know, they've sold 40 million copies of *Chicken Soup for the Soul.* And they haven't even been out to Chicago to be on *Oprah*—yet."

**Once you are on TV, don't worry too much about how you are coming across. Relax!**

Certain authors, of course, lend themselves to publicity more than others. Famous authors like Mark Victor Hansen still say, "I'll do anything!" Sure it's better to be on the *Today Show* than *A.M. Tacoma Washington,* but you've got to do it all. People listen and watch. An accountant did a small show in

Joliet, I think it was. An old lady who had five million dollars heard the show and gave him her account. You have to think in terms of, 'Have you done your local television or newspaper yet?' If you fly into Cleveland for your aunt's wedding, have you called to get booked on their local TV? The world won't come to you. Some authors have very unrealistic expectations of what I or anyone else can do for them."

"You have to practice. Would you rather practice by going on *Oprah* first or the local news?" asks Phyllis Heller.

A media appearance does not automatically lead to book sales. Even being on *Oprah* doesn't always guarantee enormous sales. "Oprah has authors on all the time," says Arielle Ford, "but they are on a panel and get a couple words in—it's not a big home run. What you want is to be the focus of the half-hour one-on-one interview where Oprah is gushing 'I love this book! It is one of my favorites! I wish I would have written this book! I keep it next to my bedside' and so on. That's ideal, but maybe 30 people a year get that."

Paul Bogaards notes, "You could have an author on *Good Morning America* or on *Today* and the book might not sell. The author might not have been effective, or the host doesn't present the book well. But if you have an author on point, a host who frames the book well—who says, 'This is a very interesting book that is going to help you.' But you can find a strong causal link between when an author appears on a show or is featured in a magazine, and the sales happen immediately. And it changes. Ten years ago Phil Donahue sold a lot of books; now he's gone and it's Oprah. Or Rosie—since she has come on the scene, she can sell a ton of books for us."

"With regard to sales, different kinds of books tend to sell well in different kinds of media," says Phyllis Heller. "If it's cooking, obviously live TV works best. For self-help, advice books, and health, do as much radio, print, and afternoon talk shows as you can. If you have a controversial spin on things, try to make it on prime time news magazines. Try to gain momentum by doing the appearances close together. You really only have 90 days from the publication date for a book to do well because books often are returned after that point.

## MEDIA APPEARANCES: YES, YOU!

Aspiring authors toiling at the computer must recognize that they will have to leave the solitude of their home offices and make appearances in the media if their work pays off. Some authors are thrilled at the prospect of being interviewed on the radio, television, or the media. Other authors are more apprehensive. However, publicists can assist authors in showcasing themselves in the media as well as possible. There are also many things you can do on your own.

Media training is a worthwhile investment. There are people who will help you with your image, appearance, and media presence. Businesspeople have caught on to this, and so should you. You do not want to only rely on your natural charm. The electronic media creates an altered perception. It can exaggerate movements and expressions. There is a good reason why many news commentators look like they have helmet hair. Television lights are not very forgiving.

"Unfortunately, by virtue of being print writers, most authors are at a natural disadvantage for media interviews that are broadcast-oriented," says Margaret Durante. "Media training definitely helps an author speak better, distill their comments and only elaborate on salient points. But after that, it's personality and body language. Authors, whether nonfiction or fiction, can be tweedy and quirky in appearance but need to create a personal link to the audience—something that will draw interest. Every successful rock star knows this."

"All of our clients, without exception, are professionally media trained," says Arielle Ford. "It doesn't do any good for us to book an incredible tour and have the authors not know how to give a sound bite. It's not a natural-born skill; it's a learned skill. Many of our authors have double media training—in verbal and nonverbal skills. The first thing I do with a client is look at their videotape with the sound off. I think, do I like them? Are they believable? Would I want to hear what they have to say?

Susan Schwartzman agreed. "I've seen authors who have been just awful on TV take a media training course and come out like pros. You have to know what to wear, how to talk, and how to maximize what you are saying in a short amount of time."

"Your publicist will be aware of the local media coaches," says Christen Brown. "A lot of writers know how to write, but they need help on speaking skills. We coach them on what to say and how to say it."

> **While promotion is a publicist's job, dream clients provide input.**

"We've done everything for our clients from setting up hair appointments and taking them shopping for the right colors," says Arielle Ford. "One of my clients sent an e-mail saying he was subjecting himself to the Arielle Ford makeover, which meant he needed a new hairpiece and did need that makeover. And it paid off. I also tell authors to do something they often don't want to do: watch the television talk shows, read *People* magazine, the women's magazines, and the *Enquirer* so they actually understand what the media wants."

"You can make yourself more marketable to the media," says Phyllis Heller, "by watching a lot of shows and having some knowledge of how they go so you're not totally in the dark. Make yourself aware of how people on the shows come across. The most important thing to realize is that, although you are getting exposure for the book, you also are getting exposure for yourself so you can become an expert in the field, if you are not already. It will spawn a bigger profile, and who knows—maybe it will spur on an idea for the next book, which may be better than the one you are on tour for right now."

## MAXIMIZE YOUR MEDIA APPEARANCES

If you are fortunate to get some media bookings, make sure you make the most of them. Be prepared.

"I have noticed that many authors aren't prepared for their interviews," comments Christen Brown. "They didn't realize that they drive the interview. Columbia University did a study and found that many people do little to no preparation for an interview. You have to be ready to lead the interview. Writers need to have a line of questions developed for them that would allow the audience to understand clearly why they wrote this book and why someone would want to read this and buy it. Media training helps authors promote themselves and their books more effectively."

"A great thing to do before any interview is to go back and re-read your book," says Paul Bogaards. "Have your publisher write out twenty questions for you and rehearse the answers so that as little as possible is a surprise. When you are out of the road, after your first couple of interviews, you'll realize there are repeat threads. Recognize what those threads are to sound out the messages people want to hear, and push those messages."

"We coach people to get comfortable with themselves," says Christen Brown. "We recommend that you don't drink cold drinks because it can constrict your throat, or have heavy meals because that pulls your energy. Don't worry about camera positioning. We have a tape to help people relax and put them in the right frame of mind. It can be ordered from On Camera by e-mailing oncamera@att.net. It gives you all the practical information about selling your book and selling yourself. The other side is about physical preparation. We teach breathing techniques and visualization techniques."

"Be gracious," says Phyllis Heller, "because if you cause problems on TV or radio, they will remember, and the next time you come through town, they might not want you. Treat producers and others with kindness. If you scream in the parking lot that they didn't cover your book well enough, just don't let them hear you."

## RADIO APPEARANCES AND PHONERS

While many authors feel television is the best media to promote books, radio is the media that gives the average author the opportunity to really sell. Radio shows generally give authors much longer time than the three-minute television segments. This allows you to discuss your book in more detail, in a more relaxed setting. Often, radio interviews are done by phone, so you don't even have to leave your own home. There are tips to make a radio appearance more effective.

"Converse with the host like you're two people having a phone conversation," advises Paul Bogaards. "It shouldn't sound rehearsed. And if it's a call-in program, always listen to the names of the callers."

"You want to talk in normal tones," says Christen Brown. "Your voice, your inflection, that energy, your vocal variety carries the interview. One needs to work on one's voice for radio. Put the power in the voice. Keep things simple; don't speak over the audience's heads, or talk too fast or too slow or mumble.

"You need to use anecdotes, give the audience a word picture, which is a lot stronger than just the words themselves. If you need to paint a picture of flea season for a book on animals, it would be better to say, 'Our dog Nellie is 14 years old and every spring, she starts scratching. That's when we know it's flea season.'"

"Keep at least three ideas in front of you that you want to make sure you cover," suggest Phyllis Heller. "Listen carefully to what you are being asked and try to answer each question. Don't ever say, 'Oh, I covered that in my book' because that is a turn-off for people, especially producers and hosts."

## TELEVISION APPEARANCES

When aspiring authors think of media appearances, they most often think of television. Appearing on *Oprah* is the pinnacle of media success for any author. But authors on TV must remember that they usually have a very short time on the air. Morning show segments are only three minutes long. Some television appearances involve the author on a panel of guests, leaving no time to discuss the book.

Phyllis Heller gives advice for authors making television appearances. "Listen and respond to the questions you are asked. Also, try to answer clearly and not too quickly. Be as receptive as you can to the person interviewing you. Make believe the interviewer is someone you know well. Once you are on TV, don't worry too much about how you are coming across. Relax!"

"Television is so visual that how you say it is important," says Christen Brown. "Consider how much energy you communicate—your gestures, your body language, your eye contact. Dress appropriately for the type of interview you're doing. Women should wear skirts that fit well. Men should wear jackets that fit comfortably, that don't pull. For television, learn when and how much nodding is appropriate and be aware of 'um's' and 'ah's.' Gestures have to match energy level, not be too fast.

> There is a kinship with print reporters that writers might cotton to.

"Black or white used to be inappropriate, but that has changed because the cameras are far better than they were 10 years ago. You can get away with most colors, but don't want to wear a lot of color or print, or overdo the movement. Even ties that are too busy will pull focus. Jewelry that moves around is inadvisable for television because it distracts."

## PROMOTION REALITIES

As Phyllis Heller points out, "Many hosts don't have time to read the book, but have producers who screen material they think would be interesting for the show. Although you may find this highly insulting, be grateful for your exposure and back yourself up with some planning. You can't expect the host to ask exactly what you are looking for, but you want to get in the essential points that will give the public a clear idea whether they want to buy the book."

"Some media coaches who will tell authors to always bring the conversation back to the book," says Paul Bogaards. "For example, the host would ask me a question and I'd say, 'You know, Charlie, on page 43 of my book on how to promote books effectively, I answer this very question.' I don't ascribe to that theory. I think you have to just communicate—be articulate, be passionate and enthusiastic about your work because people are responding to you, not just your work. They have to like you and recognize value in what you are saying. It's the job of your publisher or publicist to make sure the host mentions the book and title, so I don't think you have to worry about that."

Phyllis Heller agrees. "Don't overdo the line 'in my book' because the shows get very upset. They know they're to plug the book and show the cover on TV. Have confidence that your publicist can make that happen. Talk-show hosts have told authors on numerous occasions, 'If you say "in my book" one more time, I'm not going to air this!'"

"Television interviews are the package deal. Your voice, body language, persona, and information or story lines from the book work together. If it's successful and you're a delightful guest, they'll invite you to return. If you fail, you're dumped for a long time. It pays to do your homework," cautions Margaret Durante.

## PRINT INTERVIEWS

While authors tend to worry about how they come across on television, publicists say that print interviews can be the most difficult.

"The difference between print and radio and television is that with print you are ultimately viewed through the prism of the journalist who reviews you," says Paul Bogaards. "Whereas in television, the viewers come to their own conclusion about who you are because it happens in real time. The problem with print is that the journalist interprets you for their readership. If you are uncomfortable with that, maybe you shouldn't do the interview."

"There is a kinship with print reporters that writers might cotton to. I don't know one reporter who isn't interested in writing a book on a topic, be it fiction or nonfiction. I've always felt far too few authors are aware that reporters just might enjoy speaking with them because of that invisible 'Gee, I wished I'd written a book' bond," points out Margaret Durante.

"In print, what you say is more important than how you say it because people are going to read it," says Christen Brown. "The reporter's job is to probe. Your job is to tell your story well. Here you can use statistics and data, and you can certainly develop your message more fully because you have more time than on radio and TV. They will write about what you wear, how you sit, and how you speak to give the interview color. You can't go in Levi's and throw your legs over the table and not expect them to report that."

Many authors have been portrayed in unflattering ways because it's easier for you to let your guard down when doing print interviews. Be professional, and stick to the points you identified that sell your book. Do not make off-the-record comments.

## THE PUBLICIST'S DREAM CLIENT

Every publicist admits that some authors simply make better clients than others do. What qualities make up these dream clients? How can you become one?

Rick Frishman says a dream client does three things:

◆ *Has a good book.* We've done some stupendous promotions for authors with a great track record, but the book stunk. People send the books back!

◆ *Is a good communicator.* You can get a spot on air, but you must make people want to buy the book. You must not only be a good guest, but close the sale.

◆ *Has a good attitude.* You can't be a prima donna. You can't say, "I'm only going to be on *Oprah* or the *Today Show."* Everyone wants that, but what have you done first? You might also think doing brain surgery would be fun, but you would first have to pay your dues in medical school.

Arielle Ford looks for authors who have a lot of energy and are passionate about their books. "They must be driven to get their message out there and take 100 percent responsibility for marketing their books. All the really successful authors do what it takes; they are willing to put the time in and do interviews every single day."

"Dream clients," says Lisa Johnson, "are authors who can make themselves more marketable by thinking of angles, of areas of expertise they have, or who develop some kind of base, such as getting themselves on a small lecture circuit. While promotion is a publicist's job, dreams clients provide input."

"Nothing works like a well-written book that a host of people at a publishing company have cited as well-written," comment Margaret Durante. "While there are exceptions to every rule (and many bestsellers are trite text), more authors could create bestsellers if they put as much time and energy into writing truly creative, eclectic text that makes a difference, as they put into harassing bookstore clerks and publicists, whether freelance or in-house.

"Authors can be persistent without being annoying. Too many authors lose the opportunity to gain exposure because they are so aggressive that one would think they'd just escaped solitary confinement. Being assertive and creative are far more effective exposure tactics than harassment."

A dream client is "someone who is accessible and can be reached any time the publicist needs them," says Susan Schwartzman. "I'm working with Richard Ellis, who wrote a book *The Search for the Giant Squid.* If I get a booking for him, I call and he's there— and says yes or no on the spot. But he doesn't call me every hour and expect me to spend hours on the phone with him—the hours I should be booking him."

"Celebrities are always fun," says Justin Loeber. "The strategy of booking them is the opposite of booking an unknown, though. You have to pull publicity away from

> **Being assertive and creative are far more effective exposure tactics than harassment.**

them as opposed to begging for it, as you do with an unknown. A celebrity who did her publicity well was Cindy Crawford. I worked on her book, *Basic Face,* when I was at Broadway. She understood her place in the media. While the book was about a five-minute makeup technique, she knew it was really about the fantasy of becoming glamorous. She was very conscious of that when promoting."

Rick Frishman noted other celebrities who handled publicity well. "We've handled Howard Stern, who was a real professional. Richard Simmons is just electric, gets the whole place jumping. He is one of the world's greatest marketers. Doing publicity for Salman Rushdie was interesting. He came in with two bodyguards and I couldn't tell anyone he was there."

## SAGE ADVICE FOR AUTHORS

Arielle Ford gives authors these pieces of advice: "Authors should write a book because they have something burning inside and want to get the word out, even if they don't make money. And I always try to get authors to read books like this one, to understand how the book-publishing industry really works. It's nice to be a positive thinker and do affirmations like putting up the *New York Times* list and saying you'll become a bestselling author, but that's not what sells books. It takes publicity."

Ford also notes, "I always ask people why they're writing this book. Some want to be famous, and that's okay. But you must be about what you want people to get out of your book."

"When I meet people I ask, 'What is your goal?'" says Pat Eisemann. "Patricia Cornwell said, 'I want to be number one.' Frank McCourt said 'I just hope people will want to read this book.' And Barbara Bush said, 'I want my memoir to do better than my dog's.'"

"Above all else," Rick Frishman reminds, "have fun with this. Take a step back and enjoy it. You have published a book; you are now recorded for life."

As Eric Yaverbaum captures it best: "Imagine how many people dream of having just one book published. And you have done it!"

# Stephen Hall Harrison

Vice president of Bradley Communications Corporation and
publisher of the Radio TV Interview Report

R*adio TV Interview Report* is a magazine that radio and television
talk show producers all across the country read to find authors
who are available for interviews. It comes out three times a month,
and it reaches over 4,000 producers with each issue. What we offer
is a way, for less than $300 a month, to get five, ten, or as many as
fifty interviews each month, without having to do any work. We have
people get booked on *Oprah, Good Morning America,* NPR, and
CNN. If an author is interested in doing an ad with us, they would
call us at 800-989-1400, extension 408. First you would talk to one
of our publicity consultants, who would get a feel for whether your
topic would work well. Certain topics work well; others are not appropriate, so we turn people away every day. If we decided your topic
would work, you would send us a copy of the book and a photo of
yourself. We would have the copywriter contact you and offer ideas
for a unique hook. Then we would write the ad copy and get your approval, do the desktop publishing and the printing, and you would
be in the magazine! What's great is that you are listed as the contact,
so you'll know how well the ad does. We find when someone runs
three half-page ads, typically about fifteen radio talk show producers
request to interview them via telephone. Lots of people get many
more than that, some less, but 15 is a good rule of thumb.

We find the most important success factor is the guest—how good they are on the air and whether they are persistent promoters. Mark Victor Hansen, who co-wrote the Chicken Soup books, talks about the idea of doing one interview a day. Hansen said he interviewed Scott Peck, who wrote *The Road Less Traveled,* and Peck attributed a lot of his success to the fact that he averaged at least one media interview a day—for many, many years. That's what it takes. Mark Victor Hansen and Jack Canfield still do that. A lot of people think they will do a tour and do publicity for two or three months, but it really takes that ongoing, day-in day-out, week-after-week, year-after-year effort to really sell books.

> **You have to be able to sell without selling.**

Lots of wonderful things can help you sell your books when you appear on radio and TV talk shows. You can often give out a phone number so people can order your book directly. And you can tell people to order it through Amazon.com. You might also send postcards to bookstores letting them know about the upcoming media appearance and suggesting they order a bunch of books. It's also possible that you might end up becoming a regular guest, or having your own talk show. Sometimes listeners invite you for speaking engagements, sometimes newspapers hear about you. I call it "the publicity snowball."

We have also seen authors get new ideas for other books. Because you're in touch with a potential audience, you get feedback and hear what they're interested in. Really good guests are the kind who have you so intrigued by what they're saying that you can't stop listening to the radio—not even if you're in your driveway, with ice cream and groceries in the back of your car. You are enjoying them on the air so much, maybe because they're hilariously funny, or because they really have scared you about some problem. Ted Brower is one outstanding guest I've heard. He's a nutritionist, and when you hear him, you worry that you're going to get cancer because of the food you're eating. You really want to buy his course to avoid cancer. If you're really funny, or if people feel a certain connection with you, they will tend to buy your book. You have to be able to sell without selling.

I just got a testimonial quote from *Rich Dad, Poor Dad* by Robert Kiyosaki. It sold over 250,000 books, and several publishers have offered to purchase the rights. It became Barnes and Noble's number six bestselling business book for the year. Kiyosaki said the interviews he got through the magazine were the kick-start to his book's success.

# Arlynn Greenbaum

President of Authors Unlimited Inc.,
a speaker's bureau

Authors Unlimited is a speaker's bureau that represents over 400 authors. We get them paid speaking engagements at a variety of venues, from colleges and corporations to libraries, trade associations, and religious groups.

Authors must meet two criteria: be a good speaker and have a timely topic. It helps if the author's book is getting a lot of publicity and attention, is on the bestseller list, or won the Pulitzer Prize or other award, and if the author is well known. I do best with well-known literary authors and business authors.

Not every author is a good speaker or even wants to get into this, so the first thing they have to determine is whether they want to join what I call the "sweaty palms club." Speaking is America's number one public fear; not everybody is cut out for this kind of work. I recommend that authors who aren't used to speaking do some practice gigs for free at local libraries, schools, or associations to make sure they even want to go into this. Then if they do, they need to work on their technique and get some coaching. If they want to get really serious, they could consider joining Toastmasters and the National Speakers Association to really hone their talents. Speakers like Doris Kearns Goodwin command huge fees because they have a lot to say and are really good at speaking. The better authors get at speaking, the more marketable they will be.

Examples of authors I work with are Mary Higgins Clark, Art Spiegelman, Arthur Golden, and Judith Martin (Miss Manners).

There are dozens and dozens of speakers bureaus, so this isn't necessarily the gospel. In my case, the author or the literary agent usually comes to me, says they have a new book coming out, and asks if I'd be interested in working with them. First, I check on their topic. So if I think I can sell and market the author as a speaker, I meet with them if they are in New York, or I get their materials and a bio, a photo, and a video if possible.

My reputation depends on me recommending authors who are going to dazzle audiences, who have already been trained.

Frank McCourt is an author who dazzles. He is just so brilliant and charming, someone very special.

**If the subject matter is your passion, find a way to make your idea work.**

Art Spiegleman is great; he does a slide show on the making of Maus, so uses a lot of visuals. Usually the most popular are the ones who are very special. They have an unusual book or an important message they have gotten recognition for, so some sort of name is attached to it.

When I first started out, there was a very big book called the *Tao of Pooh,* by Benjamin Hoff. He was getting a lot of requests to speak. His publicist turned him on to me and we worked together quite successfully for a year or two, then he decided he didn't want to do talks anymore. He was very popular on college campuses, where the book was often used, and there was something very interesting about learning Taoism through Winnie the Pooh. There are no rules.

One of my best clients is a bank that has branches in a couple different parts of the country. One branch down in Florida brings an author down for a week to do five luncheons at five of their branches; they pay very good money and buy 1,000 hardcover books. I just had Arthur Golden down there, and Margaret Atwood, and David Baldacci's coming this month. They also have a sister bank in Chicago.

For authors, the book sales are great, and they get paid, too, so it's more than publicity. It's very win, win.

Spokesperson things are unusual and very interesting, and can be quite fun and gratifying. That means I work with a PR firm representing a product. They use an author, book all the media, and might actually do a multi-city tour or satellite tour. The author gets media trained on how to mention the product while on tour. For example, I worked with a firm that was representing a deodorant. I got them an author who wrote about stress. The PR firm did a 12-city tour, which was very easy because they set up the interviews with sample questions. Midway through they would ask about deodorants, relating to stress, so she was able to mention this particular deodorant as an example. I'm doing one now for prunes, if you can believe that. They have a contest, Making Dreams Come True, and I have an author who wrote a book about making dreams come true and is promoting the contest. It is an unusual way to promote your book.

> **The better authors get at speaking, the more marketable they will be.**

I once had to find an author who wrote a book on how to sell your house because the client had a product that eliminated odors. They determined that when you sell your house, it's important to get rid of the smell. So the author went on all these shows talking about how to sell your house and in the course of the interview talked about eliminating odors using this new product.

I am a member of a group called IGAB, the International Group of Agents and Bureaus (great acronym!) that provides information on other bureaus besides Authors Unlimited. The phone number is 317-297-0872. Speaking is just a wonderful way to supplement the promotion and publicity that your publisher is doing. It is not for everybody, but if you are good at it, and like it, and if you have a book getting some recognition, definitely give me a call.

# Steve O'Keefe

Internet Publicist,
Tenagra Corporation

The Internet is great for getting the word out quickly that a new book exists. The first month is when you want to make a joyous noise online to let the target audience know the book exists and give them an idea what it's about.

A lot of people feel overwhelmed by the Internet. The truth is that it's still a brand new medium, and nobody has more than five years of experience with the Web, so we are all still learning. I wrote *Publicity on the Internet* to solve a problem of mine. I spent about 25 percent of my time turning away work, explaining why certain Internet publicity campaigns wouldn't work for people, or that I simply didn't have the time to do their work. So I wrote a book as a way of giving these people information on how to run Internet campaigns by themselves.

My book is written for anyone doing publicity on the Internet, but authors and publishers will especially benefit because almost all my online experience is related to promoting books and authors on the Internet. Most of the examples in the book I've taken from my five years of experience banging my head against the wall, seeing what works and what doesn't work in terms of book publishing online.

One of the better Internet campaigns was for Cyber-punk author William Gibson's book *Idoru*. Gibson is much loved by Sci-Fi fans. I believe he invented the term Cyber-culture and Cyber-punk, so was a natural for online promotion. The publisher came to me and I said, "Why don't we take an excerpt from the book, syndicate it, and get it out to a high-traffic web site?" So we went to the *Playboy* Web site, which was getting about three million hits a day at the time. Now I'll grant you that people aren't coming to the Playboy site to read; they're mostly coming to look at pictures. But it was in the top ten high-traffic sites on the Internet, so we approached their print editors and asked if they'd be interested in running an online exclusive with this new William Gibson book, and they said yes. In fact, they just totally ran with it.

My main suggestion for authors is don't try to do everything on your own. Try to work with high-traffic Web sites. I'm not saying having your own Web site is a bad idea; it can be a very good online supplement to your work. But it doesn't approach the publicity you get with high-traffic sites. People understand this logic when they think about magazines or television show. Building your own Web site is like having an infomercial. For some people it works, but it's expensive. It's much easier to go to the *Oprah Winfrey Show* or to *Dateline NBC* or to various television shows and get them to do a story on you than to create your whole program yourself. And the same with magazines: it's better to have a small blurb in *Time* than to start your own glossy magazine and put in the money yourself. That's what publicity is all about. Every person is unique and has something to share with the online community, so they're saying, "I will come and be your content in exchange for your mentioning that I have a book out."

> **The chat tour is really a back door into publicity in traditional media, like radio, print, and broadcast.**

You can go to the high-traffic Internet sites like the search engines Lycos and Yahoo, which both have chat facilities, and try to get yourself booked into chat there. America Online represents nearly one-third of the online audience. So it's important that authors take advantage of the 30-day free trial on America On Line and promote their book in the month that it comes out. These are things authors can do independently or in connection with their publishers.

My book tells readers in painstaking (painful I would say) detail how to do all this work themselves, but a lot of people don't have time or patience for it. The Internet is very touchy regarding protocol. For example, you can't post a message online saying, "I've got a new book; go buy it at Amazon.com." You will get flamed for abuse of the Internet. But you can post a message to a selected discussion group saying, "I'm giving away a free chapter of my book; just send me an e-mail to request it." Then you can put all your promotional material in your response.

When you break Internet protocol and annoy recipients, they will filter you out. And once you're filtered out, you can never get into their e-mail boxes again. The penalties for stupidity online are severe. People don't realize that a computer mistake that might be impossible to undo can damage their company's and their own reputation in about 60 seconds. That's why I have clients. Some botched their own jobs already, and others realized it's just too touchy and too complex to handle in-house yet.

I've made mistakes that have gone out to hundreds of journalists, every bone-headed move in the book, and that is how you learn. People will give you a certain amount of leeway—enough leeway to be dumb but not repeatedly dumb.

We do author chats. Our work starts when we book a chat, then we have to promote it, which is hard work. For example, dozens of papers around the United States now run calendars of online events. *USA Today,* for example, has cyber-listings column. For example, it might say that Mary Doe, author of *Improving Your Finances,* is going to be in live chat on America Online at eight o'clock. That is worth more than the attendance of the chat, because half a million people may see that blurb in *USA Today.* The chat tour is really a back door into publicity in traditional media, like radio, print, and broadcast. A professional takes a simple thing like a chat appearance and turns it into a major media event.

For me the joy in this work comes from being able to read all these books before they come out. And I get to tell the world what wonderful things these people have done. While I've been pleased to work on some books that hit the *New York Times* Bestseller List, I like the stuff from the self-publishers just as much.

> **The Internet is very touchy regarding protocol.**

It's hard work. For self-publishers and small publishers, the deck is stacked against them on the Internet, just like it is everywhere else. They tend to think that the Internet gives them a way around doing traditional publicity, PR, and marketing, but it's just a supplement to it. I usually tell publishers they should be spending between 15 and 25 percent of their marketing budget for online promotion—the higher number for computer books and specific career-oriented nonfiction, and on the lower end for fiction.

Publishers and authors on the Internet should not be afraid to make mistakes out there because it's still brand new. What I call the "Internet Revolution" will be going on for another twenty years or so before it really integrates into mainstream society. We are all new at it. Authors shouldn't be afraid that because they haven't approached it before, they are going to be behind. They can benefit from the mistakes people like me made, and learn from our mistakes.

**CHAPTER 10**

# Getting Out of
# Your Own Way

You have done everything right. You have gotten a book published and now it is time for your success. Can you handle it? Do you realize that you can be your own worst enemy when it comes to realizing your dreams? All along the way you can find ways to sabotage yourself through your attitude, actions, or avoidance.

I bet you can't believe you could possibly do anything to yourself that would lessen your chances of becoming a successful writer. But there are things you can do and might have done all along the way. They are the pitfalls of being human. Sometimes we want something so much that we ultimately question whether we are worthy of the goal. Sometimes the goal has such an importance to our self-definition that if we get close to achieving it, we are afraid there will be no further meaning to our lives.

Well, stop all this self-indulgence. Be brutally honest with yourself if you find yourself doing things that could ultimately stand in your way. Look at yourself in the mirror and tell yourself you deserve all the success you can muster. Tell yourself you are talented and worthy; visualize your success.

## WAYS TO SABOTAGE GETTING PUBLISHED

As we discussed in earlier chapters, you first need to understand the industry to see what protocols will assist you in achieving your goals. If you do everything "by the book" when it comes to selecting a project, producing a fine manuscript, and packaging it well, you increase your odds tremendously and will be more likely to find a publisher.

But do not forget one very important factor: attitude. Writers sabotage themselves and never realize their death has been at their own hands. Remember one thing, if you haven't gathered this already: *You have no status until you have status.* Allow this fact to permeate your being.

This does not mean that you should feel terrible about yourself and sink into some sort of writer's funk. We will discuss that type of sabotage later in this chapter. This means that you have to learn the ancient art of the "suck up." It is an art, because it has to fall somewhere between being too subtle as to make you appear innocuous and too direct as to get you branded a sycophant. The proper balance is to have your prospective agent or editor feel good about the prospect of working with you while also being very excited about your project.

Many aspiring writers forget the cardinal rule of never putting the agent or editor on the defensive. The second someone shows interest in his or her query letter or manuscript, they automatically think "Hollywood." They start calling the agent or editor all the time to find out the status of their manuscript, and if they are fortunate enough to be offered a contract, they start nit-picking over every little detail.

Do not misunderstand. You should watch out for your interests. But for goodness sake, do not let on to the agent or editor that you are watching out for number one. Use some tact or diplomacy. Let your editor or agent know how important you think they are. Let them know you understand how much of your fate is in their hands. You can make your own book a huge success and do not need an agent or publishing house to get you to where you want to be. But we do not need to tell you that it sure is a helluva lot easier to get there with a good boost in the rear from people with the access and know-how to get you there. If some arrogant attitude is holding you back, you are truly getting in your own way.

Maybe you are not arrogant but rather unrealistic. When you see certain simple books take off and make someone into a millionaire, you are bound to say to yourself, "I could have written that!" It is always like that in the marketplace, no matter what the product. Who hasn't thought at least once about how they wished they had come up with the idea for beanie babies?

Some people have the Midas touch and can't fail, no matter what they do. I've seen people who I'm sure have a signed contract with the Devil stashed away in a safe along with the "Picture of Dorian Gray." Some people seem to turn everything into money and success. We are obsessed with these people's lives and all fantasize about the big "hit" that could put us on easy street.

But what we do not see is all of the work, genius, and marketing that goes behind these quirky products and books that take off and make it big. Something can hit a nerve and create a momentum of its own, but it has to be somewhere where someone can see it first or, no matter what, it is going to go nowhere.

**Writers sabotage themselves and never realize their death has been at their own hands.**

We once had a client who was highly prolific in the health field but was also a legend in his own mind. He had decent material but nothing so earth-shaking that someone was waiting to grab it up without some marketing effort. (The health field is almost as competitive as finding the one true meaning of life.) He was so certain that he was going to be an instant phenomenon that we decided not to work with him. This would seem counter-intuitive, but we could see he was too impatient. We have enough experience to know that an author like this blows a lot of steam but can't really run the engine. As you have read in many of our featured author's own words, writing success comes with a lot of planning, discipline, and sweat.

Another thing we believed about this particular potential client was that he was too married to his material. If you have already been published and have had books on the bestseller's list, you can have tremendous input into the way your book is ultimately produced. Although you have input as a new writer, part of your apprenticeship is deferring to some extent to the agents or editors who are helping you along the way. You always have the option to self-publish. But if you are going the route of having someone else publish your book, you need to be resilient enough to listen to what people have to say.

Editors and agents are not always right, but if they are earning a living at what they do, there is a high likelihood they know more about the industry than you do. Put your arrogance or insecurity aside and learn to listen and follow directions. If something is so heinous as to change the very essence of your project, search your soul and decide whether you or they have the better and more commercial idea. Not everyone is in writing for the money, prestige, or success. Principles are important too. But if you are looking for a *big* writing career, learn to play the game enough to incorporate your principles into a bigger picture.

## GETTING RID OF WRITER'S BLOCK

If you are reading this book, we know you have dreams of living the successful writer's life. You may be attending writer's conferences and may even be working on that proverbial book. We know that not all of you reading this book are ready to hand in a wonderful proposal or manuscript to an agent or publishing house. For all we know, you may be staring at your word processor as you read this, wondering what on earth you could write about that could help you achieve your dreams.

Writer's block is not a mental disorder. It is an implosion of insecurity and perfectionism. When you want something so badly and are not fully certain you deserve it, you may find yourself frozen with fear. All your negative thoughts will join forces to tell you how untalented, undeserving, or stupid you are. It is amazing how thoroughly a creative mind can implode on itself in such a destructive way. We all fear failure. Stop it. If you do not want to fail, then stop worrying about it and channel all that creative energy into banging your head against the wall so many times that something good has to come out of it.

The amazing thing about writing is that if you have such a strong desire to do it for reasons other than just the success and money factors, there is a very good chance you have the talent to carry out the process. There is a proportionate connection between desire and ability.

You will also be surprised to know that the most successful writers are not always the most talented.

## Put your arrogance or insecurity aside and learn to listen and follow directions.

The major difference is that, to paraphrase Woody Allen, "they show up." If you spend your life staring at your word processor or legal pad dreaming about your future instead of actually writing, you can kiss your beach house goodbye.

Writer's groups and conferences can be a wonderful thing for you if you want to learn your craft and gain some motivation. Just watch out for the energy vampires. If you are insecure about your writing and meet people who are highly competitive, you may be driven completely insane. Well, at least you will become nervous and anxious about your own writing, which can create a vicious circle. If there are people who insist on asking you what you are writing, always say "a bestseller."

Do not compare notes with people and concern yourself with what they are doing. If you conduct your writing career this way, you may be doomed to find yourself in twenty years comparing yourself to the same people who may actually be comparing themselves to you. In either instance, it is unlikely either of you will be getting anywhere very fast.

Everyone makes mistakes and faces rejection when endeavoring to pursue a career as nebulous as writing. It is ironic that a career that requires so much thick skin is occupied by some of the most highly sensitive people of all. You will need a lot of positive self-talk to get past the difficult times when you feel like burning everything you have ever written and joining the circus.

Rejection is a natural part of the publishing process. To become published, you need to be rejected. You will have multiple submissions to a literary agent. If you obtain an agent, he or she will make multiple submissions to publishing houses. Not everyone will want you. You do not need to have a completely filled dance card. You need one break—one publishing house to believe enough in the quality, worthiness, or commercial potential of your project to plunk down some money for it.

> **It is amazing how thoroughly a creative mind can implode on itself in such a destructive way.**

One way writers sabotage themselves is they have overly high expectations of the process. It is slow and tedious. You may not hear back right away, and if you lack any status, you may not hear back at all. If you view it from the perspective of the agent and editor, they quickly peruse the submissions for the best possible prospects, sort of like mining for gold. They are not going to carefully examine the items that do not immediately jump out at them and meet their criteria.

Just keep in mind that just because your particular manuscript or project is not suited to a particular agent or editor doesn't mean it is not suited to someone else. You need some feedback to determine if you are not finding the right mix of factors or if you are simply in need of an overhaul.

Do not be afraid to look upon the submission and rejection process as a type of information-gathering. When you write, you are pretty much existing in a vacuum. With the exception of the opinions of your writer's group, a few well-paid friends, and your spouse, you do not have any objective input. You need feedback from people who know how you stack up against what is circulating in the commercial market to help you build a truly unbeatable package.

You'll know when all the elements come together at the right time. Do not be afraid to persevere even though it seems hopeless. Sometimes you just need to outlast your rejections. Sometimes nothing can be done to improve a project. It may just need to find the right home for itself.

Do not give up because you are discouraged. Writing is a funny thing. Once you have a break, you will be amazed how many great opportunities come your way.

When you are starting out, you may want to take on projects that are not your own so you can learn the ropes from the inside. If you can, try to collaborate or ghostwrite for very little compensation so you can have some experience under your belt. There are always people looking for writers for their stories.

Staying out of your own way on your path to writing greatness is as simple as telling yourself not to give up while remembering to kick yourself in the rear if your head becomes too swollen to fit inside the door frame. Writing books is not the easiest way to earn a living, but if you can endure and jump over the right hurdles, there is nothing quite like it.

If you are one of the lucky ones who gets a book published, don't stop there. Become your own publicist, whether you hire a professional or not. Keep a very positive and passionate attitude about your book and never stop thinking of new ways to promote it.

Some people get a book published and do not know how to handle it. If you want to be successful, you have to put yourself under some kind of public scrutiny. If your goal is commercial writing, you will be unable to justify being an eccentric hermit until you have at least one bestseller under your belt.

If you can't stand attention or turn into a puddle of sweat in front of a crowd, get over it. As the publicists have told you, there are many professionals who can train you to feign confidence and presence, even if you feel like you want to crawl into a hole.

One of the most important things to remember is that you want this. You want to write and you want to be successful doing it. You have enough to contend with without having to worry about not being there for yourself. If you need to, say affirmations every night:

- ◆ I am a writer.
- ◆ I deserve to be successful.
- ◆ I have a unique voice that other people want to read.
- ◆ I believe in myself.
- ◆ I am a perfect me.
- ◆ Rejection leads to perfection; I can take it.

If you need to make these affirmations and others you create part of your daily ritual, do it. Writing can be a very lonely life with little validation from anywhere outside yourself. If you need to give yourself the extra boost of a self-propelled fan club, do it. High self-esteem can only help all aspects of your life.

## PRIDE GOETH BEFORE A FALL

On the other hand, do not become full of yourself. Call us superstitious, but when people become overly arrogant, it seems like the universe finds a way to knock them back down to size. Certainly no publisher enjoys working with someone whose demands are not commensurate with the perceived returns. If you alienate everyone at your publishing house, you will find them less interested in promoting your book and less interested in you. If you are looking for staying power, don't burn bridges.

You can't possibly learn everything you need to know without making some mistakes. You are going to mail manuscripts to publishing houses that are defunct or are going to send envelopes without manuscripts at all. You are going to speak to a crowd and find your tongue and lips locked in some type of battle for your attention. You are going to make a television appearance and when the red light on the camera signals to your brain, stare blankly and by all means say nothing.

Things that you will never even imagine are going to go wrong. One writer was on live television when a huge green spider crawled up her leg. She responded accordingly by brushing it away, but at the same time almost knocked her host's teeth out.

Don't be hard on yourself when things do not work out as planned. This is all part of the writer's adventure. If you become too serious or tense, you are going to forget that you became a writer because you wanted to write. If it is no longer fun, find an easier way to make a buck.

# The Secret Ingredients
# of Making It Big

In the world of writing and publishing, there are many winners to be found. But there is a special zone beyond that—a place where the extraordinarily successful reside, a Mount Olympus of mega-achievers whom the rest of us both envy and hold in awe.

Every business has its own unique caste system, with "just average" the bulkiest category. But whether we speak of writing or pole-vaulting, what are the elements that take the striver over the edge of the spectrum into the highly restricted ultra-zone often referred to as the "Big Time"?

Frankly, we don't know, nor do you or anyone else, including those who walk at the top. Anyone who tells you otherwise is simply mistaken. It's like claiming to know the meaning of life; the less you confess to know, the more you actually do know. If this has confused you, that's okay because we're about to move on.

While there is no replicable model for making it big as a writer, a range of characteristics, habits, thought forms, and predictable personal pathologies can be identified, analyzed, and ultimately emulated. We will attempt to classify and explain some of those traits here.

## TALENT

Being good at what you do really helps a lot. Being great helps even more. But guess what? Much of the time it ain't the best who beat the rest. Hunger, determination, the power of one's will are the forces that, when deployed with the right alchemy, will simply enable any man or woman to overwhelm those who have been merely gifted with talent. How often have you heard the one about the child who lifted the car off her mother's crushed body? It may be true . . . .

## RESPONSIBILITY

This is a tricky one, at least on the surface. On one hand, it's only logical that the most successful people are those who do not spin their wheels trying to get others to make them successful. The world is cluttered with losers who constantly berate the people and/or circumstances that victimized and diminished them.

On the other hand, the world has too many successful people who deftly deployed vampire methods to get where they are. They may be responsible in the sense that they found a way to outmaneuver life's obstacles; but they are irresponsible to the extent that they generate a trail of blood leading backwards to the origins of their endeavor. Success through exploitation is like sex through rape.

## EVOLUTIONARY

Most highly successful people carry around a bulky legacy of failures, humiliations, and dumb actions. The truly wise ones know that these potholes are not necessarily behind them. What this means is that they allowed nothing to kill their will to succeed. And while they may have made countless mistakes, it's unlikely that they ever made the same mistakes twice, once they learned the lesson.

Evolution teaches us that the universe kills stagnation and encourages mutation. Most successful people have mutated themselves many times. Their only other choice was to become yesterday's newspaper.

## PLANNING

It's very hard to get there if you haven't decided where you're going.

Successful people pretty much know well ahead of time what it is they're trying to achieve. They may not write down their goals or otherwise express them, and they may appear rather erratic and in-decisive, but at the core of their being lives an eternal vision that guides them. Plans can be latent. They may invade our conscious-ness when we least expect it but are ready to embrace it. The best-laid plans do not need to begin between the ears; they simply erupt from the forces that move our lives, if we let them.

## SHOW UP

You won't get to play if you're not on the bench. And you won't get to be on the bench if you don't go to the try-outs. And you won't do well at the try-outs if you don't prepare. And you won't prepare if you don't care. You may be among the best and the brightest, but if you don't show up, no one will care.

## PASSION

Highly successful people intrigue us because they seem more alive than the average soul. That's not an illusion. Their lives aren't just about getting through the day. To them, such a routine would be a form of death. Instead, they fill their space with a journey and pur-pose. They truly aspire to write their own scripts.

## THE WILD CARD

The number seven is one of those harmonious measurements, and this is added to respect that tradition. Fortunately, the reasons for success as a writer (or anything else) are infinitely abundant. And, thankfully, the opportunities for success are "out there" in abun-dance. Most of life's malcontents probably never truly believed in anything other than the reality of the darkness behind them and the projected likelihood of the darkness that awaits them. Successful people have faith in the plausibility and probability of their eventual success. They can "see," and they allow themselves to see the prom-ised land.

# INDEX

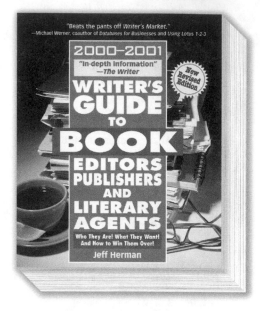